The High Magic *of*
TALISMANS
&
AMULETS

The High Magic *of*

TALISMANS

&

AMULETS

Tradition and Craft

CLAUDE LECOUTEUX

Translated by Jon E. Graham

Inner Traditions

Rochester, Vermont • Toronto, Cananda

Inner Traditions
One Park Street
Rochester, Vermont 05767
www.InnerTraditions.com

Originally published in French under the title *Le livre des talismans et des amulettes* by Éditions Imago, 7 rue Suger, 75006 Paris
First U.S. edition published in 2014 by Inner Traditions

Library of Congress Cataloging-in-Publication Data
Lecouteux, Claude.
[Livre des talismans et des amulettes. English.]
The high magic of talismans and amulets : tradition and craft / Claude Lecouteux ; translated by Jon E. Graham. — First U.S. edition.
  pages cm
Includes bibliographical references and index.
ISBN 978-1-62055-279-7 (hardcover) — ISBN 978-1-62055-280-3 (e-book)
1. Talismans—History. 2. Amulets—History. 3. Occultism—Religious aspects—Christianity—History. I. Title.
BF1561.L3813 2014
133.4'4—dc23
                                                                    2013036544

Printed and bound in the United States

10 9 8 7 6 5 4 3 2

Text design by Brian Boynton and layout by Virginia Scott Bowman
This book was typeset in Garamond Premier Pro and Gill Sans with Granjion, Gills Sans, Trebuchet, and Garamond Premier Pro used as display typefaces

Inner Traditions wishes to express its appreciation for assistance given by the government of France through the National Book Office of the Ministère de la Culture in the preparation of this translation.

Nous tenons à exprimer nos plus vifs remerciements au gouvernment de la France et au Ministère de la Culture, Centre National du Livre, pour leur concours dans la préparation de la traduction de cet ouvrage.

CONTENTS

ACKNOWLEDGMENTS

This study required so much time because access to source material was difficult. Fortunately, a large number of individuals provided me with documents that were either missing from French libraries or unobtainable, even when the collection claimed to own several different copies, the absence of which the librarians could never explain. The watchword seems to be: "We keep them under tight wraps, we do not lend them out!" My heartfelt thanks to Sandra Hanse (Bonn), Florence Bayard (Caen), Ronald Grambo (Kongsvinger), and Emmanuela Timotin (Bucharest), who provided me with valuable information about Romanian traditions, not to mention Philippe Gontier (Graulhet), who generously offered me the benefit of his knowledge and library, and Diane Tridoux, who sent me Dom Belin's treatise from Switzerland.

TO GUARD AGAINST ADVERSITY, MISFORTUNE, ILLNESS, AND DEATH

Few words are as steeped in mystery as "amulet" and "talisman," for both are powerfully associated with the supernatural, and with the worlds of legend and fable. From the beginning, the word "amulet" has brought to mind protection against all kinds of assaults, while "talisman" plunges us deep into the arcana of the East. It inspires visions of marvelous rings and swords: in our imaginations we see those predestined heroes who have successfully fulfilled their quests thanks to an object they were given, found, or won. Such visions lead us into a world like that of *The Thousand and One Nights*!

But if we look around ourselves, and especially if we travel, we shall see the use of amulets and talismans in myriad places—and it is not solely the province of primitive and animist peoples. These objects are present in all of mankind's religions, sometimes in the form of a gris-gris or a holy medal, sometimes in the form of a hand or tooth. And despite whatever we may wish to tell ourselves to the contrary, belief in their virtues is very much alive in the twenty-first century. In Europe, people frequently place Saint Christopher medals in their cars; in the Far East, taxi drivers hang talismans from their rearview mirrors. People can buy talismans in Japanese temples, where such objects often take the place of an entrance ticket. The Orientalist Henri Massé notes:

> As in Europe, the automobile has given amulets new popularity. Four years ago I saw shells (*qoss-è gorbé*) and lead figurines in several Tehran buses; a dried sheep's eye (*nazar-qorbâni*), a ball of clay, or a piece of blue glass (*kodji-âbi*) could often be seen on the radiator caps of private cars; some bus drivers wore a case on their right arms that contained a grimoire or a verse from the Koran.[1]

Good luck charms still abound. These range from the horseshoe to the rabbit's foot, from the May Day lily of the valley to the four-leaf clover. On New Year's Day in Japan, people buy a *hamaya* in the temples, which is an arrow with the power to drive away evil spirits. The seven lucky gods (Shichifukujin) portrayed in a boat are an effective luck charm; we should also note the Inu-hariko, a paper-maché dog who not only brings luck but helps women in labor, and the Akabeko, a cow or bull made from the same material that has the power to avert misfortune. Many other such charms existed in earlier times, such as the hangman's rope or a swallow's heart in Europe; the heart of a hero or a brave man in Manchuria;[2] and in Alsace, "the semen of the god Wodan," a name given to Neolithic objects, was considered to bring good fortune.[3] In the old province of Poitou, a piece of wood from a Saint John's Day bonfire allegedly protected its possessor from lightning,[4] and peasants of the Limoges region put salt on the heads of the cattle they brought to the fair "to prevent anybody from finding a way to cast an evil spell on them." In 1897, the Abbé Noguès noted:

> People wear over their chests or their bellies, or beneath their armpits, or hang from their necks an entire regiment of kabbalistic words: *abracadabra, agla, garnaze, Eglatus, Egla,* etc., as well as magical, astronomical, galvanic, magnetic—in other words, omnigeneric—amulets and talismans, which, with all due respect to the partisans of the inevitability of progress, are still highly popular![5]

In short, amulets and talismans are widespread among all the world's peoples and can be found in a thousand different forms.[6]

In France and other countries, one branch of the press is filled with advertisements for good luck medals, beneficial crosses, and so forth. In August 2000, a particular magazine offering a significant coverage of talismans could be readily purchased at any French newspaper kiosk. Among other things, this magazine provided information on how to manufacture and wear them, and what their effects would be. The magazine provided the following definition:

> The talisman is both a receiver and emitter of beneficial waves and fluids, and an insulator against evil waves. It can only work for a good purpose, and only serves good actions and never helps evil deeds. Its action is the result of a combination of letters, drawings, and beneficial phrases specific to a particular domain. It is the graphic figure symbolizing your wish or desire.[7]

Next, the magazine points out that it is necessary to wear the talisman (which seems to be stating the obvious), and that it is strictly personal and can never be given away or loaned (a claim which, as we shall see, casually contradicts all the ancient beliefs). In short, one should follow the manufacturing instructions indicated by using the illustrated figures.

> On a piece of white paper, or preferably parchment (?), draw a circle a dozen centimeters in diameter in black China ink. This circle marks out the sacred space of your wish. Copy, following the example below, the magic phrase inside it and draw the seal of Solomon [two inverted triangles]. Inside the star, draw the design corresponding to your wish.[8]

These instructions, which are devoid of scientific or magical value, are a patchwork of various esoteric doctrines, but they are interesting because they give us a glimpse of what has become of ancient beliefs that continuously adapted in accordance with the evolution of both the popular mind as well as science. There are also lavishly titled books on the market that are extremely revealing about the way in which the gullibility of our contemporaries—who, in this regard, differ little from their predecessors—can be exploited.

In order to retrace the history of amulets and talismans in the Middle Ages, it is necessary to go back much earlier and consider the earliest evidence. Prehistoric men wore amulets around their necks, such as the one found on a corpse (who was given the name Ötzi) in the Alps near the Austro-Italian border: he was wearing a leather pouch around his neck containing various objects. In Neolithic sites from the Bronze Age and Iron Age, fossilized sea urchins have been discovered with holes bored through them for hanging, which is evidence of their use as amulets; as recently as a few decades ago, peasants in the Clermont-Ferrand region could still be seen wearing them as good luck charms. An Arab legend states that, as a form of protection, Eve kept on her person the names that could be used to compel the obedience of demons. Older accounts have come down to us from the East and Middle East. The Persians, Chaldeans, Egyptians, Greeks, and Jews were all eager consumers for such objects.[9] Everyone is familiar with scarabs, knotted strings,[10] *djed* pillars, and the amulets known as the Eye of Horus or Udjat, which offered protection from the evil eye (and which curiously turn up again on the rings worn by sorcerers in the Auvergne region of France).[11] It is well known that the Hebrews crafted amulets depicting the figures of the gods or planetary bodies, and magic rings. The latter contained fragments of parchment or papyrus on which sacred letters or verses of the holy scriptures had been written. In Egypt and Chaldea, talismans corresponded to the seven major planetary spirits that ruled the earth and its inhabitants. In both Mesopotamia and Europe, archaeologists have unearthed countless amulets and talismans: seals of all kinds, intaglios, cameos (naturally engraved stones), bracteates, and so forth.[12] When rebuilding Saint Peter's Basilica in Rome, a thin gold band was discovered in the tomb of a woman named Mary, the wife of Honorius. This band bore the names

Michael, Gabriel, Raphael, and Uriel written in Greek letters. A ring bearing the commonly used expression ANANIZAPTA[13] was found in a Milanese tomb. The clergy of Aix-la-Chapelle offered Napoleon the talisman that Charlemagne was wearing around his neck when his tomb was opened in 1166. Seffrid, bishop of Chichester in 1159, owned an episcopal ring set with an Abraxas gem,*[14] which is housed today at Chichester Cathedral, and it is common knowledge that Louis XI's hat was adorned with a host of holy medals intended to protect him from illness and evil spells. Ottoman sovereigns and generals wore talismanic tunics.[15]

Oddly enough, despite the increasing number of scholarly studies about daily life and different mentalities throughout history, here in France the subject of amulets and talismans has been largely left to esotericists and occultists, as well as to charlatans who cultivate no greater understanding but instead provide a captive readership with spiritual pabulum in the form of self-assured claims. This is true not only for the Middle Ages but for subsequent centuries as well. In his excellent overview of seventeenth- and eighteenth-century folk culture, Robert Mandrou, for example, devotes one chapter to the occult sciences and sorcery, but only a single paragraph to the grimoires, which specifically passed down valuable information to us,[16] whereas one of the main studies of magic (Richard Kieckhefer's *Magic in the Middle Ages*) examines amulets and talismans at some length and considers relics as falling into the same category.[17]

Is this neglect of an area of such fruitful inquiry really so surprising? In truth, no, because certain shortsighted individuals swollen with pseudo-knowledge have discredited the subject. With scornful disdain they have banished such topics from scientific research and they accuse the academics who dare to study them of being "backward," "folklorists," or "dreamers"—thereby launching ad hominen attacks in the place of solid arguments. It so happens that those who react this way claim

---

*Abraxas is a divine name that appears in the ancient Greek magical papyri, as well as on such a large number of amulets that it has become synonymous with the latter term.

to be researching and documenting the history of mentalities. Yet one need only glance at what scholars outside France are doing to see that they have fully grasped the value of these subjects, as my bibliography attests.

With regard to the history of mentalities and the daily life of our ancestors, amulets and talismans provide an extremely rich supplemental area of study that is highly revealing about how individuals confronted adversity, misfortune, illness, and death. They are also quite revealing of a certain vision of the world, as well as the hopes and desires of those who lived in it. When all "normal" means have failed, the human being turns to magic and the supernatural. What is frequently revealed can teach us much about the most dreaded afflictions and fears. Do we not still see patients today who, in despair at science's inability to heal them, turn to the ultimate recourse of a pilgrimage or a saint? To not take these elements into account, to remain satisfied with glossing the analyses and commentaries of others, and to treat gestures and representations as if they were entirely disconnected from the irrational is to remain blind to what the documents are saying. Alas, many people do not take the trouble to read the actual documents and simply project their own fantasies upon what they assume they know.

A few words must be said about these documents. For the period from antiquity until the inception of the Holy Roman Empire, the sources are essentially archaeology and the Greek magical papyri, Pliny the Elder's *Natural History*, and the writings of the church fathers. For the Middle Ages up to and including the twelfth century, we have at our disposal the information from the penitentials and clerical texts, along with several texts that fall under the heading of scholarly literature—herbals, lapidaries, and medicinal and pharmaceutical codices. From the beginning of the thirteenth century onward, we have a plethora of texts translated from the Arabic; often these can be traced back to Greco-Egyptian or Chaldean traditions. The number of treatises on amulets and talismans gradually grew, and this growth was exponential until the end of the sixteenth century, which could be considered a veritable "golden age of the irrational" if we were to consider it from this angle. Is it a coincidence that the first *History of Dr. Johann Faust* appeared in 1587—a work that symbolically reflects the concerns of a century alarmed by its audacities and gnawed at by its contradictions, committed to the future but still dependent on its past?

Medieval Westerners were familiar with all kinds of amulets and talismans. Our knowledge of them essentially comes from clerical literature, treatises on natural history (herbals, lapidaries) and medicine, inventories, and finally regulations.[18] In 1263, the statutes of the religious hospital of Troyes stated that no nun could wear rings or precious stones unless she was sick. In 1380, Charles V owned a "small box inside of which hung a small gold chain in two pieces that was effective against venom: suspended from one chain was a small black snake's head called *lapis Albazahan,* and from the other a small square white knucklebone." Jean de Roye reports that at the time of the execution of the constable of Saint-Pol in 1475, the condemned man turned to one of the attending monks and said, "Good father, see this stone that I have long worn at my throat and deeply loved for its great virtues. It protects against all venom and spares one from all pestilence."

The inventories of the nobility frequently mention talismanic objects. Charles V's inventory mentions "a stone, set in gold that cures gout. A king is carved on one side and Hebrew letters on the other." The inventory of the Duke of Burgundy, dated 1414, describes a tar-coated cup with "a unicorn and other things good against poison" on the bottom. The inventory of the Duke of Berry, drawn up in 1416, includes "a gilded stone, called *banzac,* for protecting against venom, hanging from three tiny gold chains." The high lords clearly feared being poisoned; in 1483, Charlotte of Savoy owned a bracelet set with stones that were likewise effective against such attacks. But the individuals taking the inventory did not always explain what the protective power of the amulet was. In Charles V's inventory, a gold clasp is mentioned that is adorned with four rubies and four diamonds and is meant to be worn over the chest. It also bore the names of the Three Magi. Relics, too, could serve as amulets—Jeanne d'Evreux wore a silver apple hanging from her belt containing a "small round of unicorn horn carved in the form of a Madonna holding her child, similar to the medallions worn by the Dukes of Burgundy."

In more recent times, documents have also been provided by ethnographical studies. In the seventeenth century, medals of the Great Comet of 1680 were believed to be potent phylacteries. The front of the medal depicts the comet with the date (the year 1680); the reverse side bears the following inscription: "The comet threatens evil things / Place your trust in God / He will do what must be done." Folk tradition maintains that an amber necklace placed around the neck of a child will protect her from convulsions, sore throat, and whooping cough, and the stone called trochite protects her from spells and diseases. Set in gold and worn on the left hand, peridot will drive away demons and ghosts. Up until the beginning of the twentieth century, the shepherds of the Cévennes region believed that variolite pebbles would protect their herds from sheep pox, and they hung small leather pouches of it from their sheep's necks when they took them up to their summer pastures in the mountains. In Italy, as protection against evil spells, people made amulets out of coral depicting a closed hand with the pinky and index fingers extended to form horns. In his 1745 *Essai de médecine pratique pour l'usage des pauvres gens de la campagne* (Essay on Practical Medicine for Poor Country Folk), Vignon, doctor to the Duke of Orleans, was still prescribing "amulets against fevers that can be hung from the neck." It is only a little more than a century ago that Bretons were still hanging starfish over the beds of their children who were beset by "night terrors" (nightmares).

It is obviously impossible today to catalog all the different kinds of talismans and amulets found in the period extending from antiquity into the Middle Ages. To do so would demand a lifetime as, among other things, it would require scrutinizing every medical text that was produced during this span of time. And there exist other difficulties, such as making precise identifications. Pliny, for example, speaks of an amulet that drives away sleep, which can be taken as something to prevent drowsiness. But when he describes another as facilitating teething, is that truly an amulet? Here we are reaching the limits of the definition. And when we examine the texts, we encounter a consistent difficulty time and again: objects referred to as amulets that do not provide protection but instead are supports for magic or give their owner certain advantages.

Paul Sébillot cites several customs that fall into the category of phylacteries, or in other words, protective objects. In the sixteenth century, a spider sealed alive inside a walnut and hung from the neck was said to protect its wearer from fever. In the Renaissance, a piece of wild garlic hung from the neck of the sheep leading the herd allegedly would protect the herd from attack by wolves. To be free from fear, people carried a wolf's tooth or a dried wolf's eye on their person, and to avert evil spells, the people of the Berry region carried a mole bone under their left armpit or placed the head of a stag beetle on their hat string. In Upper Brittany, a rabbit's or hare's foot was good against toothache. In the region around the Creuse River in central France, people placed ladybugs by the throats of their children as a kind of amulet.

Plants have also been utilized for a fair share of these practices. At the beginning of the thirteenth century, Gervase of Tillbury noted that a branch of *agnus castus* placed beneath the pillow would spare the sleeper from fantastic visions. Wearing a gorse flower in Brittany is said to drive brownies away, whereas in the Beauce region, a small ash twig and a piece of elm bark sewn into a vest protects one from the evil spells of witches and sorcerers. In Saintonge, on the morning of Saint John's Day, farmers place a bouquet of walnut leaves around the necks of their sheep to counter the curses of evil spellcasters.

Little by little, the talisman supplanted the place of the amulet in people's minds, for the amulet came to be considered a more primitive or rudimentary form of magic. At the time this book was written, the results of an Internet search turned up 56,700 references to amulets versus 222,000 for talismans! The "talisman" seems to have become the *nec plus ultra* of magical objects, as demonstrated by its incorporation into various areas of literature and art, from the works of Sir Walter Scott to those of the painter Paul Sérusier. "Talisman" was also the name of a boat that plied the waters around 1883, and the name given to a mutual fund launched by a French bank in 2003. One can search in vain for a similar usage of the word "amulet." It is the name for a teenage rock group and an interactive game (Amulet Quest).

This book expands upon and makes more explicit what was presented in my earlier work *The Book of Grimoires*. We shall start by examining the cultural and linguistic aspects of the subject, and then we will study the practical aspects involved in the use of amulets and the crafting of talismans. Many faulty assumptions exist about these unique objects. My purpose is to present amulets and talismans in a new light to reveal their complexity and show how deeply they are anchored in the way we see things.

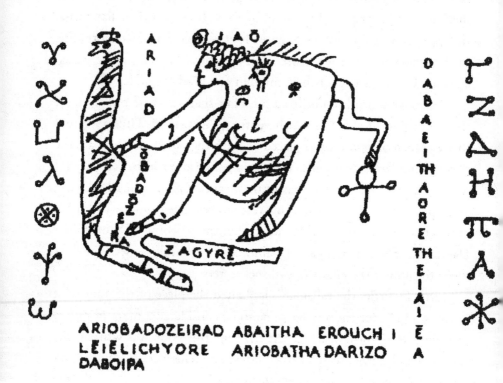

Fig. I.1. A Greek amulet against anxiety and dread.
It guarantees victory, favor, and reputation.

PART ONE

A Scarcely Catholic Tradition

Fig. 1.1. Greek amulets

1

ON THE WORDS "TALISMAN" AND "AMULET" AND SOME DEFINITIONS

If we turn to dictionaries and encyclopedias for the definitions of the words "amulet" and "talisman," we most often find the one word used to describe the other and vice versa, and our thirst for knowledge remains unquenched. If we examine the scholarly studies touching on this subject, we find the same thing. In an 1867 article, Wilhelm Froehner noted:

Greek and Latin alone offer more than forty expressions for designating a talisman. Sometimes it is the shape or material that gives it its name (Latin: *lamina litterata, breve annulus*); sometimes the inscription (its *letters* or *characters*), the way it is worn or carried (Latin: *ligamina, obligamenta, ligaturae, suballigaturae;* Greek: *periapta, periammata, periartémata, katadéseis, katadesmoi*) either on the neck (Latin: *suspensiones colli*) or over the chest (Greek: *kardiophulákion*), or finally its intended purpose (Latin:

servatorium, amolitum = amuletum, amolimentum, praevium;
Greek: *phylaktérion, amuntérion, apotreptikos*), which is to provide defense against an illness or the effects of a charm. The
types of amulets that neutralize the influence of the evil eye are
called *fascine* or *praefiscini* in Latin, and *abáskanta* or *probaská-
nia* in Greek.[1]

Jean Marquès-Rivière makes a distinction between the amulet, a
natural or minimally worked object that is naturally endowed with a
prophylactic virtue; the talisman, which is manufactured; and the pentacle, which is a more evolved form of the talisman.[2]

In 1987, another scholar, David Pingree, suggested an interesting
distinction that is a clear advancement over Froehner's list:

> I define an amulet as a stone of inherent supernatural powers that
> may be engraved and/or consecrated, and that is either used as a
> seal or worn as a phylactery. I differentiate this from a talisman,
> which is an image either made of metal (though sometimes wax, or
> even mud, is used) in the round or engraved on a metal plate, over
> which a ceremony of incantations and suffumigations is performed
> in order to induce a spirit to enter the talisman and to endow it
> with power; if that spirit is one drawn from a celestial body, the
> instructions for forming the talisman and for empowering it . . .
> involve astrological considerations.[3]

On the one hand, this definition is reductive and does not take into
account, for example, plants whose magic virtues result from a strict
and precise harvesting ritual.[4] On the other hand, the support materials
were much more widely varied than Pingree assumes when he reduces
the talisman to a seal and the amulet to a stone.

In 1984, Brian P. Copenhaver suggested that amulets are stones
or other objects attached to or hung from the body that do not contain any sign, word, or image, whereas talismans are "the same class
of objects decorated with artificial marks."[5] This amounts to saying

that amulets work by themselves by virtue of their intrinsic powers, while talismans are the result of a human intervention that, by means of magical operations, invests an object with superior power.

The ethnologist Dominique Camus, whose field work researching magic and witchcraft put him in contact with contemporary talisman and amulet use, provides the definition that comes closest to reality:

> The talisman is a shield imbued with the "force of the cosmic powers" it has harnessed. In addition to the fact that it is, therefore, infinitely more effective than the amulet, it is not solely a protector. By condensing the active "universal forces" through transference, it puts them at the disposal of its owner.[6]

In 1697, Valentin Löscher resolved the matter in his own, simple way: "Amulets are licit; talismans are superstitious and illicit."[7]

With the help of textual accounts, we are going to try to recover the meaning these names held in ancient times.

AMULETS

The first attestation of the Latin word *amuletum* is in the work of Varro (first century BCE). It is derived from the verb *amoliri*, "to drive away, to protect," and designates a phylactery: a portable, personal tutelary object (such as a figure, medal, or seal) that has been attributed with a preventive virtue against illnesses, afflictions, accidents, and evil spells. The word French word *amulette*, which appears in the fourteenth century, was feminine but became a masculine noun the following century (it would not be until 1877 that the Académie française definitively established its grammatical gender). This type of object has many names. Some familiar examples include: the African gris-gris; the relics, scapulars, and medals used by Christians (because sacred relics were also regarded as talismans!); and the ancient Egyptian scarab, a beetle amulet (generally in the form of a ring) that was also known to the medieval West thanks to the Romans. Some amulets are simple good luck charms, while others hold a unique function, such as the "hand of Fatima," which in the Maghreb allegedly provides protection from the evil eye.

Pliny the Elder, the compiler of the largest treatise of information in classical antiquity, a rational and enlightened thinker, fulminated endlessly against the impostures of magicians and the gullibility of his contemporaries. He mentions amulets on several occasions, which allows us to learn that all sorts of objects could be used this way. Less frequently than the word "amulet," he also uses the noun *sphragides*, "seal, tablet," which corresponds to Greek and Oriental tradition and reappears in the Middle Ages at the end of the thirteenth century—a time when the authors of magic and astrology texts spoke regularly of seals (*sigilla*).

In Pliny's *Natural History,* the great scholar uses "amulet" less than ten times and in starkly different contexts, which allows us to discover some of its aspects. Moreover, he cites cyclamen root and basilisk blood as amulets that are supposed to provide protection against evil spells and bats. The large notched horns of scarabs are also a phylactery for Pliny; these are used to protect infants just like amber, which should be placed around their necks. But amber, either ingested or attached, is also a remedy against urine retention, he says, echoing Callistratus.[8] More amazing, according to Pliny, is spit: to spit in one's urine or in one's right shoe before putting it on is an amulet![9] It is readily apparent that the general sense of the concept is not necessarily connected with a manufactured object.

What first emerges from Pliny's account is that the function of amulets is protective, and second, that almost anything can be used to craft one. An amulet is carried on the person, attached to the neck or to a limb, and Pliny almost exclusively uses the verb *adalligare*, "to bind, to attach to," in all its grammatical forms. In the Middle Ages, the verb *gestare*, "to carry," was used. Amulets reflect a medical and magical knowledge that was the property of magicians; this knowledge concerned the hidden virtues of everything that surrounds us. Pliny provides only a single example of pure magic, the use of two Greek letters written on a parchment, without giving us any clue as to what they mean in this context.

Scholars and writers were perfectly familiar with the linguistic heritage of classical antiquity. In the seventeenth century, Jean-Baptiste Thiers provided us with a list of synonyms for the Greek *phylaktérion*: "in Latin, *Phylacterium, periaptum, periamma, Pictatiolum, conservatorium, servatorium, ligatura, amolimentum, amuletum,* or to better put it, *amoletum,* according to Vossos, who derives it from the verb *amolior.*"[10] These are superstitious remedies condemned by the councils and the church fathers. One ties and attaches them "to the neck, the arms, the hands, the feet, the legs, or to several other parts of the bodies of men and beasts, to drive away certain diseases or to avert certain accidents." In 1674, Grimmelshausen tallied up the commonly used terms and provided us with the then-current synonyms for "amulet": *periaptes, fascinas,* and *praeficines.*[11]

Julius Reichelt, whose dissertation was published in 1676, mentions an amulet called "shield of David" (*scutum Davidis*) and takes the opportunity to describe the object as

> anything that is attached to the neck or a part of the body or to clothing, or is placed in certain spots to repel illnesses and strengthen the body, whether in natural and licit fashion or in a superstitious manner.[12]

In 1696, Johann Daniel Schneider shared his thoughts on the subject, comparing pentacles (the word is also written as "pantacle";* its synonyms are "pentagram" and "petalpha"),[13] *periapta* (one of the names for amulets), and amulets. His definition tends to merge the latter two, whereas the pentacle is defined as a kind of talisman:

> **Pentacle:** large medal made of a magnetic base set between two crystals surrounded by a gold or silver setting, or in a circle; famous

---

*Those who spell the word this way claim it derives from the Greek root *pan.*

figures are engraved on the outside. Or else the pentacles are sealed within two pieces of cloth, like an *Agnus Dei*[14] or a scapular, among the common folk. They are carried between the outer garment and the shirt, in the area of the heart.

Periapta: these are buttons, sachets, or medals, pierced from the outside and filled with powders, animals, or a magnetic substance, hung around the neck with a ribbon.

Amulets: they are similar. They are worn at the throat, or on the arm like a bracelet, wrapped in fine linen or taffeta. There are many protective bracelets, for example, those against epilepsy or falling sickness, and which are made from oak mistletoe or the callus from an elk's hoof.[15]

In 1710, Martin Frederick Blumler provided a suitable definition of amulet:

Anything that men attach to their necks or any other part of their body, binding it there in some way, or carry in their clothing to ward off illness, strengthen their constitution, or to acquire something is called an amulet, whether it is made in a licit and natural manner or a superstitious one. In the strict sense the word designates an object covered with letters, images, or figures serving to guarantee its singular effects with the help of celestial forces (*virtute quadam coelesti*). There are painted, carved, and written amulets, amulets claimed to have fallen from the sky or dug up, or discovered by chance. They are old and new, large and small, obscure, made from metals, paper, or stone.[16]

In 1728, the amulet was defined as "any remedy that, by means of a forbidden power, protects from illness or war, and is worn at the throat or on the body." Finally, the meteorites used as amulets were called "Apollo's Drop," "Seeds of the Sun," and "Seeds of the Rainbow."[17]

TALISMANS

"Talisman" comes from the Arabic *tilsam* and designates an object (stone, ring, and so on) bearing sacred signs to which magical properties of protection and power are attributed.[18] The Arabic *tilsam* is itself derived from the Greek *telesma,* which encompasses a wide semantic range. For Clement of Alexandria and Gregory of Nazianzus, it had the meaning of religious ceremony; for the Byzantines, it designated a ghost (*stocheio*); and for Andrew of Crete, it referred to a diabolical work. The verb *télo* means "to bring to an end," and the compound *télétourgia* means "the rite." It therefore appears that the talisman is an object that is sanctified, probably ritually, which invests it with an effective and beneficial magical power. During the Byzantine era, it was believed that such objects were the dwelling place of various demons that had been incorporated into them by a magical ceremony (*téleté*).

In ancient times we also find the terms Abrasax or Abraxas, meaning a stone with all or part of one side engraved with this word in Greek letters, often accompanied by a human figure with a rooster's head and two snakes for legs. Another variant features a human-headed serpent surrounded by rays, which is the decan Chnoubis of the ancient Egyptians. Sometimes the other side is carved with extravagant figures accompanied by names like Sabaoth, Adonai, Ostris (meaning Osiris), or Harpocrates. Analyzed numerologically, the Greek letters of Abraxas equal the sum of 365. According to the Gnostics of the Basilidian sect (second century),[19] this name is that of God, the indescribable and unspeakable father out of whom emanated the 365 spirits (*pneumata*) and kingdoms. Abraxas gradually came to mean those amulets carrying magic symbols intended to reinforce the therapeutic action of a gem. We also find the word Ablagatagalba, which can be read identically right to left or vice versa, and is hence a palindrome.

The talismans *telesmata* were akin to haunted objects (*stoicheioména:* "inhabited by a *stocheio*"), for which there are three categories depending on the intended purpose and the procedure used to induce the *stocheio* to enter. We will consider two of these: the objects that incorporate beneficial demons, for the protection of a city for example, like those constructed by Apollonius of Tyana; and those that are connected to the life of important men, or even families, who perish when the talisman is destroyed. These two types of talismans have long been the stuff of legend.

The inhabited object can be of any size, and it does not necessarily have to be carried on the person. It is simply owned individually or collectively, and it has more extensive properties than the amulet: it makes it possible to defend, to attack, or to produce marvelous effects. The best known example in the Western world is the Palladium,[20] a statue of Pallas that fell from the sky near the tent of Ilus when that hero was building Troy. The Trojans saw its possession as the pledge for the safety of their city. The Romans' palladium was the Ancile, a sacred shield that fell from the sky during the reign of Numa Pompilius (714–671 BCE).[21] Although scholars continue to classify these objects among the talismans of cities, it should be recognized that their magic and protective nature in fact makes them amulets, since no particular preparation for the objects is mentioned.

Another very famous magic object is Solomon's ring, a circular talisman engraved with two equilateral triangles that cross to form a hexagon, in the center of which is carved the name of God. According to Hesychius, Pisistratus placed a bronze grasshopper on the Acropolis as a charm against the evil eye, and numerous stones with engravings of this insect can be found in the collections of major museums.[22]

Talismans must be prepared according to a complicated ritual by the same individual who will make use of them. For Jean Albert Belin, writing in 1658, talismans are astral figures.

> The talisman is nothing other than the seal, the figure, the letter, or the image of the celestial sign, Planet or Constellation, created, engraved, or carved on a sympathetic stone, or on a metal corresponding to the Astral Body, by a worker with his spirit fixed & attached to the work, & at the end of his labor, without being distracted or dissipated by other extraneous thoughts, on the day

Fig. 1.2. Abraxas

Fig. 1.3. Gnostic gem with the decan of Chnoubis

and hour of the Planet, in a fortunate place, when the weather is fine & calm & when it is in the best place in the Heavens so that he may, in order to attract its influences more strongly, for an effect depending on the same power and virtue of its influences.[23]

A little later, Belin adds, "The purpose of the talisman is to attract the influences of the higher bodies for particular effects." In 1679, Jean-Baptiste Thiers defined talismans as "certain figures that are the invention of Arab philosophers. . . . They are made on stones or on sympathetic metals, which respond to certain constellations."[24]

We should keep in mind this definition of talisman as a planetary seal,[25] for it corresponds exactly to what medieval manuscripts tell us in treatises entitled, appropriately enough, *De sigillis* (On Seals). On the other hand, Thiers sees no superstition in the *gamahees* (cameos), the term once used for stones bearing a natural engraving.

In a 1697 dissertation, Johann Sigismund Koblig distinguishes several meanings for the word "talisman":

Talisman has three meanings. For Jewish rabbis and the Arabs, it means a kind of amulet. Next, strictly speaking, it designates the type of amulet manufactured in accordance with the rules of the astrologers who supply it with the energies of the astral bodies. Finally, according to philologists and antiquarians, it designates ancient coins and gems as well as the monuments of antiquity adorned with astrological and magical characters. . . . An amulet inscribed with characters is called a pentacle.[26]

Writing in 1728, an author writing under the name Sperander informs us that the talisman is "a metallic image . . . an item or a particular figure made under certain constellations or aspects of the stars, on stones or metal, that some superstitious people use for all kinds of actions that go against nature, and which they wear around their necks."[27] We should note, incidentally, that during the Middle Ages, "image" (*imago, ymago*) was the most common name for astrological talismans.

Reading these definitions allows us to easily see that the difference between amulet and talisman is not especially pronounced. The amulet is an object possessing natural virtues whose use in the Middle Ages was licit under certain conditions. The talisman is a manufactured object that has been invested with magic powers, thanks to a ritual compelling astral influences to condense within it. "Manufacturing" should be understood here in a broad sense. If the support material was a stone or gem, it was carved or engraved; if it was a piece of metal, it was hammered into a thin strip and inscribed with a spell, figures, or symbols (*characters*). If one chose to use wax, it had to be "virgin" (that is, not permeated with foreign properties that could form an obstacle to the reception of the astral virtues). For parchment and paper, it was necessary to use an appropriate quill and ink. At the end of a fairly complex operation, as we shall see later, the object is capable of having multiple effects. These include inspiring love or hate; causing death or destruction; driving away enemies, animals, demons, or diseases; healing certain afflictions; procuring grace, honors, and consideration; and providing victory in war or in the courtroom.

A talisman can be an amulet, and vice versa; it is a question of its size and use. The same object can be presented as either one. The following example is illustrative: "Carried on one's person, the beak and tongue of the vulture are good for traveling at night," states the *Kyranides,* "as they drive away demons, wild beasts, all serpents, all misfortune, and to sum it all up, they procure every victory, abundance of wealth, and let the one who bears it obtain just causes, glory, and honor."[28] The first part of this description corresponds exactly to the definition of amulet, while the second refers to the talisman.

Christ's Epistle to Abgar, written on parchment and carried on one's person, is an amulet, but if the text is written on the walls of a city (as was the case in Philippi in Macedonia), or if it is fixed to the door-posts of a house, it becomes a talisman in accordance with the opinion of the ancients on the matter. The talisman is, among other things, an incantation, a magic word, a charm set down in writing instead of being recited. Depending on its purpose, the person either carries it or not; it is a personal object that, in order to be effective, should take into account everything concerning the individual for whom it is intended. This explains the important role that the heavenly bodies and astrology play in the crafting of a talisman. It should be prepared based on the configuration of the stars and planets. It can be passed on from one individual to another without losing its powers, notably by means of a wax impression. Talisman is, therefore, another name for a seal (*sigillum*). In the Middle Ages, it was not uncommon for families to maintain possession of an object that was viewed as the guarantor of their well-being and prosperity.

To make it simple, we should remember that the amulet is primarily a protective object, while the talisman, which also offers protection, is an object that creates or furnishes something. In the first case, the important element is the material; in the second, it is the ritual preparation. However, the truth is a bit more subtle here, since the above description, although philologically exact, does not quite correspond to the reality of the facts. And in modern times we can see that "talisman" has come to designate any magical object, as shown by a section in Luzel's *Contes populaires de la Basse-Bretagne* (Folktales of Lower Brittany) that is quite simply titled "Tales of Talismans."[29] And what can we find there? A cap, a staff, a pair of Breton bagpipes, a purse, a napkin, and so forth—all magical objects, which testifies to a semantic shift of the concept.

CHARACTERS

*Characters,** or magical signs and symbols, represent one of the most interesting conceptions in the lesser-known history of medieval beliefs. In his treatise on the Christian doctrine (II, 20), Saint Augustine notes that the power of amulets and phylacteries depends on these symbols.[30] Tertullian maintains that they were inspired by the demon.[31] There are multiple designations for these symbols—we can find *signum, signaculum,* and *figura* all sharing the same meaning—but they should be understood as corresponding to a single category.

Augustine also tells us the name of the "specialist" who crafts them: the Caragi, from the Latin *caraxare,* "to carve, to write." The ancients also called them "Ephesian letters," "unknown barbaric names," and "Solomonic script."[32] It was the obscure nature of the signs and their unintelligibility that brought about the condemnation of *characters* in the Christian world. The church in fact feared they implied a tacit pact with the devil. The Rev. Father François Placet used a pretty phrase: "The demon slithers in the *characters* like the Serpent beneath the flowers."[33]

A capitulary from around 774 defined phylacteries as amulets covered with writing and magical signs, which men wear around their necks, with who-knows-what written words.[34]

A tenth-century manuscript informs us that *characters* are "secret

---

*In order to avoid any confusion, I have italicized the term throughout the book when it refers to magical writing.

letters." Some of these turn up again today in what are called kabbalistic words or esoteric symbols. Others fall under the category of secret alphabets, as magicians often encrypted their texts,[35] while a final group is connected with astral magic and offers symbolic or schematic representations of the planets, constellations, zodiac signs, and decans. And because angels and demons are reputedly connected to each heavenly body, their names are depicted by symbols that also fall under the category of *characters*.[36]

Charlemagne's *Admonitio generalis* of March 23, 789, a prominent edict of ecclesiastic regulations, forbade naming or creating the names of the unknown angels and only tolerated the names of Michael, Gabriel, and Raphael. The eighth-century *Homily on Sacrileges* notes that the figures of angels and Solomon were used, and the collection of sermons known as the *Pseudo-Augustine* (§19) mentions that Solomonic letters (*solomonicae scripturae*) were drawn on charters, parchment, and strips of bronze or other metals. Similarly, Thomas Aquinas made a distinction between *characters,* astronomical images, and *nomina* (unknown and sacred divine names), as opposed to the sign of the cross and relics of the saints, which were the only authorized talismans. He tolerated Christian amulets on the condition that they contained no unknown name, they bore no singular form of writing, and no special procedure (in other words, ritual) was involved in their attachment. He accepted the wearing of Christian symbols such as Christ's "triumphal title" I.N.R.I, or Christ's chi-rho monogram, or even the Greek letters chi–mu–gamma, which signify "Christ born of Mary." He did not object to use of the Alpha and the Omega nor even the word ἰχθύς.

From the fourteenth century on, *characters* were regarded as Hebrew, Samaritan, Arab, and Greek letters, and one famous author, Henry Cornelius Agrippa of Nettesheim (1486–1535), considered to be the greatest occultist of the Renaissance and disparaged by Jean Bodin, who dubbed him "the great doctor of the Diabolical Art,"[37] reproduced alphabets that he called Chaldean, Celestial, Malachim, and Crossing the River (*Transitus Fluvii*), as well as the secret alphabet of Pietro d'Abano.[38] The names can be explained by the fact that it

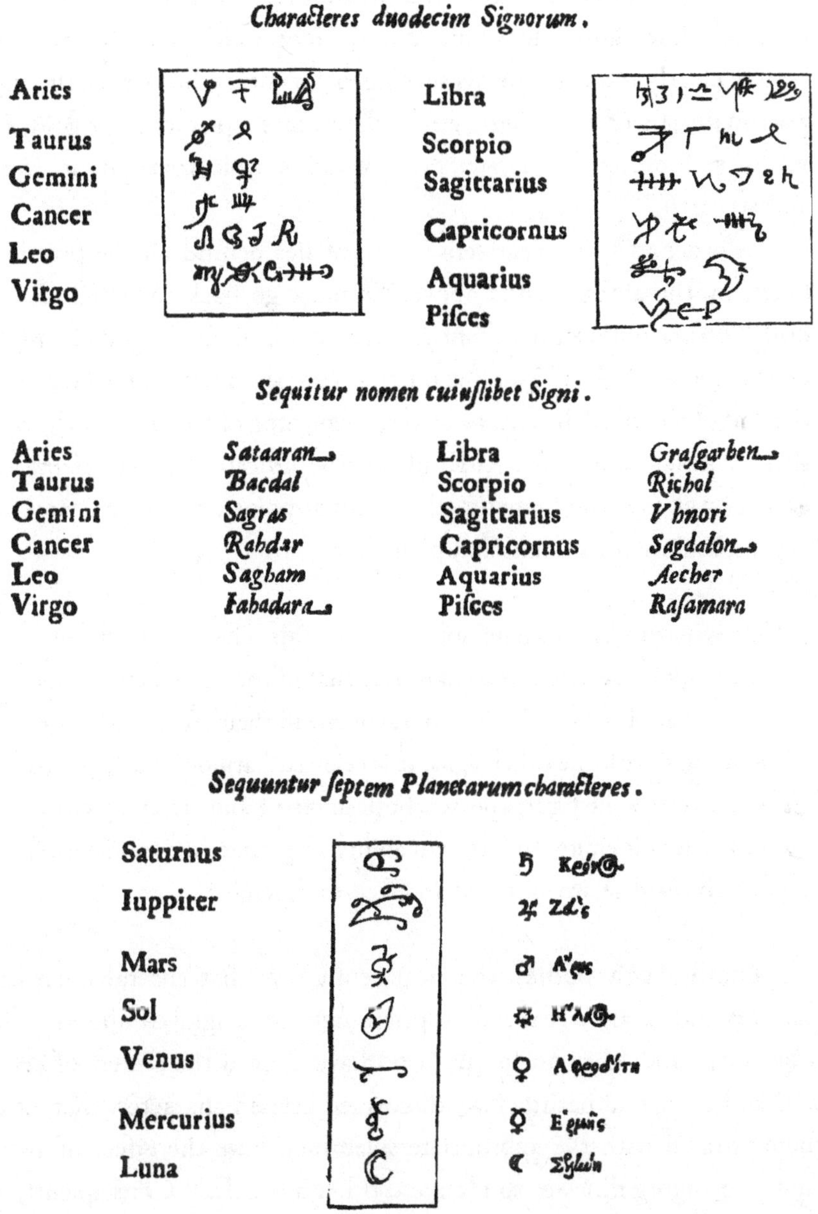

Characteres duodecim Signorum.

Aries		Libra	
Taurus		Scorpio	
Gemini		Sagittarius	
Cancer		Capricornus	
Leo		Aquarius	
Virgo		Pisces	

Sequitur nomen cuiuslibet Signi.

Aries	*Sataaran*	Libra	*Grasgarben*
Taurus	*Bacdal*	Scorpio	*Richol*
Gemini	*Sagras*	Sagittarius	*Vhnori*
Cancer	*Rahdar*	Capricornus	*Sagdalon*
Leo	*Sagham*	Aquarius	*Aecher*
Virgo	*Iahadara*	Pisces	*Rasamara*

Sequuntur septem Planetarum characteres.

Saturnus		♄ *Keiv@*
Iuppiter		♃ *Zd's*
Mars		♂ *A'ρης*
Sol		☼ *H'λι@*
Venus		♀ *A'φροδίτη*
Mercurius		☿ *E'ρμῆς*
Luna		☽ *Σηλωίη*

Fig. 1.4. Coded representations of the signs of the zodiac and the seven planets
(Athanasius Kircher, Œdipus Ægyptiacus)

was Latin translations of Arab or Jewish treatises at the very beginning of the thirteenth century that introduced talismans covered with
unintelligible signs and symbols and Hebrew letters. Jean-Baptiste
Thiers clearly indicates in his seventeenth-century book that the support materials of these signs were "plates, or strips rather, of gold, silver, copper, bronze, steel, iron, brass, wood, marble, jasper, bone, ivory,
and so forth."[39]

In order to get a clear sense of what lies behind all the positions
taken by the authors cited above, we must go back to Al-Kindi (ca.
800–866), a philosopher from the entourage of the Baghdad caliphs
al-Ma'mûn and al-Mu'tasim, who left a treatise translated into Latin (at
the end of the twelfth century or very beginning of the thirteenth) entitled *De radiis* (On Rays). Al-Kindi clearly indicates that the *characters*
exert power over the elements, the cardinal points, the heights and the
depths, and man, animals, and plants.

> Drawn with appropriate solemnity, certain characters reinforce
> the work of Saturn, other characters that of the other planets, and
> some that of the fixed stars. Some concur in their effect with Aries
> and some with the other signs. It is celestial harmony that governs
> the diversity the figures possess both in virtue and effect, by virtue
> of the rays it emits, and its own ability to produce a movement on
> which the diversity of forms and figures depends.[40]

The heavenly bodies, therefore, emit rays that the talisman can
harness and catalyze if the appropriate signs are engraved upon it. The
sages, Al-Kindi goes on to say, "who have pierced the secrets of celestial and elemental nature, have discovered certain characters that, after
being drawn with the appropriate solemnity, have the effect of avert-
ing or bringing illnesses to man and other animals."[41] Consequently, it
should come as no surprise to find numerous medical recipes accompanied by symbols we find incomprehensible today. One last paragraph
from this treatise is worth citing:

As each star and each sign possesses its own name and own characters, which conform to it in virtue and effect, it is necessary, at the beginning of every intentional action, to pronounce the names. If they are in agreement with the star or the sign, they will naturally guide the operation to a successful conclusion.[42]

Words, figures, images, and sacrifices are necessary to obtain and use the power of the astral rays.

The *Liber solis* (Book of the Sun), attributed to Hermes, recommends writing on each planetary image, meaning on each talisman, the *characters* of the planet concerned in the magic working.

In his treatise *De legibus* (On the Laws), William of Auvergne (1180–1249), the bishop of Paris, mentions *characters* and classifies them in the category of idolatry. His treatment is particularly interesting because he draws up a nomenclature of talismans in the first phrase and brings in the notion of the demonic pact.

The idolaters of stars have established four kinds of figures in the planets: the seals, the rings, the *characters,* and the images, which bear no resemblance to the planets. They are symbols or codes for us.

He then goes on to say:

It is thus necessary to destroy the idolatry of characters and figures, stigmata and impressions. We would, therefore, say that the foolishness of certain men and their imbecility [*stultitia quorundam hominum, eaque imbecilitas*] has given them to believe that painted, carved, imprinted, or written figures possess a divine virtue that makes it possible to perform obviously impossible marvels. . . . Such characters and figures do not achieve these amazing working by their natural virtue but thanks to a pact concluded with demons.[43]

Implicit in the background are notions of natural, licit magic and illicit black magic. The latter is illicit because it utilizes elements that do come together under natural circumstances and, in the opinion of the church, are necessarily demonic. William's classification can be seen again in the work of Nicolas Oresme (1325–1382), the bishop of Lisieux, and an intimate of Charles V.[44] The notion of a pact, meanwhile, will be commonly repeated throughout the sixteenth century.

Michael Scot (died 1235), court translator for Frederick the Great and editor of a *Liber introductorius* that earned him the reputation of a magician and a place in Dante's *Inferno,* indicates the primary function of *characters:* they are links. In a long analysis of the hours of the day and night, Scot notes that each corresponds to a particular devotion. We shall leave out the nocturnal hours as they are reserved for demons:

> On the first hour of the day, men pray to God and it is a good thing to bind the tongues by images, characters, and conjurations; on the second hour, prayer is made to God's angels, and it is good to make images, characters, and conjurations for love and harmony.[45]

Scot specifies that it is also appropriate to make each hour attributable to a planet. In Jupiter's hour, for example, images, characters, and conjurations are made for love or for convoking the spirits.[46]

Another man of letters who came to be labeled a magician, Roger Bacon (1214/1215–1292), a professor at the College of Arts in Paris during the 1240s, notes that false astrologers, "desiring the aid of demons, make charms, characters, and sacrifices by following what they are taught by pernicious books, some of which have been written by demons."[47] The books to which he alludes are those that were translated in Spain and gradually spread from there into the rest of Europe. These were treatises on astrology and magic, a list of which we can find in another book by Bacon, *Letter on the*

Secret Works of Art and Nature and On the Invalidity of Magic. In this pamphlet, the scholar presents *characters* as "words composed of figures that serve the function of letters . . . or are made in the image of the stars."[48] Bacon notes, however, that they can be used to treat the sick.

A name was given to the science of *characters* in the fourteenth century. Thaddeus of Parma, a professor in Bologna from 1318 to 1321, called it *altigraphia* and defined it as a necromantic discipline that worked with *characters* and signs.[49] The term turns up again in the writings of Giorgio Anselmi, a professor at the College of Medicine of Bologna in 1448–1449, who specifies that the knowledge and use of *characters* is part of the science of the composition of images (in other words, talismans), which itself has two components: *altigraphia* and *altiphitica.* According to him, *altigraphia* is the art of achieving one's desires by means of the images or impressions of things (in other words, seals), with the help of the super-celestial bodies (*supracoelestium corporum*) and incantations;[50] *altiphitica* is the art through which one attempts to influence the body of an individual or another living being by using ceremonies (*cum ceremoniis*) or the image by itself.

Clerics considered all claims about the efficacy of *characters* as senseless, and in his 1405 work *Tractatus de superstitionibus,* Nicolas de Jauer (or Jawor) noted, "We cannot compel demons to appear, speak, and act with simples, circles, images [talismans], charms, words, characters, figures, signs, and adjurations." Such opinions were diametrically opposed to those of the magicians, who either claimed the opposite or maintained a prudent reserve on the subject. For example, Johannes Trithemius (ca. 1462–1516) declared, "With rings, pentacles, talismans, exorcisms, and conjurations, they say they can summon evil spirits together to appear in a circle, a crystal, or another container, where they will answer all questions directly."[51]

Characters, therefore, form part of a whole that includes many elements—prayers, incantations, and so on—which we shall examine in our analysis of how talismans are manufactured.

LIGATURES AND PHYLACTERIES

In the Latin texts of the Middle Ages, strictly speaking, the most frequent names for ligatures are *ligatura, ligamen, ligamentum, gestamen, suspensio, tutamen, filacterium,* and more rarely *servatorium.* The first three names simply indicate the way a person should wear what is used as an amulet: it can be attached to a part of the body, wrapped around a limb, or suspended to be worn around the neck. *Gestamen* simply means "carried object," and *tutamen* "protection." The word *filacterium,* "phylactery," was coined from the Greek *phulaktérion,* "protector," which likely derives from the verb *phulassó,* "to protect," and therefore denotes a function. It designated a small square box containing strips of parchment on which Bible verses had been inscribed, or else these same strips were carried in the hand or worn on the brow. The protective function of the amulet is confirmed by three terms we find in Greek theological writings: *periammata,* coined from the verb "to protect, to defend," *periapta,* from "to attach around," and *probaskanion,* which literally means "anti-evil spells."

In the Gospel of Matthew (23:5), for example, we find the observation "They make broad their phylacteries," and in Deuteronomy (6:8–9) these words of God are quoted: "And thou shalt bind them for a sign upon thine hand, and they shall be as frontlets between thine eyes; And thou shalt write them upon the posts of thy house and on thy gates." This makes them talismans.

In his *Commentaries,* Saint Jerome rejects this custom as superstitious. He states that this box is called *pictatiola,* which is the diminutive form of *pittacium,* "a piece of leather or parchment," on which the Decalogue is written. He also mentions the superstitious women of his time who had a habit of making small, portable Gospels.[52] For Pope Gregory the Great, *phylakterion* was the name of the Christian amulets made from sacred texts and relics. What we have here overall, then, is a group of very straightforward designations. This would tend to show there was no need for obscure magical-sounding terms in order to make clear what was going on.

It is probably because Saint Augustine used *ligatura* to designate medical amulets, and because *phylacteria* was taken from the Bible and reused by clerics and theologians, that these two terms are ten times more common than the others I have cited. The penitentials also use these two terms as synonyms in a recurring phrase: *diabolica ligatura et phylacteria*. These same texts tell us that the preparers of ligatures are sorcerers or magicians who answer to the name *herbarius*, which basically means "specialists of simples," or else *pharmacus*, which implies knowledge outside of the ordinary.*

BREVETS, BRIEF TEXTS, NOTES, AND LETTERS

The Middle Latin word *brevia*, "brevet" or "brief text," designates a magic formula copied onto parchment or paper. This is carried in a sachet (either by itself or together with other objects, such as relics) that is kept on one's person, or else in an object one uses, such as a sword.[53] It is therefore a kind of amulet. According to Julius Reichelt, the brevets contain crosses, the beginning of the Gospel of John, the name of the Virgin, Jesus, the Trinity, *characters,* and the following phrase:

> He who carries this note shall not die by land nor by water nor by the sword.[54]

Reichelt also describes a brevet against sword strokes, poisoned arrows, and mortal wounds that includes pentacles and kabbalistic signs and is wrapped in red silk and hung around the neck on a purple silk string.[55]

The use of these short magical texts was widespread throughout the Middle Ages, and churchmen considered it a heresy, even long after this period. Johannes of Freiburg considered these brevets to be charters

---

*In ancient Greek, *pharmakos* had the sense of "sorcerer."

covered with *characters*, uncommon names, and the ineffable names of God, and also adorned with the following observation:

> Whosoever carries this brevet on his person shall run no risk.[56]

Brevets, or short magical scripts, were essentially used to protect against illness and the bite of bladed weapons. Over time, this panorama expanded to include firearms. For example, Antonio Guaineri (died ca. 1412), the doctor to Amadeus VIII of Savoy, mentions brevets in his treatise *On the Plague*, when examining and listing means for sparing oneself from this affliction. It is necessary to carry brevets or prayers on one's person (*brevia sive orationes super se portare*), and he places them on the same plane as relics.[57]

During certain time periods, these brevets were also called "letters." This usage of the latter term should not be confused, however, with the extraordinary letters (*epistolae*) that were said to be written by God or a biblical figure. The most famous example is the Himmelsbrief (Heaven's Letter), an amulet against fires, diseases, accidents, and wounds. Another well-known example is Christ's Epistle to Abgar, first used by the Copts. It offers protection against all kinds of danger but was banned in the fifth century by a decree of Pope Gelasius, which did nothing to halt its diffusion. The Inquisitor General Nicholas Eymerich was aware of its existence in 1376.

In 1600, the Cardinal of Sourdis, Archbishop of Bordeaux, declared as excommunicate any priests and clerics who gave out brevets, belts, or notes in which there were herbs, words, or other things condemned by holy decree. This kind of interdiction can be seen earlier in the synodal statutes of Cahors in 1368 and again in those of Sens in 1658, Evreux in 1664, and Agen in 1673. Jean-Baptiste Thiers, the Champrond parish priest, tells us:

> It is clear that this condemnation should be extended to all the notes and brevets, of whatever material they are made: cloth, linen, paper, parchment, bound, attached, hung, rolled, folded, sliced,

cut, alone, or sealed inside feathers, wood, bone, gold, silver, ivory, and so forth.[58]

It is dangerous to carry just anything. Thiers cites the case of a young Avignon man who was possessed by the devil because someone had placed a brevet containing unknown words around his neck.[59] Despite all these warnings, people continued to carry these short texts. "The inhabitants of the Limousin region called it *brivé*," Gaston Vuillier said in 1899. "The *brivé* is the amulet, the talisman. All people have placed their faith in them since the beginning. They are most often today sacred invocations mixed with appeals to the devil, bizarre, incomprehensible words, fragments from old grimoires. Sometimes it simply includes holy phrases, perhaps supplied by a priest."[60] In all likelihood, the custom has still not died out.

The accounts examined here, which span more than a millennium, employ words whose meaning we should know if we truly wish to understand what their authors are saying. And since I am obliged to use them in the course of my study, it is necessary to familiarize the reader with these concepts, which have very precise definitions in the world of magic.

2

AMULETS AND TALISMANS IN MEDIEVAL CULTURE

We have to wonder about the increasing frequency of the church's condemnation of the crafters and wearers of phylacteries and amulets, and the levying of heavier and heavier penalties between the thirteenth and seventeenth centuries. Such a reaction presupposes the existence of a threat. What was it?

While remedies that fall under the category of ligatures and phylacteries turn up sporadically in medical works, pharmacy codices, herbals, and lapidaries, there are other influences that began to make themselves felt around the beginning of the thirteenth century and whose impact we should not underestimate. Through the intervention of the translator schools of Toledo, Montpellier, and Palermo, the medieval West suddenly discovered the Arab and Jewish tradition, which spread rapidly in the form of specialized treatises.

THE MAJOR TREATISES

Arab scholars recycled Greek information—some of which has reached us in highly fragmentary form, notably in the lapidary of the magician

Damigeron—and passed this on, blended together with other remnants. From the earliest years of the thirteenth century, Toledo, an important cultural hub of three cultures, Arab, Jew, and Christian, was famous for its magic schools. Numerous manuscripts, many of which were inventoried by Lynn Thorndike and Pearl Kibre,[1] did not enjoy the good fortune of being published but attest to the popularity at that time of astrology and talismanic magic.

The *Speculum astronomiae* (Mirror of Astronomy), whose attribution to Albertus Magnus is not certain, provides us with a list in chapter 11 of these treatises and the names of their authors:[2] Hermes, Belenus (Jirgis ibn al-ʿAmid), Toz the Greek, Solomon, Mohammed, Raziel, Aristotle, Thebit, and Ptolemy.[3] We will repeatedly come across these names right up to the seventeenth century. Combined with other anonymous works, they form the key elements of a scholarly tradition that spread almost everywhere, and certain treatises are sometimes casually attributed to one or another of these authors. In 1456, Johannes Hartlieb (died 1468), Albert III of Bavaria's personal physician, dedicated his *Puch aller verpoten kunst, ungelaubens und der zaubrey* (Book of All the Forbidden Arts, Superstition, and Sorcery)[4] to Duke Johann of Brandenburg and notes from the outset that "numerous books of black magic exist that teach how to summon demons with plants, stones, and simples, such as the *Kyrammdorn* book [= the *Kyranides*], which teaches us how to assemble herb, stone, fish, and fowl together in an appropriate metal." After mentioning the seven black arts, the best representative of which is necromancy, he cited the most widely known books of his time: *Sigillum Salomonis* (The Seal of Solomon), *Clavicula Salomnis* (The Key of Solomon), the *Jerachia,* and the *Shem Hamphoras.* Hartlieb states that they are filled with magic characters and unknown words that make it possible to ally oneself with the devil. He then goes on to say:

There are many more books on this art, such as those of Thebit, Ptolemy, Leopold the Austrian, Arnold, and all those numerous books on the images, which say how to make a figure at a certain

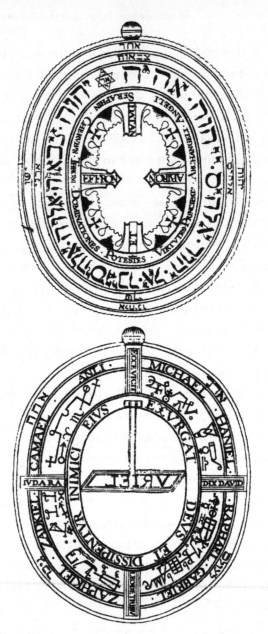

Fig. 2.1. Crystal pendant (Reichelt, Exercitatio de amuletis*). In the outer circle: "Jeschu, Elohenu, Jehova, Echad" (Deuteronomy 6:4); in the second circle: "Adonai, Shadai, Althach, Gibor, Leolam" ("God you are eternally powerful"); the names of the ruling intelligences of the planets can be read in the second circle; in the third, their characters with their planetary domicile; in the fourth, there is a quote from Numbers 10:35; on the strips, another from Revelation 5:5.*

time in conformance to the planets and the stars; figures that then possess a great power for love and grief, victory and happiness. . . . There is one called *De annulis inpensis,* which has been attributed to Arnaldus de Villa Nova and teaches great things. But all these books are filled with disbelief.[5]

Another art is called "Notorious Art": with words, figures, and characters (magical) it teaches you how to acquire all the others. . . . Another book is called *Book of Raziel;* it teaches very surprising things in these arts and presents them as if they involved holy angels for whom one fasts, who must be beseeched, and to whom sacrifices should be made. There is yet another remarkable book on the necromantic art. It begins like this: "For the glory of God and the very glorious Virgin Mary" and is called *Picatrix.* It is the most accomplished book I have ever seen on this art.

We should note incidentally that the *Book of Raziel* discussed by Hartlieb is in fact the *Liber institutionis,* which deals with magic rings, among other things, and that the *Picatrix* is an Arab treatise, *Ghâyat al-hakîm* (The Goal of the Sage), which is a vast compilation of magic spells mistakenly attributed to the mathematician and astronomer Maslama ibn Ahmad al-Majrîtî (died ca. 1005–1008). This book was translated into Castilian around 1256–1258, and then into Latin during the reign of Alfonso X the Wise, king of Castile. It contains orisons for addressing the planetary spirits and their images, and magic rings, and it reproduces a myriad of *characters* and figures.[6] This book had considerable impact, especially among alchemists and occultists of the sixteenth century.

As for Leopold of Austria, he has been attributed with the authorship of the *Compilatio de astrorum scientia* (Compilation of the Knowledge of the Stars),[7] which appeared in 1271. This is a presentation of astrology in ten treatises;[8] the ninth of these, which is largely inspired by the treatise of Thebit ben Corah, is devoted to talismans. In it, Leopold describes crafting methods and the different kinds of talismans: for acquiring or recovering something, making a place a source of good fortune, obtaining honors and the favor of the great, inspiring love or hatred, and driving animals away. He states that the name of the rising sign should be inscribed on the talisman, along with that of its ruler, and that of the ruler of the day and the hour, and the name of the moon (for good purposes on the front of the talisman, and for evil on the reverse side, after which the talisman should be buried).

The two most important Greek authors, who are the source for a plethora of Arabic treatises, are Hermes and Ptolemy, translated into Arabic by Thebit ben Corah (Thâbit ibn Qurra, 835–900), astrologer for the caliph of Baghdad.[9] It so happens that in the twelfth century, an English Benedictine, Adelard of Bath (ca. 1070–1146), translated Thebit's treatise into Latin under the title *Liber prestigiorum Thebidis secundum Ptolemaeum et Hermetem*. A translation of another book by Thebit on seals, *De imaginibus* (On Images), was made by John of Seville and Limia. This text is particularly interesting because it presents seven talismans and the method to craft them.[10] It will be noted that the talismans here are three-dimensional and therefore more like statuettes. To produce them it is necessary to create a mold with the shape one wishes to give to the metal poured into it under a specific astrological configuration. Once this has been done, the talisman is buried in the center of the area where one desires it to have an effect. In this way it is possible to repel scorpions, destroy a town, locate lost or stolen items, succeed in one's undertakings, conquer a city, influence a king, or excite love or enmity between two people. The *Opus imaginum* (Book of Images), mistakenly attributed to Ptolemy, has great resemblance to Thebit's treatise but is organized by decans of the zodiac.[11]

The first traces of Eastern influence can be detected in the work of the German encyclopedist Arnoldus Saxo, who, at the very beginning of the twelfth century, wrote about seals (in other words, engraved stones), and then in the work of Thomas of Cantimpré and Vincent of Beauvais, to mention just two highly influential authors. Scholar Albertus Magnus (died 1280) was interested in talismans and discussed them in his treatises *De mineralibus* (On Minerals) and *Speculum astronomiae*,[12] although it is not entirely certain that he actually authored the latter booklet. More than once, Albertus cites Costa ben Luca, who lived in ninth-century Baghdad and was the author of *Letter to a Son on Incantations and Invocations* and a treatise on medical ligatures.[13] In *De fato* (On Fate), written by Albertus Magnus in 1256, there is a justification of astrological talismanic images based on aphorisms nine and twenty-two from the *Centiloquium*, a collection of "one hundred sayings" that is mistakenly attributed to Ptolemy. The ninth aphorism states, "The figures of this century are subject to the figures of the heavens, and this is why the sages observe the entry of the stars into the celestial figures and then do the working required." The twenty-second aphorism relates that it is necessary to take the positions of the stars into account when putting on or making new clothes. The justification that appears in *De fato* is the following:

> Just as a periodic radiance imprints the placement of the order of the being and its duration in natural things, so does it imprint artificial objects. This is the reason why it is forbidden to manufacture the figures of magical images in accordance with the aspects of the stars.[14]

Between the end of the thirteenth century and the middle of the fourteenth, disputes over astrological images raged in the universities. One name that stands out is that of Peter of Auvergne (died 1304), rector of the University of Paris, who—along with his colleagues—questioned their natural effectiveness and concluded:

> Here is why, if a celestial figure has a determined virtue that acts upon the inferior bodies which are subject to it, and if an image has also been imprinted, it will have the virtue of this figure to some extent.[15]

The *Sefer Raziel* (Book of Raziel) was attributed at the beginning of the thirteenth century to a Jewish scholar, Eleazar of Worms (Eleazar ben Yuda ben Kalonymos, 1176–1238).[16] This book was allegedly transmitted to Noah by the angel Raziel (whose name means "secret of God") at the time when Noah entered the ark. It is particularly important because "there is no question that it supplied to the practical Kabbalah, and to Jewish superstition in general, its richest arsenal of amulets, talismans, propitiatory or healing spells, magical mixtures, and love potions."[17]

The *Libro de las formas & ymagines* (Book of Forms and Images),[18] dedicated to Alfonso X, is a compilation created in Castile around 1276. The only part of the book that survives is the table of contents— but this alone amounts to forty parchment folios! It indicates the ten authors included in the book as well as the number of chapters or sections borrowed from each of them. I will cite a few of them to give an idea of the abundance of the material: Abolays (360 chapters); Timtim the Indian (360) and Pitagoras (360)—no relation to the Greek author Pythagoras!—discussing zodiacal talismans degree by degree; Yluz (36) on decanic talismans; Utarit (7)—who could be Utarid the Babylonian or Utarid the Scribe, who is undoubtedly Hermes—on the planetary spirits;[19] and so forth.

There are two highly important fourteenth-century authors: Arnaldus de Villa Nova (died 1311), alchemist and doctor of Peter III, king of Aragon, and Pietro d'Abano (1250–1316), Italian doctor and alchemist in the service of Pope Honorius IV. They left us texts on astrological and, notably, zodiacal talismans. They indicated how to manufacture them using the map of the heavens, and what powers they held. The manuscripts of these scholars are also beneficial as they feature illustrations of the talismans. It is worth noting the ambiguous status of magicians during this time: they were feared but people turned to them nevertheless. Such was the case with Charles VI. His madness, which was interpreted as the result of an evil spell, drew about a half-dozen magicians to the court between 1393 and 1403. The royal family charged these magicians with the task of breaking the spell. In August 1398, the magician Jean de Bar was arrested and condemned after a hastily expedited trial. In his confession, among other things he declared:

I have several times made and sought to make a pact expressly with the Enemy in order to give him certain things through action and speech, because I offered him two wax images, one white, the other red, and another in copper, all baptized and consecrated with conjurations of the devils and in their names. . . .

Furthermore, in my invocations I used the blood of beasts like the hoopoe, goats, and doves, and from it I made letters and characters, and anointed myself with it just as I anointed some of the images I described earlier.[20]

The word "image" used here could describe either a malefic talisman or a *voult,* which is a wax figurine made in the image of the person one wishes to curse; it is impossible to determine exactly which is meant in the text. As for the use of blood to draw *characters,* this is quite common in magical medicine.

Three major names arise in the fifteenth and sixteenth centuries. First we have Heinrich Cornelius Agrippa of Nettesheim (1486–1533/1534), Charles V's kabbalistic doctor and historiographer, famous for writing *The Occult Philosophy,* published in 1503. This book, which was placed on the index of forbidden works by the church, gave birth to all kinds of legends in which its title was reduced to the *Agrippa.* It was commonly said:

Originally, only priests could own *Agrippas.* Each had his own copy. The day after their ordination, they would find it on their night table on waking, knowing not of whence it came or who brought it. During the great revolution, many priests emigrated. Several of their *Agrippas* fell into the hands of simple churchmen who had learned how to use them at school. These clerics left them in turn to their descendants. This explains the presence of this strange book in some farmhouses.[21]

This book was believed to be dangerous and it was hung by a chain from the strongest ceiling beam in a room reserved for that purpose;

this beam had to be twisted. When placed upright it was the height of a man and its pages were red. Whenever it was not being consulted, it was necessary to keep it closed with a padlock. The *Agrippa* was said to be a living book that hated to be consulted and hid its *characters* until it had been compelled, by beating it, to reveal them.[22]

The next of these important figures is Johann Heidenberg, known as Johannes Trithemius (1462–1516), a Benedictine abbot of Sponheim from 1485 to 1506. In about 1500 he finished writing the *Steganographia,* which is a treatise on secret alphabets,[23] mainly those that appear on talismans and pentacles. With some confidence we can state that he read everything on this subject, and he deserves immense credit for drawing up a list of all the authors who concerned themselves with astrological talismans in a small treatise titled *Antipalus maleficiorum* (I, 3). Here is a quick overview of the works on the list, with their titles translated into English:

The Book of Glamors, by Thebit ben Corah

The Images and the Rings and the Seals of the Dozen Signs (of the Zodiac), by Ptolemy

Book of the Twelve Signs of the Zodiac, attributed by Trithemius to Arnaldus de Villa Nova

Book of the Seals of the Seven Planets, by Balenitz, also known as Abolemiten or Apollo

Book of the Rings of the Seven Planets, by Behencas, in *Figures of the Seven Planets,* by Geber

The Composition of the Images, by Hermes

The Crafting of the Rings According to the Houses of the Moon and *Lucidary of Necromancy,* by Pietro d'Abano

The Book of the Seals the Israelites Made in the Desert, by Zahel[24]

Some of these names belong to well-known astrologers. This is the case with Geber of Seville (Gebir ibn Hayyan), a twelfth-century Arab astronomer, and Thebit ben Corah.

Among the important authors of this pivotal period between the late Middle Ages and the Renaissance, we finally have the father of hermetic medicine, Philippus Aureolus Theophrastus Bombastus von Hohenheim, better known as Paracelsus, professor at the University of Basel from 1526 to 1528, who died by poisoning after what could be described, to say the least, as an eventful life. Paracelsus took an interest in magic and even wrote a treatise on talismans. Magic, he informs us in his *Astronomia magna oder die ganze Philosophia Sagax der großen und kleinen Welt* (Great Astronomy, or the Whole Wise Philosophy of the Great and Little World), includes six kinds. The third kind of magic, *magia caracterialis,* teaches the way to form and pronounce effective words, the science of *characters,* that is, drawn or carved signs that have the same power as the words and protect against vexing events. The fourth kind of magic, *gamaheos,** teaches how to engrave the image of planets and constellations on gems in order to obtain protection against wounds and disease, monsters and demons. These stones also confer the power of invisibility and so forth. Paracelsus gives the following example: "It is a powerful magician who knows how to draw the sign 'Tau,' or other signs, with an eye to forestalling certain events."[25] The fifth kind of magic, *altera in alteram,* is the art of crafting talismanic images and conferring on them the same properties as those of the astral body depicted on them; they then have the power to heal or make sick, to protect or harm. We must keep constantly in mind that for Paracelsus, as for his predecessors, amulets and talismans brought sidereal powers into play.

Paracelsus dedicated several studies to this subject, and his reflections on the natural and licit aspect of talismans warrant our attention:

In pursuing the justification for other modalities of magic, we come to the art related to inscriptions and talismans. This should come as no surprise! Here is the reason: if nature has spontaneously endowed plants and stones with magical virtues, how many more it could make if asked to do so! In fact, we do not find stones,

---

*For Paracelsus, this word meant "cameo."

simples, and similar things everywhere. . . . It is because they are lacking that it is necessary to resort to magic. Nature will therefore confide its forces and words in the same way it grants them to simples and plants, and confides them to images or talismans.

The mage has the ability to enclose numerous plains of heaven in a small stone and call it a talisman, figure, or mark. These objects are like receptacles into which seals and keeps the sidereal forces and virtues.[26]

In the treatise he devotes to remedies,[27] Paracelsus revisits the "heavenly seeds." He borrowed this concept from the ancient Egyptians and Persians, who, he said, "were the first to recognize the power of the firmament and its influence, and they imagined it as a seed that can be buried in the ground or in a stone."[28] Yet the art of magic plants this seed specifically into the stones called cameos (*gamaheu*), a term that, in fact, designates a gem bearing a natural carving.[29] "He who, as a magician, has the intelligence of the celestial power, is capable of imprisoning this sidereal influence into an object. . . . The Egyptians who bore these stones suffered these influences and these diseases. Conversely, stones have likewise existed that spared those who carried them from such illnesses."[30] And Paracelsus offers examples to support his statement:

People have made, in the same manner, cameos depicting arbalests [crossbows] that are beneficial in the art of shooting; people have also carved swords on them with an eye to striking blows and wounding, but it is pointless to go on at length here. The reason why I have come back to this is that mages have prepared stones or other objects, and those who wore them have seen their fevers or other illnesses vanish.[31]

What emerges from the preceding material is that amulets and talismans are objects invested by the force of the stars and that, among these objects, gems hold the most important place, probably because they already each possess virtues sui generis. Another fact that stands out in Paracelsus's explanations is that images, whether in the form of intaglio, drawing, or characters, are essential for the object to be effective. Furthermore, there is a fundamental law involved here: the law of congruency. It is out of the question to carve just any image on just any support material once the stars come into play—this is something we shall see later.

The picture would remain incomplete if we did not mention Marsilio Ficino (1433–1499), whose *De vita coelitus comparanda* (On Obtaining Life from the Heavens) "is presented like a veritable medico-philosophical, astrological book."[32] Ficino devotes chapters 13 through 20 to the talismans whose virtues come from the stars. He knows the "great classics" of the Middle Ages such as *Picatrix,* and it is upon his work, and that of Giovanni Pico della Mirandola (1463–1594),[33] that sixteenth- and seventeenth-century scholars like Reichelt, Wolff, and Apre base their positions on talismans.

I would like to mention a few further individuals who are deserving of our attention.[34] Abraham Gorlaeus (Abraham van Goorle, ca. 1549–1609), an antiquarian and numismatist from Antwerp, states in the beginning of his book *Dactyliotheca* (Catalog of Rings)[35] that rings exist that are used as phylacteries and worn on the fingers to protect their owners from illness and danger; to grant them success in their endeavors; to increase their facility at certain tasks; for gaining the friendship of certain people; for learning secret things; and to produce certain effects that surpass those of nature. We should note that Pope John XXII, with his bull *Super illius specula* (ca. 1326), declared a sentence of "excommunication ipso facto" for those who make such rings, those who have them made, and those who use them.

In the same vein as Gorlaeus's work follows a treatise by Georgius Longus on engraved rings and the rituals to observe (1615), another by Johann Kirchmann on the same subject (1623), and one by Johann Macarius on the Abraxas (1657).[36] Passeri also touches on them in his treatise on the Basilidian gems, published in 1750 in Antonio Francesco Gori's *Thesaurus gemmarum* (Treasury of Gems).[37]

During the fifteenth century in Italy, and then one hundred years later in France and Germany, amulets and talismans enjoyed huge popularity. Scholars compiled and discussed all that their predecessors had written on the subject; one such compendium by Jacob Wolff, for example, amounts to more than seven hundred pages.

Now that I have introduced you to those who were the primary transmitters of the tradition, let us now examine the position of the ecclesiastical authorities on the subject.

THE POSITION OF
THE MEDIEVAL CHURCH

Origen (died 254) was one of the first to testify about the aversion of the early church against all amulets. In his *Homilies on the Book of Job*, he mentions "the evil spells, the protective items, the plates covered in characters" that are snares and delusions of the devil, remnants of idolatry, illusions, and "scandals of the souls."[38] He notes that his contemporaries used ligatures and protective items whenever they suffered any inconvenience, and that they wrote certain *characters* on paper, lead, or tin and bound them to the afflicted part of the body. Eusebius of Caesarea (died ca. 399) mentions parts of the Gospel worn like amulets (*periamma*),[39] and Saint Augustine (354–430) states that wearing phylacteries—objects he labels as "diabolical"—is stupid because they draw their functional power from the signs.[40] He who resists the temptation to turn to these means in the event of illness is a *martyr in lecto*.[41] In the fifth century, Tatian of Mesopotamia spoke of tendons, bones, layers of skin, herbs, and roots that his contemporaries placed in leather pouches to make amulets. Regardless of whether it is Cyril, the patriarch of Jerusalem, Saint Basil, or Saint Gregory of Nazianzus, the accounts are unanimous in their conclusions: a Christian should have nothing to do with amulets and charms. Saint Ambrose dramatically declared in one of his sermons that eternal damnation awaited their makers and their wearers.

Saint John Chrysostom, who lived in Constantinople in the fourth century, was ideally positioned to criticize the wearing of amulets by the inhabitants of a city that was heir to Middle Eastern traditions. He informs us that his contemporaries bore medals of Alexander the Great as talismans, and he mentions the interesting example of a woman whose faith was stronger than the pagan tradition:

> A child fell ill, and its mother refused to place an amulet around its neck. She was considered to be a martyr because she sacrificed her son for her convictions. In fact, even if these amulets are useless and smack more of deceit and glamor, what difference would that make? There were enough people to attempt to persuade her that they were truly effective, but she preferred to see her child dead than to tolerate idolatry . . . because using amulets is idolatrous.[42]

We should note, incidentally, that thick, round, and concave objects were used as amulets up through the seventeenth century. They have been called "Drops of Apollo," "Sperm of the Sun," "Sperm of the the Rainbow," "Rainbow Flowers," and "Asterisks," just like the talismans mentioned earlier.[43]

Scattered throughout Chrysostom's writings are threats like the following: "If someone makes himself culpable, I shall not spare him, if he uses an amulet, a charm, or another sortilege!" He would tolerate only the spiritual weapon: "You are Christian? Then make the sign of the cross and say 'this is the sole weapon, the sole remedy I have, I know no others!'" The bishop of Milan, Saint Ambrose, believed that those who trusted in amulets would be damned.

In the middle of the fourth century, the Synod of Laodicea forbade churchmen to act as mages, wizards, seers, and astrologers or to make amulets, and it recommended that those who wore these protective devices be excluded from the church.[44] The Council of Rome of 494 classified all phylacteries (*phylacteria omnia*) as the art of demons (*daemonum magis arte conscripta sunt*). The same position was taken in 506 at the Synod of Agde, where it was also declared that phylacteries are great obligations of the soul, which relates to the notion of

Fig 2.2. Bronze Greek amulet, Byzantium, third to ninth century, with fishes, Christian symbols, and the magic square accompanied by the letters "I.C." (= Jesus Christ)

a pact with demons (Saint Augustine had earlier said that amulets are a means of communicating with demons). Similar statements turn up again in the twelfth-century collection of canon law known as the *Decretum Gratiani*.[45] In 692, the Council of Constantinople set the punishment for these churchmen as six years of excommunication and condemned repeat offenders to excommunication for life. Some clerics took on a role that made them akin to sorcerers or enchanters, and such persons were a continual target of criticism from the ecclesiastical authorities.

Martin of Braga (died 580) took the same position when he declared that making ligatures amounted to binding the soul.[46] Here it should be kept in mind that the early medieval church viewed amulets as a means that allowed the devil to take a person back into his clutches.

Caesarius of Arles (died 542) provides us with information about the wearing of amulets during his time. Belief in phylacteries was so deeply rooted in the mentality of that period that he was obliged to remind people of their interdiction: "May none hang on his person or that of others, phylacteries, diabolical characters, or any kind of ligature" (*filacteria aut diabolicos caracteres vel aliquas ligaturas*);[47] "flee, enchanters [*praecantores*], like a poison of the devil! Do not hang upon you or yours diabolical phylacteries, characters, amber and herbs, for he who has committed this evil action should have no doubt he has committed a sacrilege!"[48] He ceaselessly warned the faithful against the clerics who gave out such amulets, and went on to say:

> Even if you are told that the phylacteries contain holy things and holy verses, let no one believe it![49]

Christian phylacteries therefore gradually replaced pagan amulets. The Roman "protective bull," for example, a capsule of precious metal containing an amulet—one of them is a thin leaf of silver covered by eighteen lines in Greek accompanied by numbers[50]—that children wore around their necks was a pagan custom. But this phylactery was authorized once relics, pieces of the true cross, and pieces of Bibles replaced its former content and Christian symbols were engraved in the capsule.[51] Christians also wore a pendant (*encolpion*) as an amulet.[52] Hung around the neck, it contained certain pages of the Gospel or of a psalter. It could also be hung in barns and stables. Gradually the cross, holy images, and medals (such as pilgrimage and guardian angel medals) were used as substitutes for pagan amulets, and we can say that the belief had certainly not been eradicated but rather transformed and integrated into the Christian world. Gregory of Nazianzus declared, "Your child has no need of amulets and charms through which the Evil One makes, so to speak, his entrance, depriving God of his glory among enlightened spirits, but give him the Trinity, this great and glorious mystery."[53]

Relics, real or fake, were used as amulets and talismans, but since these are Christian objects recognized by the church, they were licit once their value was recognized; otherwise the inventories of the nobility would never mention them as such. Gregory of Tours (died 594) relates a bit of news that confronts us with the reality of his time. In 580, a man came to the city of Tours "carrying a cross hanging from which were vials of what he claimed was holy oil. He claimed he had come from Spain, and he revealed the relics of the blessed martyrs Vincent the Deacon and Felix the Martyr." The bishop Ragnemod was suspicious and had him thrown in prison. When he inspected the imposter's sack, he found in it "roots of various herbs, the teeth of a mole, and the bones of a mouse, as well as the claws and fat of a bear. Considering that all these things were components for evil spells, he ordered them thrown in the river."[54] Gregory does not say whether the man was selling these alleged relics. Comparative evidence from other texts shows that the items listed are recognizable elements from which it was possible to craft ligatures and amulets. Almost five hundred years later, an account from Rodulfus Glaber, author of five books of *Histories* probably completed at Cluny around 1048,[55] reveals that nothing had changed in this regard. A commoner, who constantly changed his name and address to avoid recognition, secretly exhumed the bones of the recently dead, placed them in different kinds of small cases, and sold them in large quantities to people as relics. He had moved into the Alps under the name of Etienne and was pursuing his regular commerce but was unmasked by the ecclesiastical authorities. Rodulfus adds, "But since then, many folks with common sense failed to see the abomination of this detestable deceit, and it did not prevent the peasant mob from revering in the person of this corrupt peddler the name of a man . . . and to persist in this error."[56] Saint Thomas and other doctors of the church did not oppose the bearing of relics on the condition that no *character* or unknown word was affixed to them.

The Synod of Rouen of 650 forbade the enchantment of bread and herbs to be hid in the trees at crossroads to protect herds from disease or to encourage an epidemic to strike a neighbor's livestock. In 721, the first Roman council held under Gregory II pronounced anathema upon those who used phylacteries (*phylacteriis uses fuerit*), and the Venerable Bede (died 735) spoke of the bishop Cuthbert who "toiled to turn the people away from their mad customs and encourage them to love the joys of heaven." He then provided a glimpse of the aforementioned "mad customs":

> For many profaned the faith which they held by their wicked actions; and some also, in the time of a pestilence, neglecting the mysteries of the faith which they had received, had recourse to the false remedies of idolatry, as if they could have put a stop to the plague sent from God, by incantations, amulets, or any other secrets of the Devil's art.[57]

In 741, Saint Boniface (died 754) in a letter to Pope Zachary deplored the fact that women wore, in pagan fashion, phylacteries and ligatures on their arms and thighs. He noted that they could be easily purchased because they were offered for sale in public.[58] The sovereign pontiff responded that these phylacteries were pernicious and detestable.

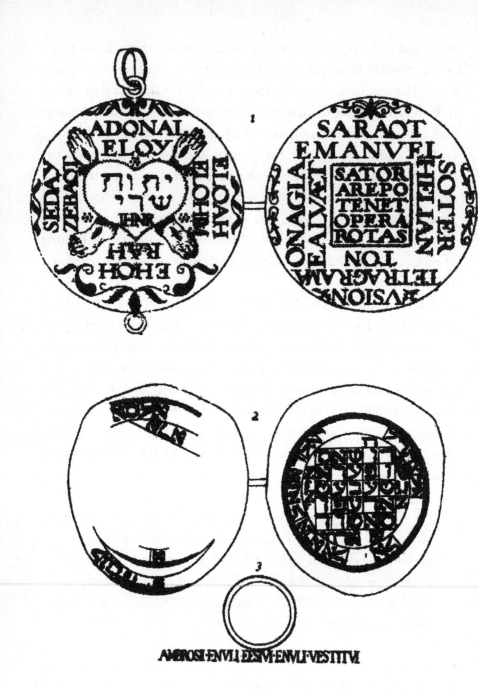

Fig. 2.3. Talismans
(*Reichelt*, Exercitatio de amuletis)

Saint Pirmin (died 753) recommended that one give no credit "to phylacteries or devices of this kind."[59] The *Homily on Sacrileges* fulminates against the wearing of snake tongues and condemns whoever draws "Solomonic characters; writes magic signs on a page of parchment or a strip of copper, iron, lead, or on something that has been consecrated; or writes and hangs them around the necks of men or beasts."[60] In their capitularies, Charlemagne and Louis the Pious forbade both laymen and churchmen the use of phylacteries and ligatures "because they are signs of the magical art" (*quia magicæ artis insignia sunt*), and the *Indiculus superstitionum et paganiarum* (Small Index of Superstitions and Paganism), the table of contents for a lost capitulary from the eighth century, refers to a chapter devoted to them.[61]

In the ninth century, there are lines in the Pseudo-Eligius collection of sermons that deserve a brief mention. Here the faithful are advised not to turn to Caragos or Caraios—a name for amulet crafters taken from Saint Augustine—who speak incantations over herbs (*herbas incantare*), hang pieces of amber from their neck (*succinos ad collum dependere*), or attach ligatures to the necks of men or animals, adding that they should be wary "even if they were made by churchmen claiming they are holy objects and contain sacred words, because these remedies do not come from Jesus Christ but the Devil." In 813, the Third Council of Tours forbade the wearing of dead animal bones and enchanted herbs; commanded priests to warn the faithful that in no way could ligatures heal sick men or animals, the lame, or the dying; and declared that ligatures "are bonds and snares of the ancient enemy" (*esse laqueos et insidias antiquis hostis*), through which the Devil seeks to bring about the perdition of the human race.[62]

We also come across prohibitions in the penitentials, but they all say the same thing and represent a tradition that is scanty in its details.[63] The Penitential of Egbert forbade the wearing of diabolical phylacteries, herbs, and amber, which can also be found in the work of the Pseudo-Bede. The Merseburg Penitential states that it is reprehensible to speak incantations over herbs used to make ligatures, and the Pentitential of Theodore recalls that priests should not make them any more than should laymen. The penance to be performed if this prohibition were transgressed was for two years, one of which was on bread and water. The penitential known as the "Corrector," which Burchard of Worms inserted into his *Decretals,* written between 1008 and 1012, mentions the same actions but also refers to the "diabolical characters" that some are in the habit of drawing, and the penance is ten days on bread and water.[64]

Saint Thomas Aquinas (died 1274) holds a fundamental place in the battle led by the church against amulets, phylacteries, and ligatures. Relying on Augustine of Hippo and John Chrysostom, he literally codified the matter and established the rationale that was then ceaselessly employed until the seventeenth century. According to him, amulets fall into the category of magic and, more specifically, that of the notary art (*ars notaria*), which is illicit. This art uses things that have no natural virtues in themselves to produce supernatural effects, mainly by means of certain *characters* or certain words. These practices are forbidden when the effects expected of them cannot be attributed to God or nature and have not been instituted by the church. According to Thomas Aquinas, whoever uses phylacteries or ligatures is signing a tacit or deliberate pact with the devil, for example by granting particular powers to words from the Bible or the divine office on the condition that they are written in a certain way, on a certain material, at a certain time and hour. Here is a revealing passage from his *Summa theologiæ* (*Secunda secundae,* question 96, article 4) on the sacred phrases hung around the neck:

Objection 1: It would seem that it is not unlawful to wear divine words at the neck. Divine words are no less efficacious when written than when uttered. But it is lawful to utter sacred words for the purpose of producing certain effects (for instance, in order to heal the sick), such as the "Our Father" or the "Hail Mary," or in any way whatever to call on the Lord's name, according to Mark. 16:17–18, "In My name they shall cast out devils, they shall speak with new tongues, they shall take up serpents." Therefore it seems to be lawful to wear sacred words at one's neck, as a remedy for sickness or for any kind of distress.

Objection 2: Further, sacred words are no less efficacious on the human body than on the bodies of serpents and other animals. Now certain incantations are efficacious in checking serpents, or in healing certain other animals: wherefore it is written (Psalms 57:5): "Their madness is according to the likeness of a serpent, like the deaf asp that stoppeth her ears, which will not hear the voice of the charmers, nor of the wizard that charmeth wisely." Therefore it is lawful to wear sacred words as a remedy for men.

Objection 3: Further, God's word is no less holy than the relics of the saints; wherefore Augustine says (Lib. L. Hom. xxvi) that "God's word is of no less account than the Body of Christ." Now it is lawful for one to wear the relics of the saints at one's neck, or to carry them about one in any way for the purpose of self-protection. Therefore it is equally lawful to have recourse to the words of Holy Writ, whether uttered or written, for one's protection.

Objection 4: On the other hand, Chrysostom says (Hom. xliii in Matth.): "Some wear round their necks a passage in writing from the Gospel. Yet is not the Gospel read in church and heard by all every day? How then, if it does a man no good to have the Gospels in his ears, will he find salvation by wearing them round his neck? Moreover, where is the power of the Gospel? In the shapes of the letters or in the understanding of the sense? If in the shapes, you do well to wear them round your neck; if in the understanding, you will then do better to bear them in your heart than to wear them round your neck." I answer that in every incantation or wearing of written words, two points seem to demand caution. The first is the thing said or written, because if it is connected with invocation of the demons it is clearly superstitious and unlawful. In like manner it seems that one should beware lest it contain strange words, for fear that they conceal something unlawful. Hence Chrysostom says that "many now after the example of the Pharisees who enlarged their fringes, invent and write Hebrew names of angels, and fasten them to their persons. Such things seem fearsome to those who do not understand them." Again, one should take care lest it contain anything false, because in that case also the effect could not be ascribed to God, who does not bear witness to a falsehood. In the second place, one should beware lest besides the sacred words it contain something vain, for instance certain written characters, except the sign of the Cross; or if hope be placed in the manner of writing or fastening, or in any like vanity, having no connection with reverence for God, because this would be pronounced superstitious: otherwise, however, it is lawful. Hence it is written in the *Decretals* (XXVI, qu. v, cap. *Non liceat Christianis*): "In blending together medicinal herbs, it is not lawful to make use of observances or incantations, other than the divine symbol, or the Lord's Prayer, so as to give honor to none but God the Creator of all."

Reply to Objection 1: It is indeed lawful to pronounce divine words, or to invoke the divine name, if one do so with a mind to honor God alone, from Whom the result is expected: but it is unlawful if it be done in connection with any vain observance.

Reply to Objection 2: Even in the case of incantations of serpents or any animals whatever, if the mind attends exclusively to the sacred words and to the divine power, it will not be unlawful. Such like incantations, however, often include unlawful observances, and rely on the demons for their result, especially in the case of serpents, because the serpent was the first instrument employed by the devil in order to deceive man. Hence a gloss on the passage quoted says: "Note that Scripture does not commend everything whence it draws its comparisons, as in the case of the unjust judge who scarcely heard the widow's request."

Reply to Objection 3: The same applies to the wearing of relics, for if they be worn out of confidence in God, and in the saints whose relics they are, it will not be unlawful. But if account were taken in this matter of some vain circumstance (for instance that the casket be three-cornered, or the like, having no bearing on the reverence due to God and the saints), it would be superstitious and unlawful.

Reply to Objection 4: Chrysostom is speaking the case in which more attention is paid the written characters than to the understanding of the words.[65]

We know, for example, that men of the Middle Ages wore the beginning of the Gospel of John—*In principio erat verbum*—written on virgin parchment rolled up and sealed with a goose quill on the first Sunday of the year, one hour before sunrise, in the thought that the amulet would make them invulnerable and protect them from a thousand evils. The apotropaic virtues of this Gospel are confirmed by the witch-hunters' manual *Malleus Maleficarum* (Hammer of Witches), in which we can read the following:

> There were also three companions walking along a road, and two of them were struck by lightning. The third was terrified, when he heard voices speaking in the air: "Let us strike him, too." But another voice answered: "We cannot, for today he has heard the words, 'The Word was made Flesh.'" And he understood that he had been saved because he had that day heard Mass, and at the end of the Mass, the Gospel of Saint John.[66]

Saint Thomas forbade the use of certain unknown words to produce a desired effect and the use of figures like those we have seen in pentacles and on a number of objects.

Bernard Gui (1261–1331), a Dominican cleric who was in charge of the Inquisition in Toulouse from January 16, 1307, wrote a manual called the *Pratique de l'inquisition* (Practice of the Inquisition), in which he provides a list of the questions to ask those who are suspected of witchcraft. Some of these articles are relevant to this subject of study. For example, such a person should be interrogated

> About enchantments and conjurations by means of incantations, fruits, plants, ropes, and so on.
>
> What does she know about the healing of illnesses by means of conjurations and incantations?

What does she know about harvesting plants while kneeling and facing the East, and while reciting the Dominical orison?[67]

What is being referred to here concerns preparation of future ligatures, whether accompanied or not by magical words. What Bernard Gui says can be compared to an account condemning "those who wear a chicory root as protection against evil spells, which has been touched with gold or silver, on the day of the Nativity of Saint John the Baptist, shortly before sunrise, which they tore from the ground with an iron tool and much ceremony, after exorcising it with the sword of Judas Maccabeus."[68]

A Middle High German manuscript from 1393 recommends the following:

Those remedies created diabolically are to be avoided. But he who would write the twelve commandments of the faith on the healing plant and the Our Father on a brevet, then place it upon the patient so that God, creator of all things, was honored, does nothing illicit and condemnable as long as none of the lies and forbidden things I've described are included.[69]

Written toward the middle of the fourteenth century, *Das buoch der tugenden* (Book of Virtues) offers a good glimpse of current practices and the way the church looked at them.[70]

Is it a sin to hang good holy words around one's neck against evils, or against misfortunes, or against the Devil?

When a man wishes to wear just any kind of writing on his person, he must keep in mind two things. First he should be careful about what is written on these brevets, because if they are words used to summon the Devil, it would be a magic brevet. Next, he should make sure that no word on the brevet is incomprehensible, so that no illicit meaning is hidden upon it. [71]

He should also make certain that there is nothing in these brevets that is not true. In the contrary case, the brevet will receive none of God's virtue, because God will not be the witness of lies. The man should also make certain that illicit things are not added to the good words of these brevets, like these figures drawn on the brevets of swords that are called characters in Latin, because such figures of circles are odious to God; the only thing that should be there is the cross. Like such circles found today on these brevets, they are forbidden.

It can also happen that the man attaches particular importance to the writing in which he places his trust, as if he believed the brevet would be ineffective if not written in red letters, or else after noon, or in a church, or if it is worn on the right arm and not the left, or around the neck, or on the belt. Everything that may be added that is vain and not appropriate to the reverence owed to God is naught but superstition. When these elements are absent from brevets, good Christians may wear or hang them on their persons.

It should be known here that the brevets written in church and bearing naught but good divine words, are good and holy. But when it is believed that such brevets are ineffective unless they were written while reading the Gospel, or that they have more power if written during the Gospel than if they were not, this is nothing less than an error and a superstition.

Is it a sin to wear a relic around the neck?[72]

When a man wears one on his person or around the neck, and does so with all the faith he has in God and the sacred nature of the object; it is not illicit and therefore authorized. But if he adds magic to it, by saying, for example, that the capsule in which the relic was carried had to be triangular and not round, or other similar things, it is illicit, offends God, and is nothing other than superstition.

On September 19, 1398, the theological college of Paris gathered to correct widespread errors and put the faithful back on the right path.

Tabula III.

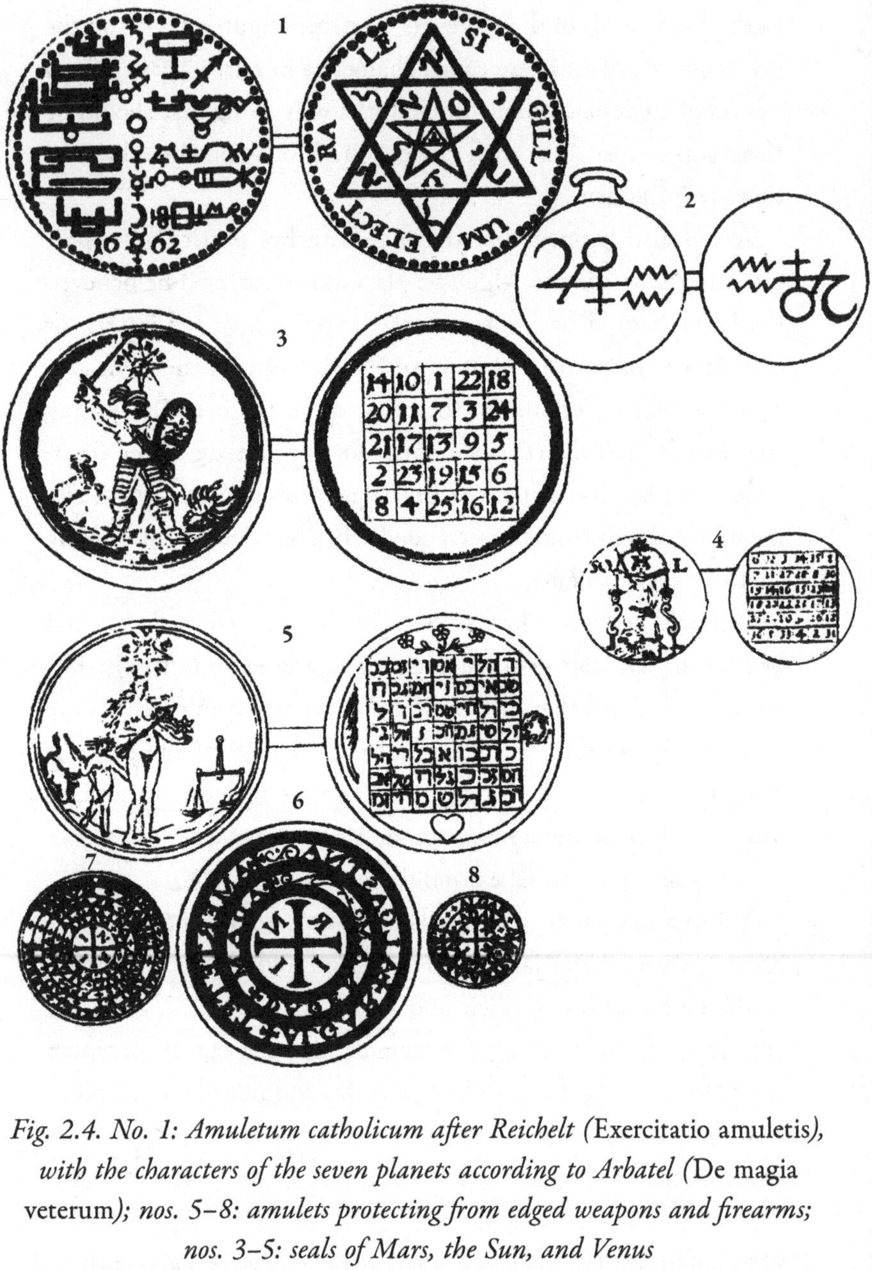

*Fig. 2.4. No. 1: Amuletum catholicum after Reichelt (*Exercitatio amuletis*), with the characters of the seven planets according to Arbatel (*De magia veterum*); nos. 5–8: amulets protecting from edged weapons and firearms; nos. 3–5: seals of Mars, the Sun, and Venus*

Of the twenty-eight articles of protocol, there are three that relate to our subject:

> **Article 19.** To say that the good angels are contained in stones, that they consecrate images and garments, or do things attributed to them by magic, is an error and a blasphemy.
>
> **Article 20.** To say that the blood of a hoopoe, a goat, or some other animal, that virgin parchment, lion hide, and similar things have the power to compel or drive away demons, by means of magic and evil spells, is an error.
>
> **Article 21.** To say that images of brass, lead, gold, white or red wax, or some other material possess the admirable virtues that books of magic attribute to them once they have been baptized, exorcised, and consecrated, or rather conjured, according to the rules of magic and on certain days—is an error in the faith, in the natural philosophy and in the veritable astrology.[73]

The angels mentioned in article 19 are foreign to Christianity. If we take certain lists that have come down to us at face value, their number is immense, and they preside over the days and the hours, as well as over all the moments of life.[74] If their name or their "signature" was inscribed on an object, this allegedly invested the latter with magical power. The same is true for images: the signs and figures that are drawn or carved on them furnish virtues to the support materials—provided that the latter are well chosen, hence the enumeration of various materials, and that they are manufactured at propitious moments, which means based on the alignment of the stars. Article 20 alludes to phylacteries, and "expelling demons" or compelling them reflects an ancient belief that viewed demons as being responsible for every disease.

In the fifteenth century, the preacher and inquisitor Martin von Amberg (1340–1380) indicated that his contemporaries wore amulets (he speaks of phylacteries and ligatures) written on various objects against fevers, pains, and afflictions of men and beasts.[75] Stephan von Landskron (1412–1477), prior of the collegiate chapter of Saint Dorothea in Vienna, states that these amulets are written on apples, laurel, lead, a host, and blessed wax and worn around the neck or on a limb against headaches, toothaches, eye problems, and afflictions of various parts of the body. He mentions the brevets that protect against fire, water, and sword wounds.[76] Since at least the very beginning of the thirteenth century, "sword brevets" (Latin *litterae gladiorum;* Middle High German *swertbrief*) have been widespread. They were placed inside or around the part of the hilt above the guard. Around 1210, the poet Wirnt von Grafenberg alludes to this in his *Wigalois:* "The priest knotted around his sword a brevet that reinforced his courage; it had the property of acting against all spells."[77] Such brevets also possessed the ability to prevent wounds caused by an edged weapon.

Wear this brevet on your person. No sword, no ax, no knife shall bite you.

Examples of these could be collected up until quite recently. Here are two such texts, one dating from 1780 and the second written around 1850, which will illustrate how this sort of thing evolved and distorted over time:[78]

1780

Sole / Mando / Ocsilutas / Saba / Spesis / Sera : habat : Tabenta / Doza / Sanas / Qvadua / Dimas / Pulmonorumfamma / Sciccf – esapas / Crema / Alfuit / Debæmus / Seara / Sierasla volo / Seuruto – Babi / Colubos/ je Nominematris / Silius Spiritus Amen

1850

Sola mande ós sebudt os Sabra Sviris seri gabel labent daslit sansax Qvadur Simuch Gilmorum sounl Ferfipapai levenekol suit beult se are serosta Neilo aabi labulax in Nomine Pateris lehimis Spiritus amelus.

In his treatise on the Ten Commandments, written after 1418, Nicolaus von Dinkelsbühl (1360–1433), rector of the theology college of Vienna in 1405, looks at magical healings in the context of sins against the first commandment. He attacks amulets in particular.

> Sinning against the first commandment are those who wish to heal the sick with incantations, crazy charms, by writing brevets that they hang around their neck, or else that add things that are worthless and possess no natural virtue. They say or write some phrases that none know or understand. Or else they paint characters or write on an apple, a laurel, and claim to help folk this way.[79]

Those who wear amulets are thereby lending to the glory of the devil, he adds, before proceeding to enumerate these superstitious errors.

> Arising from this error or thought . . . the amulets worn around the neck and all these false remedies that one gives folk and are contrary to the doctrine and art of doctors, whether they are administered with charms or characters, whether they are written or other objects are used that are hung or attached.[80]

Nicolaus closely follows the reasoning of his predecessors but adds a singular detail of which I know no other example: "Many people, I've heard say, keep the head of a dead dog at home with which they work, for example by healing the sick, and other illicit things. Of all the follies, this is the worst."[81]

He also responds to the question of Christian amulets, those covered by "good and holy words," which are worn around the neck or "in a purse." His response allows us a glimpse of the context in which a phylactery is created, because in forbidding it, Nicolaus cites what is commonly done. One should never, he says, inscribe any magical sign; only the sign of the cross is authorized. It is illicit to write inside a circle with red or blue ink, before sunrise, beneath a walnut tree, seated in a field. If the cord used to attach the amulet be red or green, or if it was threaded by a virgin, or if the brevet or note be as round as a circle, or if it be a certain length, or made of this material and not another—all this is forbidden. Healing is performed by applying these phylacteries and ligatures (*per applications rerum*). If "phrases" are used (by this he means incantations, as his use of the verb *ansprechen* shows), these should only be those of the Credo and the Paternoster.[82] Found objects should not be used as amulets for foretelling the future—good or bad—he states, echoing Saint Augustine.[83] Every amulet is a sign of complicity with the devil.[84]

The priest Ulrich von Pottenstein (died 1416/1417) completed his exegesis of the Ten Commandments around 1411–1412, and what he says about amulets allows us to see the existence of a veritable ecclesiastical tradition regarding them, with authors copying one another and relying on the treatises of Saint Augustine and Saint Thomas Aquinas, which they annotate and round out by citing the practices of their contemporaries. "Many folk wear notes around their necks," Ulrich says, "that have been written in church during the Gospel: many wear amulets against sword blows so that no weapon shall wound them."[85] It will be noted that the Gospel itself, and especially the Gospel of John, was long considered to be an actual grimoire and has been used that way continuously until quite recently. This is typically done by copying down passages to be carried on one's person as protection against all kinds of mishaps. Ulrich indirectly cites Saint John Chrysostom (the "Golden Mouthed"), who says:

> Some persons wear round their neck some written portion of the Gospel; but is not the Gospel read every day in the church and heard by all? How then shall a man be helped by wearing the Gospel round his neck, when he has reaped no benefit from hearing it with his ears? For in what does the virtue of the Gospel consist—in the characters of its letters, or in the meaning of its words? If in the characters, you do well to hang it round your neck; but if in the meaning, surely it is of more benefit when planted in the heart than when worn round the neck![86]

Like all his contemporary ecclesiastics, Ulrich deplores that "many are those who visit a sorcerer and a magician when they fall ill, who turn to seers or send for enchanters, or hang notes around their necks including figures or signs." The most scandalous thing, however, is that churchmen are involved in such commerce.

> Sometimes, they receive such ligatures from monks or priests, but these are minions of the devil and not monks or priests! My very dear brothers, I urge you to not accept such objects, even if offered to you by monks or priests. They contain no Christian remedy but poison from the devil, because the body will not by healed by this agency and the sword of the devil shall slay the ill-fated soul. You have also been told that these brevets are covered with holy and good words, but no one should believe that they will cure you. And if some people have been cured on some occasions, may it be know that this is due to the ruses of the devil who removes the illness of the body in order to slay the soul.[87]

The stakes are clear, as is the underlying notion that a pact with the devil is involved. This is an idea that the church has repeated nonstop since Saint Augustine.

Ulrich informs us that sorcerers and magicians observe the day when they hang these notes and brevets around the necks of people or animals; he also authorizes only phrases like those from the Credo and the Our Father. These medical practices are "diabolical," as are "the incantation or figure that one writes, hangs around the neck, or attaches." When asked if the wearing of relics is forbidden, he follows the tradition set forth by Thomas Aquinas and John Chrysostom:

> Many people compose and write Hebrew names and attach them to folk. They should not do this! The writing should not include any lie, otherwise one cannot hope to obtain divine aid as God is only a witness to the truth. It is necessary to avoid adding vain

things to the divine word, such as those figures called characters, except for the sign of the cross.[88]

Ulrich then refers to a certain William (Willelmus), who says:

You have not forbidden the brevets on which only the words of the Gospel are written. But if someone believes that they shall have less power if they were written at another time than when they were read at church, I am opposed because that is a superstition. And when one writes singular names, thinking they are the names of God that none dare name, and when figures and characters are drawn on these brevets, and that he who wears them is protected against this or that, then that is charm and incantation. And he who writes these brevets and carries them on his person, gives them, or teaches them to another, if he is ignorant, has an excuse, but if he is aware (of what I am saying) he is not excused.[89]

As for relics, they need never be worn in gold or silver or in a triangular pouch: to give attention to these details is vain and superstitious.

Thomas Ebendorfer von Haselbach (1387–1464), a dean of the theological college in Vienna and canon of Saint Stephen's Cathedral, lists in his sermons those who sin against the first commandment, and among a myriad of superstitions, we find several references to talismans. He declares as anathema those who burn incense for Jupiter or Saturn on the fifth day of the holy time (meaning Thursday for Jupiter's days) and on the nights of Saturday (Saturn's day). This is almost certainly aimed at suffumigations intended to consecrate talismans, as I shall show in the chapter about their manufacture. Later, Thomas mentions "those who seek protection from wounds, thanks to unknown words, or *characters* [italics added], or even sword brevets which they carry on their persons." He tells us that these *characters* are carried on apples or hosts or are steeped in wine that a person drinks to prevent illness.[90] None of this is anything new, to be sure, but these references indicate the spread of the use of amulets and talismans during this time.

In 1445, the acts of the Rouen provincial council cite "those who hang notes and brevets around the necks of men, horses, or other places" and condemn them to a month of fasting in prison.[91] In one of his sermons, the cardinal Nicholas of Cusa (1401–1464) calls idolaters those who carry brevets with *characters* and diabolical and unknown names; those who seek their salvation in these things that the medical doctors condemn are, in fact, making sacrifices to the devil. Nicholas mentions the use of blessed candles and a cross made from a branch to protect from certain evils; offerings placed on an altar; and stones for Saint Stephen or arrows for Saint Sebastian. He authorizes only the wearing of "the Gospels, the Lord's Prayer, and the relics of the saints," provided they are not accompanied by superstitious practices, such as attaching importance to the way they are worn, what they contain, and so forth.[92]

The author of another exegesis on the Ten Commandments dating from 1459 examines the same subject more briefly and simply notes that "those who wear roots or herbs on their persons, or keep them in their homes for good luck and good fortune," go against the first commandment. He adds that people should not turn to unknown saints like Ainpet or Grünolt.[93] The modern editor of this text gives an example of one of the "unknown names" (the *ignota nomina,* to which all the ecclesiastical authors refer): "Brevets should not bear unknown names like ananisapta thedragramaton."[94]

In the beginning of the fifteenth century, Johann Herolt touched on this subject when describing the thirteen kinds of existing magic. According to him, amulets are part of scriptomancy, and he cites a phylactery of his own time: a ring made of three needles found by chance protects from illness. In a short passage, Herolt tells us that time plays an important role in the crafting of amulets.

You should not believe in the short notes in swords or magical brevets. Many folk write them on the day of Ascension, saying they are good words; a man can revere them. But it is believed today that they will be more effective written at this or that time, and rather during the Mass than afterward. This is a superstition. So say I.[95]

The fifteenth century witnessed a veritable outpouring of books by theologians fighting with all their might against the belief in the virtues of amulets. The anonymously authored *Der Spiegel des Sünders* (The Mirror of the Sinner), printed in Augsburg around 1470, for example mentions apples bearing inscriptions—what the French reformer Jean Gerson, who lived earlier in the fifteenth century, calls *pommis inscriptis*—short texts or bones worn around the neck; objects over which a mass has been said; the use of stoles or other objects from the priesthood, the service, or the holy sacraments; and the bearing of *characters* (folio 35a).[96] The book also asks the sinner if he has immersed brevets or coins; thanks to other accounts, we know that objects meant to be used as amulets were plunged into the water of baptisteries. A century later, the notion of the pact with the devil was dominant in all the condemnations levied against sorcerers and magicians who claimed to heal using phylacteries. Examination of the acts of the provincial councils of Milan (1565), Reims, Tours, and Bordeaux (1583) reveal an interesting evolution: there was a gradual transition from sorcerers to laymen and churchmen, as these latter had long been devoted to the incriminating practices.

Jacob Sprenger (died 1496) and Heinrich Kramer (died 1505), who were in charge of the Inquisition in the Rhineland, included amulets and phylacteries in their witch-hunting manual, *Malleus Maleficarum*. Borrowing a definition of enchanters from Isidore of Seville, they tell us:

> As for incantations made on weapons with written words or songs that are carried on the person, it is up to the judges to see if they contain unknown words or these characters and signatures other than the sign of the cross.[97]

Following a consistent position regarding unknown words and brevets that goes back to Thomas Aquinas, the inquisitors command "that no faith be placed in the manner of writing, reading, ligature, or any other detail of this kind." It is licit "to reverently wear the relics of the saints." The same is not the case with "the images called astronomical, whose effectiveness relies on certain written characters that have no effect in the order of natural operations. . . . The objects crafted by astrologers only include a tacit pact by virtue of the symbolic inscriptions and drawings they contain."[98] The preceding declaration is a reference to the crafting of talismans on which are carved the "signatures" of the planets, constellations, or decans, as we shall see in the second part of this book. Numerous other authors repeat exactly the same sentiments, which spares us the necessity of citing them.

In the sixteenth century, almost all the synods and councils deliberated on these beliefs. In 1528, the Provincial Council of Bourges ordered priests to denounce to the bishop or his high vicar those who gathered herbs and those who made or wore *characters*. In 1565, the Council of Milan imposed severe penalties on those making or selling rings or other things for magical use. These are clearly the talismanic rings that we can see in numerous European museums. They are often engraved on the inside or outside, or sometimes on all sides if the band is squared off in form.[99] An April 30, 1611, decree from the court of Aix-en-Provence mentions rings "with inept and crude figures and letters." In 1579, the decrees of Jean-François Bonhomme,[100] the apostolic envoy of the towns of Novare and Como under Gregory XIII, commanded:

None shall use paintings, images, rings, nor orisons written or as spoken ordinarily, brevets on which there are unknown words or characters, to heal the illnesses of men or beasts. None shall remove them by evil spell, charms, or ligatures with certain practices, nor with other strange and foreign medications.[101]

Everywhere the church fulminated with its anathemas, and on account of their recurring frequency, we might ask whether an explosion of magic practices had taken place. Let us consider a statement from the Council of Tours, which was convened in 1583. Here we read, among other things, "There are many people . . . who at great peril to their souls, wear phylacteries or protective charms, rings, brevets, characters, and certain phrases of prayers conceived in unknown terms."[102] The unknown always inspires the church with fear, and this is why these indecipherable words and figures can only be hiding the devil's snares.

In the seventeenth century, Jean-Baptiste Thiers, the priest of Champrond, made reference to amulets and phylacteries on numerous occasions, creating a synthesis of the church's positions on them. He classified the wearing of such objects under the category he called the "observance of sacred things or relics" (*observantia reliquiorum*), in order to produce effects they do not intrinsically possess.

> This would be the wearing of the Gospels, relics, short notes, or brevets, belts and bracelets on which sacred words or Crosses have been written, with the assurance of never dying suddenly nor without confession, by fire or water, to never be wounded in war, to always hold your own in the graces of the Great ones of this world, to obtain health of the soul and that of the body, or some other extraordinary effect.[103]

The range of effects is quite large and confirmed by countless witnesses. For Thiers, the wearing of such objects was sinful for four reasons: first, because it is the result of a pact with the devil; second, if these phylacteries are accompanied by unknown words like Authos, Anostro, Noxio, Bay, Gloy, and Alphen; third, if they are combined with some falsehoods, "like someone wearing the alleged Orison of Pope Leo";[104] and fourth, if magical characters are found on them "written or carved by a certain individual, on a certain day, at a certain time, in a certain way, on a certain paper or parchment, or some other material." The same holds true for reliquaries, which should not be made in a certain way or with a certain figure.[105]

When a person uses this kind of object for his health and that of his animals, we fall into the superstition called the "observance of soundnesses of health" (*observantia sanitatum*). Here Thiers cites synod statutes and provincial council acts spanning the period from 1515 to 1673, anticipating the punishment of "magicians and others who convince themselves or promise others they can by means of ligatures, knots, characters & secret words, dismay the minds of men, and give or heal illnesses."

To eradicate these beliefs and practices, the church offered a number of measures intended to replace them. Those who were ill, cursed, or in distress should double their prayers, make penance, and confess their sins ("which are often the cause of evil spells"), take communion, fast, give alms, practice patience, request the help of holy persons and holy life, and use licit exorcisms, holy water, the Agnus Dei, and the sign of the cross.

> Despite these age-old efforts, the church never managed to extirpate the belief in the powers of amulets, and Thiers has to concede that despite the effort applied by the church & what arms if has implemented to exterminate the Superstitions, this has not prevented them from sinking deep roots into people's minds & they still cause strange disorders today.[106]

If we cast a glance at modern times, we see that mentalities have scarcely changed. Today anyone can easily procure amulets and talismans, sometimes without even having to get up from their living room—the Internet is teeming with specialized websites for such products. These websites often presume an astonishing level of naïveté or gullibility on the part of their customers. The enduring nature of such beliefs can be confounding. As the historian Jacques Le Goff once remarked in an interview, "We never left the Middle Ages."

I am now going to provide examples of the Christianization of these beliefs and cast a little light on the phenomena of substitution.

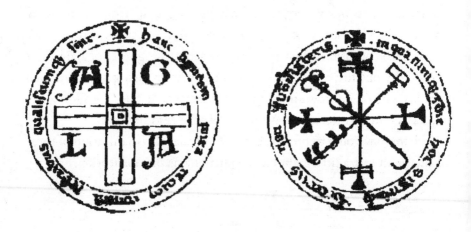

Fig. 3.1. Christian amulets
(clockwise from top left) against eye disease; against thunder and lightning;
against violent death; against fever

3

SOME CHRISTIAN AMULETS AND TALISMANS

It might seem shocking to see the words "amulet" or "talisman" preceded by "Christian," but this would be a display of ignorance concerning earlier mind-sets. The fact is that magic was not always foreign to the Christian world, even if people prefer to describe it in different terms, such as "miracles."[1]

Clement of Alexandria, who lived in the second and third centuries, only accepted certain images as being symbols: the palm branch to represent peace, a boat in sail as a symbol of the church, a dove as a sign of peace, and an anchor as a sign of hope.[2] The fish, which appears frequently on Christian objects, would be later added to this list. In his *De corona militis* (On the Military Garland), Tertullian (died after 220) recommends the cross and indicates that it can be inscribed on doors, clothing, shoes, bathtubs, tables, lamps, beds, and chairs. As an apotropaic symbol, the simple cross or the ansate cross (ankh), and the tau of Ezekiel (9:4) are extremely widespread. In 1658, for example, Dom Jean Albert Belin wrote:

Yes, I would daresay (however using this comparison with respect) that the Son of God has left two divine Talismans for Christians to share, which, charged with the influence of his grace, include every virtue imaginable. Has he not left us the precious figure of his Cross, which was publicly marked with his blood on Calvary on the day dedicated to Venus because he wished to reconcile us with Heaven & establish peace over the entire World, which by itself includes infinitely more virtues than all the Talismans of natures as it drives away Demons, it gives victories, it subjects all the powers to us, it extinguishes fires, it moves the earth, it changes the air, it calms the waters, it stops the lightning, it tames the storms, it causes all to tremble & provides true honors, true greatness & true wealth.

Have we not left in second place the rich nature of his name to achieve through its virtue everything we wish in order to obtain all our requests, to drive away Demons, to crush serpents, to soften the effect of venoms, to heal all kinds of illnesses.[3]

Christian amulets have the exact same therapeutic and prophylactic functions as their pagan counterparts, but they no longer possess strictly magical virtues. They can be found everywhere and I will limit myself to providing a few examples of this amazing variety.[4]

The simplest Christian amulets consist of prayers or the names of God worn on one's person. Here, for example, is the text of an amulet written in runes on a piece of wood that was found in 1870 beneath the floor of the Borgund church in Norway. I will provide a parallel transliteration and translation in order to give a sense of how corrupted the text is.[5]

Messias soþer	Messias Sother
Imanuel sabaoþi aþio	Emanuel sabaot Adonai
nai usion agioss oþan	Usion Agios Athanatos
naþos ælæison	Eleison
alfa æþ o	Alfa et O(mega)

filæhs artifæhas	Filex artifex
deus iesus saluat	Deus jesus salvator
or agios oþonna	Agios Athanatos
þos ælæison aæl	Eleison a Elka (?)
kaagelai agela	Agla Agla

In the seventeenth century, people would write the name of Saint Bernard and swallow it for protection against edged weapons, wounds, and ever being captured: the recipe above ends with the traditional *probatum est* (it has been proved).[6]

In Norway, the Our Father was used as the basis of the following text. This transcription is from a thirteenth-century amulet made from a lead strip on which the prayer was written in runes:[7]

† patær nostær kuiæsinnceliss : s / anktificetur nomen tuum adeveniaþ r / egnum tuum fiaþ uoluntas tua sikuþ inn celo æþ inn terra panem nostrum kotid / ianum da nobis odie æþ dimitte nobis debita nost / ra sikuþ æþ nos dimittimus noss / triss æþ ne nos indukas inn tæntacionæm sæþ li / bera nos a malo amen † Johannes maþ / uss maþþeuss markuss lu(k)ass.

The effigy of the Virgin Mary or the drawing of a cross on a coin or medal provided protection against the evil eye. Women wore "belts of the Virgin" that had been sprinkled with holy water and held relics in the lining, and to be prepared for any danger, pregnant women would also gird on the belt of Saint Marguerite.[8] People would also wear pilgrimage medals, pious images, and so forth. The old antiphon to the Mass of the Holy Cross, *Ecce crucem Domini, fugites partes adversae,* has been found on a copper strip from the beginning of the modern era, and on a magic nail, as well as on a wide variety of amulets.[9] (Attributed at a fairly late date to Anthony of Padua, the church censored this hymn for such uses.) The Church of York used an amulet listing the thirty-eight names of God that ended with "May these names protect me from all the ills of body and soul."[10]

When the Roman Catholic William Jackson was convicted of murder and executed in January 1648 or 1649, in Chichester, it was discovered he wore a linen pouch at his neck containing a note that read:

Sancti tres reges
Gaspar Melchior Balthazar
Orate pro nobis nunc et in hora
Mortis nostræ.

These notes have been touched to the three heads of Their Holinesses the Kings in Cologne. They are for travelers against the misfortunes of the roads, headaches, falling sickness, sorcery, all manner of evil spells, and sudden death.[11]

In the twelfth century this phrase was already in use, mainly by travelers to escape all danger,[12] and against falling sickness (epilepsy) starting in the thirteenth century.[13] It is presumed that the popularity of the Three Magi evolved from the discovery of their relics in Milan in 1158, and after their transfer to Cologne in 1164.

The cross and medal of Saint Benedict were widely used by Christians as amulets and played an important role in the seventeenth century, the time of the great witchcraft trials. Both held protective and healing virtues for men and animals, and they offered protection against enchantments of all kinds. People would even immerse them in the water they used to drink or bathe in. They were worn on the person, attached to animals, attached to objects, hung in dwelling spaces, or buried beneath the threshold of the house. Regarded as an object that nourished superstition, the medal of Saint Benedict was harshly criticized by the clergy, but following repeated requests of the abbot from the Benedictine cloister in Brevnov, Bohemia, Pope Benedict XIV authorized it in 1741. Only the abbot and his successors enjoyed the right of consecrating it. This certainly means they also had the right to make and sell it!

The initial letters of words forming a conjuration were written on the cross and medal:

VRSNSMV   CSSML
SMQLIVB   NDSMD

These stand for the Vade Retro Satana formula:

Vade Retro Satana Nunquam Suade Mihi Vana Crux Sacra Sit Mihi Lux
Sunt Mala Quae Libas Ipse Venena Biba   Non Draco Sit Mihi Dux

The first phrase was etched on the perimeter of the medal; the second as the title of the cross in its four corners, in which can be read C S P B, "Holy Cross of the Patriarch Benedict." On the reverse side of the cross, the twenty-five initial letters of the Benediction of Zechariah can be found.[14]

Fig. 3.2. The medal of Saint Benedict

A Latin pamphlet, banned in 1678 by the Benedictines, tells the legend of this Christian amulet.[15] During the 1647 trial of Bavarian witches in Natternberg, the accused allegedly stated that they were not able to cause harm to the Metten Cloister because the cross of Saint Benedict was hidden there. A search was made and eventually a manuscript was turned up with a gold cover encrusted with precious stones and relics, in which the phrases cited above were found.

A brevet against the plague is worth describing here because it informs us how the number of safeguards invoked for obtaining a powerful object gradually increased. It contains a seraphic Saint Francis (meaning one experiencing an ecstatic vision) and displays a double cross with the initials of the benedictions of Zechariah and Saint Benedict, as well as the names of Saint Roch and Saint Sebastian above the caption *contra pestem* (against the plague), the *Note of the Three Kings,* and the effigies of Saint Anthony of Padua and Saint Ignatius. Beneath is a Latin prayer against demons in which a drawing of the flowers of the common hair moss (*Polytrichum commune*) is inserted, and the effigy of Saint John of Nepomuk above the words "plague leaf" written in German. Next we see Saint Francis Solanus, and the head of Saint Anastasius, placed over the prayer of Saint Agatha and that of Saint James of the Marches. The small arrows of Saint Sebastian can be seen in the center of this short magical text along with the nails of the Holy Cross, coins, a "tongue of Nepomuk," pieces of saints' clothing, the cross of Saint Benedict, the Agnus Dei, palm branches, corn gromwell seeds (*Lithospermum arvense*), a red rag, a triangular note with a Latin prayer, and an image of the Virgin placed on top of it. This is a veritable accumulation of independent methods that, taken separately, protect against plague. The closer we get to the modern era, the more this kind of talisman* resembles a compilation, which tends to show that our ancestors assumed that the effectiveness of these phylacteries depended upon the number of prayers, saints, symbols, and objects that they employed.

We should note that the "tongue of Nepomuk" is a small stone tongue, set in silver, which one wore as protection against gossip and slander, by virtue of the principle of analogy. "Saint Sebastian's arrows" are metal darts that a person wears as protection against plague. Because Sebastian was nicknamed "God's arrow," he was invoked during the great plague of 680 in Italy. As for Saint Roch, he had been turned to for his anti-plague virtues since 1414, and his image was painted or hung on

---

*These are clearly talismans because they have been consecrated.

houses. Legend maintains that Zechariah's relics drove away the plague of 1547, but his Benediction did not begin to spread until 1647.

Starting in the sixteenth century, we find an amulet called the Measure of Christ, which has multiple powers.[16] It circulated in various forms and was accompanied by different depictions of said measure. The oldest known text in our possession is filled with lacunae but is still worth studying:

> It is the measure of the cross of Our Lord iesu crist. It was XLVI times as long as the measure presented here, and whoever wears it out of devotion shall be delivered from all perils and can die from neither evil death nor sudden death. Neither by water, nor by fire, nor by lightning, nor by thunder, nor by famine, nor by evil man, nor by evil woman. Nor by false testimony, nor by the judgment of false judge. Nor can the devil cause him any harm. And if any woman wears it upon her person and writes or has writ this orison that follows below, when she wishes to birth a child she shall not die in childbed.
>
> This measure was brought to Constantinople in a gold cross by the hand of the angel Gabriel to the emperor Charlemagne in order no enemy could lay harm upon him in battle.
>
> † Christus rex venit in pace † Deus homo factus est † Jesus autem transiens per mediorum illorum ibat † Si autem me queritis sinite hos abire † Agios † Agios † Tetragrammaton † Athanatos † [lacuna].

Another measure immediately follows in the manuscript and it also relates its history and virtues.

> It is the measure of the Benedict wound of the cross of Our Lord Jesuchrist which was brought from Constantinople by the noble emperor Charlemagne in a gold chest like a precious reliquary so that none could harm him in battle. And its title said that he or she who sees said measure from afar or wears it

on their person without swearing shall not die a sudden death. Neither by fire . . .

Then comes the orison that should be repeated to activate the talisman along with the following details:

*The man or woman who has fever writes the verses here after following them in order. Nam et si ambulavero in medio umbre mortis non timebo mala; quoniam tu mecum es domine deus meus.**
   This brevet was found by Joseph of Arimathea on the wound of our Lord Jesuchrist in gold letters.

Part of the text bears a strong resemblance to what appears in the *Enchiridion manuale precationum.* This is a grimoire better known as the *Enchiridion of Pope Leo,* which legend claims was offered to Charlemagne, thus situating it in the eighth century. A *Letter,* or more accurately a brevet, runs beneath the name of the great emperor and protects its bearer against all kinds of dangers.[17]

Falling more into the category of a talisman by virtue of its presentation, the Benediction of Zechariah was often combined with that of Saint Benedict. It consists of a succession of eighteen letters and six crosses arranged as follows:

† Z † DIA † BIZ † SAB ZHGF † BFRS

This inscription can be found in German-speaking countries, carved above the doors of houses. The meaning of this enigmatic inscription is known to us thanks to a work by Gelasius de Cilia published in 1709.[18] The inscription contains the initial letters of phrases taken from the Bible, such as

---

*[The Latin text in the brevet basically follows that of Psalms 23:4. It translates to "For though I should walk in the midst of the shadow of death, I will fear no evil, for thou art with me, Lord, my Lord." —*Trans.*]

May the seal of Your house free me. O God, my God, drive off the plague! In your hands, O Lord, I place my spirit. God existed before there were heaven and earth and His power can free me from the plague. It is good to wait in silence for the aid of God so that he may take the plague away from me. I wish my heart to lean toward respecting Your precepts. I see the sinners in peace and the unjust men that annoy me, and I place my hope in You. I am Your savior says the Lord. The abyss calls the abyss, and Your voice has expelled the demons. Free me from this plague! Blessed are those who place their hope in the Lord! May I be filled with the zeal of God before I die! May my tongue cleave to my palate if I do not laud You. Darkness covered the entire earth at your death. Blessed is he who seeks not vanities! The Lord is my refuge, look at me, Lord, my God Adonai! You are my hope, heal me and I shall be healed!

A series of amulets known as Egerland (Switzerland) amulets offer a fairly good synthesis of what Christians wore as protection against all manner of things. Waldemar Deonna studied the one in the Geneva Museum, which dates from the eighth century and provides protection against evil spirits and attacks from enemies, charms, and the plague. The amulet looks like a pouch with Christ's monogram JHS on one side, surmounted by a cross with a three-branched floweret beneath the H, and on the other side a fiery heart in a hexagon with curved sides and plant motifs.[19] Inside the pouch there is a folded page detached from a breviary, which is wrapped around a copper engraving decorated with spells and figures on both sides. A small piece of cardboard with various small religious objects is glued to the center of the front. This is divided into nine squares arranged in three rows. I will only provide a brief summary here because all the details can be found in Deonna's article. In the first row, from left to right, we have Saint Francis of Assisi with a prayer, the Immaculate Conception of the Virgin with a caption, and Saint Anthony of Padua. These three images allegedly offer protection against demons and diabolical spells. The second row has a copper medal stamped all over with sketches: on the upper left, Saint Hubert before the stag, on the right Saint Florian(?), Saint Ignatius on the lower left, and Saint Francis Xavier to the right. There is also a Saint Benedict medal, a piece of paper folded into a triangle with a spell, and the initial letters of spells on both sides arranged in the shape of a cross.

V

F + E

C

(= Verbum Caro Factum Est)

F

I + N

H

(= Et habitavit in Nobis)

S

S + F

D

(= Sanctus Deus, Sanctus Fortis)

S

M + N

I

(= Sanctus Immortalis, Miserere Nobi)

We find the large Cross of Lorraine, marked with letters refer-ring to prayers or passages from the holy scriptures. For example: EMT = *Ecce Mater tua* ("Behold your Mother"); PIMTCSM = *Pater, in manus tuas comendo spiritum meum* ("Father, into your hands I commend my spirit"); or even CE = *Consommatum est* ("It is completed"). In short, this kind of document gives us an excellent glimpse into what Christian amulets contained. In his 1693 study *Curiosus ameletum scrutator,* Jacob Wolff provided a list of curious amulets. One of them bore a tau with a ribbon, on which was writ-ten DEI TETRAGRAMMATON on one side and EMANUEL ANANIZAPTA DEI on the other.[20]

Another exceptional piece of evidence, known as a *sachet accoucheur* because it helped pregnant women deliver their babies,* is a veritable compilation of Christian phylacteries. Among the most noteworthy elements we find in this linen pouch are a cardboard reliquary; two oval metal medallions; seven rosary beads; a red ribbon representing the Measure of Christ; pieces of virgin wax;[21] a bundle of four vellum manuscripts, and one on paper; and a printed work, also on paper, dating from the beginning of the sixteenth century. It also contains a powerful prayer. This states that all men and women who keep it in their homes shall never be caught by surprise by the Evil One, nor shall fire or storm touch them, and when a woman is having trouble giving birth, she should place this letter on her in devotion and she will be delivered immediately.

We find here an orison in verse that specifies it should be said over wheat bread to be given to a sick individual to heal him.

The documents on parchment are much older. One consists of thirty medallions placed in five horizontal rows of six, with four miniatures (these depict the crucifixion, a Virgin and child, Saint Marguerite emerging from the body of the dragon, and the beheading of the latter), a passion of Saint Marguerite, the list of the phylactery's beneficial powers, the names of God, and a brevet against fevers (the charm of Saint Peter).

The other document contains thirty-six squares representing amulets against the perils of the sea, all mortal danger, nosebleeds, toothache, leukoma, epilepsy, thieves, evil spirits, and snakes. There are others for reconciling with one's master, gaining victory in court, and so on. Finally, there are twelve magic circles; seven should be kept on one's person for protection against enemies, the "dropsy," fevers, demons, perils, lightning, the evil eye, having one's throat slit, and a danger spelled out by what appears to be the first letters of words (p. s. a c. B. t. N. m. r.), while one should be present on a pregnant woman before she gives birth, one includes a prayer and a request for assistance, and one is for procuring eloquence.[22]

---

*[The word *accoucheur* refers to someone who assists with a birth. —*Trans.*]

The phrases in the *sachet accoucheur* are taken from the Old and New Testaments (Gospels of John, Luke, and Matthew). Appeal is made to the seventy-two names of God and to the angels Michael, Gabriel, Uriel, Barachiel, and Tubiel; to the names of God in Hebrew; and to a large number of magical *characters*. Repetitions are frequent, which shows that each text existed independently of the others for a time before they were all collected together.

Passages from the Gospels are used: words on the mounting of a cameo of Charles V, *Iesus autem transiens* (taken from Luke 4:30), and the first verse of the Gospel of John, the beginning of the entire Angelic Salutation (*Ave Maria gratia plena Dominus tecum*) or in abbreviation (AVE M), followed by HIS, sometimes distorted into IPS, and W. We also find the charm of Saint Agatha reduced to its core phrase on rings and even bells:

> ✠ MENTEM ✠ SANTAM ✠ SPONTANEUM ✠
> HONOREM ✠ DEO ✠ PATRIA ✠ LIBER

Occasionally only the initial letters of the words are present.[23]

Relics have also been used as phylacteries, and an impressive multitude of reliquaries in the form of jewelry are displayed in the collections of European museums. Reproductions can be found in the copiously illustrated book by Liselotte Hansmann and Lenz Kriss-Rettenbeck.[24] Joan Evans has discovered others listed in wills and inventories; for example, she cites Elizabeth Fitzhugh, who in 1427 left her son a ring with a relic of Saint Peter's finger, and the Countess Philippa of March (died 1381), who left a bequest of a gold ring in which a piece of the true cross had been set. On the ring was written *In nomine patris et Filii et Spiritus sancti. Amen.* Pope Gregory I even sent Theodelinde, queen of the Lombards, a fragment of the holy cross and a gospel in a tube to be used as a phylactery for her son.

Among the phrases we find that are quite comprehensible and derive from the holy scriptures, the following are perhaps the most common:

Christus vincit † *Christus regnat* † *Christus imperat*[25]

Christus natus est † *Christus passus est* † *Christus crucifixus est* †
Christus lancea perforates est

Vincit leo de tribu Juda, radix Dauit, alleluia[26]

The above phrases are the ones found most frequently on countless seals, medals, rings, and tokens.

Sacred names play a very important role in Christian amulets and talismans. It is well known that works of medieval magic and medicine offer lists of seventy-two names for God, although the lists can vary.[27] Among these names, the most important is "agla."

There are a few possibilities for what this name likely represents. These four letters may stand for four Hebrew words—*aieth, gadol, leolam, Adonai*, or *Atlah Gabor Leolam Adonay*—which form a phrase meaning "You shall rule for eternity, Lord." This phrase appears in a Jewish prayer, the Shemoneh Esreh. On the other hand, agla could also be a distortion of the Greek *hagios* ("sacred, holy").[28] Like many magical words, agla is found in countless spells and is used in the crafting of various phylacteries.

To stop a hemorrhage for example, it is necessary to write *Consummatum est* † *agla*, with one's own blood,[29] something seen again in the charm of Longinus, where it must be written on the hand and accompanied by two crosses: † *agla* †.

Agla is used against fevers in the following manner: One must take three hosts and write on the back and perimeter of the first † *on* † *Jhesus* † *on* † *leo* † *on* † *filius* †; and then † *A* † *g* † *l* † *a* in the middle. On the second, † *on* † *omg* † *on* † *aries* † *on* † *agnus* † should be written, and on its center † *te* † *tra* † *gra* † *ma* † *ton* †. Written on the third should be † *on* † *pater* † *on* † *gloria* † *on* † *mundus*, with *Jhesus nazarenus* † *crucifixus* † *Rex* † *judeorum* † *sit medicina mea* on the back. The grimoire also recommends, "You will recite five Our Fathers and five Ave Marias every day."[30]

A fifteenth-century manuscript includes the following magical prescription against poisoning.

For whomever is poisoned. Write the following words on three virgin parchment sheets and swallow them; one in the morning, one at noon, and one in the evening. And if someone has sought to poison you, the poison will leave immediately, it will be healed. Here are the words:

† *Agla* ††† *effrecga* ††† *agla* † *refoa* †††[31]

For a difficult birth, agla appears in the charm of Saint Susan, combined with a very common phrase:

Christus vincit † *Christus regnat* † *Christus imperat* † *a* † *g* † *l* † *a* † *Amen.*[32]

The aforementioned *sachet accoucheur* from Upper Auvergne, which was discovered in 1925, includes texts that date partially from the early Middle Ages. The expression turns up there in the following form:

† *a* † *G* † *l a agyos* † *o theos* † *yskyros* † *emanuel* † *omnipotens virtus in terra celum omnipotens olimphi . . .*[33]

In the charm of Saint Job intended to kill worms (in other words, certain illness-causing entities), agla appears in this final phrase:

in nomine Patris alaia agla † *et filij messyas* † *et Spiritus sancti* † *sorchistin* † *Amen.*[34]

Barring some lucky discovery, we may never be able to identify the meaning of the word "sorchistin."

In a seventeenth-century divination ritual cited by Jean-Baptiste Thiers, it is necessary to say "Aglati, Aglata, Calin, Cala" when summoning the angel Uriel.[35] Thiers provides other spells featuring agla such as those offering protection against all kinds of dangers[36] and against weapons.[37]

Tab.V.

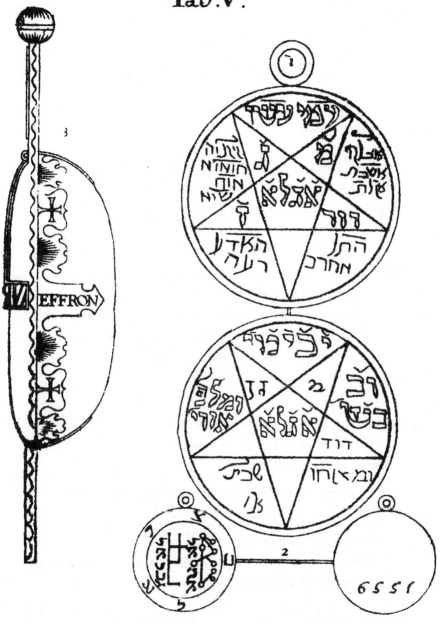

*Fig. 3.3. Amulets. On the right is the famous Shield of David
(Reichelt, Exercitatio de amuletis).*

Agla was used to dull the blade of a sword. After saying the conjuration in the name of the blood of the Lord, it was necessary to say four times

† *pantheon* † *genton* † *Aglay* † *pater noster*[38]

In a Dutch spell against fire, Agla appears in the incantation as one of the names of God:

HELI, HELOIM, SOTHAR, EMANUEL, SABOATH, AGLA
TETRAGRAMMATON, HAGIOS, OTHUOS, ISCHUROS,
ATHANATOS, JEHOVA, ADONAI, SASAY, MESSIAS,

which should be written on the house and sprinkled with holy water.[39]

But the same expression, in somewhat richer form, can be found in the *Thesaurus exorcismorum* (Treasury of Exorcisms) and is used to determine if a person is being tormented by unclean spirits (*vexatur a spiritibus immundis*).[40] The following conjuration can be read in a German manuscript written in Latin from the fourteenth or fifteenth century:

> Take the head of the possessed individual in your left hand and place the thumb of your right hand in his mouth while saying the following words in both his ears:
>
> > *Abremonte abrya, abremonte consacramentaria ypar ypar*
> > *ytumba opote alacent alaphie.*
>
> Then hold it firmly and repeat these conjurations:
> I conjure you, evil spirits, by the terrible name of God Agla and by the very powerful name of God Agla Helen . . .[41]

In another fifteenth-century exorcism ritual, the possessed individual is placed on a cross drawn in chalk in front of the altar and surrounded by magical words (*characters*): Agla, Gaba, Emanuel.[42]

Agla is used against spells and demons. It can be found in the lengthy prophylactic charm *agla* † *ende tetragrammaton* †, the "sacred words" (*heijlich woort*).[43]

To communicate with a spirit, it is summoned and "the sacred words are spoken": *ala drabra ladra dabra rabra afra brara agla et alpha et omega.*[44]

A sixteenth-century charm for exposing a thief made use of this magic word, together with the help of a sieve or a colander and a pair of scissors. The spellcaster directs a triple conjuration at the utensil and to the three figures of the Trinity, then to the Virgin Mary, the patriarchs, prophets, apostles, evangelists, martyrs, confessors, virgins and widows, then finally to the four elements and the four cardinal points. The coercive phrase then comes in: "I command you by the powerful name Agla."[45]

The *Agrippa,* a magic booklet that was once widespread in the French countryside and became the stuff of legend, provides us with an "Exorcism of Aerial Spirits." Here we gain two interesting bits of information. The biblical figure Lot allegedly heard the name *agla,* which thereby saved him and his family (*per nomen Dei Agla quod Loth audivit, et factus salvus cum sua familia*). Agla also serves as one part of the three secret names (*per haec tria nomina secreta Agla, On, Tetragrammaton*).[46] These two details can also be found in the *Grimoire of Pope Honorius,* printed in Rome in 1670.[47] Agla turns up again in the *Agrippa* as part of a ritual for summoning the angels of the four corners of the world. Their names must be inscribed inside a magic circle and then the following spell recited:

O vos omnes, adjuro atque contestor per sedem Adonay, per Agios, Otheos, Ischyros, Athanatos, Paracletus, Alpha et Omega, et per haec tria nomina secreta, Agla, On, Tetragrammaton, quod hodie teneatis adimplere quod cupio.

("I implore you, all of you, and call you by the throne of Adonay, by Agios, Otheos, Ischiros, Athanatos, Paracletus, Alpha and Omega, and by these three secret names, Agla, On, Tetragrammaton, so that you may appear today and perform my will.")

Lastly, the *Agrippa* uses this magic name, deformed into Agia, in a charm intended to protect the flock. A pentacle must be created on virgin parchment, and "AUTHEOS, ANASTROS, NOXIO, BAY, GLOY, APER, AGIA, AGIOS, HISCHIROS" written on it along with an orison, after which a mass must be said over it. Then "the sheep must be rubbed with it, then it should be placed between boards at the exit of the sheepfold, so that the flock crosses over it, then take back said parchment and keep it properly."[48]

The *Enchiridion of Pope Leo,* generally attributed to Pope Leo III, elected to the Holy See in 795, uses agla in a charm intended to ensure a good journey. It opens this way: "Agla, Tetragrammaton, on athanatos, Anasarcon, on, Pantateon, Janua . . ."[49] An orison from this same collection is preceded by the following detail: "and it must be observed that in this is held the name of Christ, which is Agla, which is used to be armored in ice against all adversities, which being seen, so it is said, and carried each day, one cannot die an evil death or suddenly"[50]—thus, despite its lack of eloquence, it is a sacred phylactery! According to the *Grimoire of Pope Honorius,* Agla is also used, along with other sacred names, to expel the demons in hell,[51] to summon Bechet, the demon of Friday,[52] and to cause Lucifer or one of his acolytes to appear "in fine human shape, without any mishaps or ugliness, to answer the true will of all that is asked of him without having the power to harm either my body or my soul."[53]

A very widespread amulet in the West was the Himmelsbrief (Heavenly Letter, or Letter Fallen from Heaven),[54] which among other things promises invulnerability. It is for this reason that many soldiers carried it on their persons up into the twentieth century. According to legend, a stone fell from the sky to Jerusalem or Rome; when opened, it contained a letter from Christ. Another legend tells us that it was found in a column of a Greek monastery. In Romanian traditions, there is even a manuscript that states

And for the prophets, for the martyrs, and for Saint John the Baptist, the one receiving this letter must, even if he is a priest, deacon, or scribe, send it to the East and West, and all their towns and cities, and all his sins shall be forgiven.

And the wrath of God shall withdraw from his house, his sons, and all will be healthy, and no one shall suffer illness again, or blindness, or lameness, or be tormented by unclean spirits.[55]

One of the versions of this Himmelsbrief can still be found in circulation today. It is sold in the bookshop of the Râsca Monastery in Romania.

Finally, there is a famous Christian amulet, the Agnus Dei, which was still in use during the twentieth century. I have an example of one that came down from my great-grandmother. This particular "Lamb of God" looks like a small disk made from the wax of the Easter candle mixed with holy chrism; the image of the Easter lamb standard-bearer can be found on the disk. Such Christian amulets were blessed by the archdeacon and distributed to the faithful on the first *sabbato in albis** of a new pontificate, with the ceremony repeated every seven years. They were carried in a reliquary or a sealed leather pouch. They could also be mounted in crosses and glass capsules, and the important families had goldsmiths put them in settings. Since the sixth century, kings have received an Agnus Dei from the pope and Charlemagne's can be seen in Aix-la-Chapelle. This phylactery offers protection against hail, storm, and illness, and pregnant women hang them from their rosary or bed.

For the sake of thoroughness, I should also mention the amulets intended for animals, although these are often the same as the ones for human beings. As a general rule, they are prayers or fragments of liturgical texts and blessings, which act like Christian charms. The charm of Job, for example, was hung around a horse's neck to protect it from contracting worms.

The mentality underlying the use of Christian amulets predates Christianity itself. It constitutes an interesting form of syncretism that

---

*[On the Catholic calendar, this refers to the first Saturday (or in some countries, Sunday) after Easter. —*Trans*.]

combines the elements of the dominant religion with older structures. The texts casually ignore the clergy's recommendations, as I have shown earlier, and disobey the ban on using incomprehensible words and magical signs (*characters*). One of the best examples of this can be found in a manuscript from the Laurentian Library in Florence. The ninety psalms of David are used for all manner of purposes and contain a large number of secret figures.[56] The seventeenth-century French scholar Jacques Gaffarel fulminates against these uses:

> Let us say, following our discourse, that in the manufacture of these figures all words are irrelevant & only serve to amuse the most simple, such as when Albinus says that to cure tertian and quartan fevers, pains of the nerves, ventricle, & the shameful parts, one must carve the image of the scorpion on gold or silver, when the Sun is in its own house & the Moon in Capricorn, & while carving it, one must say, *Exurge, Domine, Gloria mea: exurge psalterium & cythara; exurgam diluculo* & then recite again the Psalm: *Miserere mei Deus, miserere mei, quia in te fonfidit anima mea.* A thousand superstitions have been born of this, & people have begun seeking to heal illnesses with simple words, without taking into consideration the stars, or any other thing.[57]

It is important not to just single out Christians in this regard. The Jewish method for crafting these is the same and they take from the Hebrew Bible the phrases they carve on their amulets and talismans. We might note, incidentally, that Hebrew letters are considered to be greater in virtue than Roman ones.[58] In 1693, Jacob Wolff emphasized that the words from this language are more eminent, more sacred, and more effective than those from other tongues, and he subsequently remarks that the majority of people wearing these amulets do not understand a word of what is carved upon them.[59]

The Arabs provide us with a very interesting example. The *Ghâyat al-hakîm* cites *The Preserved Book* by a certain Ja'far al-Basri (who is otherwise unknown), in which the Koran is used.* This author divides up the suras (chapters) of the Koran among the seven planets and states that this distribution allows the true name of God to be discovered. Furthermore, the twenty-eight letters of the alphabet represent a perfect individual—in other words, comprised of one body and one soul—because he is equal to the sum of his factors. Fourteen letters appear at the beginning of the suras; the other fourteen that do not appear represent the stations of the moon. Ja'far al-Basri then attributes the suras to the planets in the following way: Taking the first, *al-fâtiha,* with seven verses, he tells us the first falls under the jurisdiction of the Sun and the last under that of Mars; in the 205th, *al-baqara,* the first returns to the Sun and the last one the Moon, and so forth. So it should come as no surprise to find the verses of the Koran on amulets and talismans in the Arab world.[60] The suras 112 to 114 are called the "protectors." A religious literary genre was even developed called "the benefits of the Koran," or even "the singular powers of the Koran," which exploits this text. Constant Hamès cites the 114th sura—which contains the words *djinn,* "genie," and *was-wâs,* "devil"— as an example: "He who recites it every night," writes Shaykh Mâl'aynîn (died 1910), "shall be protected from the djinns and *was-wâs.*"[61]

---

*The passage is missing from the Latin translation of *Picatrix!*

4

THE MEDICINE OF AMULETS AND TALISMANS

Gramine seu malis aegro praestare medellam
Carmine seu potius: namque est res certa saluti
*Carmen ab occultis tribuens miracula verbis.**

MARCELLUS EMPIRICUS OF BORDEAUX[1]

IN ANTIQUITY

The oldest accounts of medicine from classical antiquity inform us that this discipline made wide use of amulets. Alexander of Tralles used them in Caria in the sixth century, and they were prescribed by Archigenes of Apamea during the reign of Emperor Trajan.[2] Thanks to Plutarch, we know that the ailing Pericles hung an amulet around his neck.[3] Pliny

---

*Translation: Whether you wish to heal a patient with a plant or if you prefer to do so with a charm, the salutary method of the cure is the charm that performs wonders through its obscure words.

the Elder tells us that a tick taken from a dog's left ear and attached to an amulet (*adalligatum*) relieves all pains (*Natural History*, XXX, 82). He also claims toothache can be cured by wearing a tooth torn from a living mole (XXX, 19); those who wear a fox tongue on a bracelet will never suffer eye problems (XXVIII, 172); and that magicians recommend wearing a hare's heart before an attack of fever (XXVIII, 229). We have numerous Greek phylacteries, such as one that consists of a small papyrus (approx. 14.5 x 5.5 cm), folded three times widthwise and twelve times lengthwise, and containing a spell that evokes God and the archangels.

Echoing Saint Augustine, the Council of Carthage in 398 noted that medicine reproves and condemns all remedies consisting of enchantments or of certain *characters* belonging to magic, but beliefs that have already been established for centuries cannot be eradicated by a simple canonical decision. *Poimandres,* the first treatise of the *Corpus Hermeticum* and the most important, which has been dated to the second century AD, offers us a glimpse of what was then used against illness. It is an odd blend of exorcisms, charms, and spells.

Angelic hymn for protecting your said servant, given to Moses by God on Mount Sinai while telling him:

Take and bear this hymn and have no fear of diabolical phantoms. May he who possesses this phylactery clearly read in the name of the Son and the Holy Ghost: I conjure you, evil spirits and signs, to leave said servant of God who wears this phylactery, and his children, whatever demon you may be . . . in order you cause no wrong or harm nor approach said servant of God who wears this phylactery, nor his house, nor his vines, nor his lands, nor his livestock. I conjure you to return to the wild mountains and flee there in the name . . . I conjure you, evil spell . . . so that you take fear and be bound far from said servant of God who wears this phylactery, and his house and his children, so that you may take from him all pain and suffering, from his brow, eyes, and mouth, and from his neck, shoulder, arms, chest, intestines, penis, fundament, knees, thighs, legs, and brain . . . and may you dwell in the house of his enemy and may you stop and muzzle his mouth so that he may say nothing against me. . . . Give to God's servant his victory over his visible and invisible enemies.[4]

We can see that the phylactery was intended to produce several effects. It protects and cures by driving the demons of illness and the ill will of men far away, but it is also malefic to the enemies of the wearer. We also see that the amulet's protection extends to all the possessions of its wearer.

Alexander of Tralles also provided some interesting thoughts in his *Therapeutics* about his contemporaries' reactions when they were ill:

But if despite many, varied interventions, the patient remains afflicted with none of the remedies of the art having the capability of putting an end to a rebel illness, it is not at all absurd to resort to natural amulets to save him. It would in fact be impious to neglect something like this and form an obstacle to the [forces] capable of ensuring the patient's salvation; this is why the very holy Galen and his predecessors used them. In his eight-volume book . . . the very wise Didymus wrote: "Many are the things not to be scorned, everything is to be put to work." But as some benefit from natural [remedies] and amulets and request to use them and, in truth, they find success in this manner, I have deemed it appropriate to introduce some points of this matter to my apprentices, so that the doctor will be well-armed on every side for bringing aid to the ill.

As some [patients] are incapable of following a dietary regime with any kind of perseverance or are unable to tolerate the remedies, they oblige us to use natural remedies and amulets against gout so that the best doctor will be well-armed on every side and thereby able to help patients in multiple ways. This is the reason I have presented this point. As these elements that allow us to take action are many in number, by virtue of my long experience I can describe the remedies with which I have experimented.

But as many patients under treatment—the rich in particular—refuse to swallow the smallest amount of medicine or to take an enema to relieve their belly, they oblige us to use natural amulets to soothe their pains.[5]

It is amusing to see that patients prefer magical medicine to possibly unpleasant medications such as purges! Whatever the case may be, the mental attitude of these individuals shows the confidence they had in traditional remedies. This is why all the ancient pagan medical treatises contain thousands of remedies that our modern medical schools would condemn. Many fitting examples can be found in the treatise titled *De medicamentis* (On Medications) by the practitioner Marcellus Empiricus, who lived in Bordeaux around 400; among other things, he mentions a spider placed in virgin parchment that is hung around the patient's neck by a linen thread on a Thursday.[6]

IN THE MIDDLE AGES

Before they became the subject of specialized treatises like the one by Costa ben Luca, phylacteries could often be found in the medical literature. Hildegard von Bingen, for example, provides us a recipe for healing a possessed individual (an epileptic):

If a person is in the power of an evil spirit, another person should place a sapphire on some earth, then sew that earth into a leather sack, and hang it from his neck. He should say, "O you, most wicked spirit, quickly go from this person, just as, in your first fall, the glory of your splendor very quickly fell from you."[7]

What smacks of magic to the theologians is often the remnants of iatromathematics[8] and astrology. Jean Bodin noted in 1580:

Because the Arabs knew the strength of celestial forces on the body, they did not want any doctor accepted if he did not also possess knowledge of Astrology & and those who possessed both arts were called Iatromathematicians in Greece.[9]

In the *Sacred Book of Hermes to Asclepius,* it is said that each sign of the zodiac rules over the part of the body belonging to it and causes an illness in those surrounding it.[10] If one wishes to be spared, one must carve the forms and *characters* of the decans in the stone that belongs to each one and add to it its plant. Once this has been done, one wears it like an amulet and thus has at his "disposal a powerful and auspicious remedy for the body." This treatise gives us the names of the decans and their corresponding stones and plants. For example, for Aries we have the following:

Decan	Body Part	Stone	Plant	Metal
1st	Head	Babylonian	Isophrys	Iron
2nd	Temples, nose	Siderite	Watercress	Gold
3rd	Hearing, glottis, teeth	Bostrochyte	Calf's tongue	Whatever you please

We will revisit this topic.

Anthony of Florence (died 1459) drew up a list of the most widespread superstitions of his time in Italy. He provides information that shows we are dealing with universally held beliefs that touch on magical healing. He asks:

Have you recited incantations or had them recited to obtain health? Have you written on an almond, a host, or any other things, speech [words] intended to protect against fever and worms? Have you recited incantations or had them recited against pains of the teeth, head, belly, or eyes, with a fava bean and the Our Father, or something similar? Have you crafted or had crafted amulets or talismans smacking of superstition, either by their words, or by their signs, or by the materials from which they are made, or by the way they are placed on patients, or by the way they are worn, or by the time and place in which they were written? If they smack of superstition, they must be burned and whoever refuses to so shall not be absolved because they are committing a mortal sin. Have you, as an amulet, worn a piece of parchment called Saint Cyprian's Charter, or a charter of unborn or virgin parchment, in other words vellum, or some similar thing to recover your health, or for some other superstitious reason which does not naturally fall under the jurisdiction of the medical art or any other?[11]

"Unborn parchment" is parchment made from the skin of a stillborn animal; some ancient authors go so far as to claim it was the skin of a stillborn child!

Michael Herr, municipal doctor of Strassburg in the first half of the sixteenth century, left an interesting account in his "New Bestiary" in which he describes common animals and the remedies that can be taken from them.[12] He tells us that the paw cut from a still-living rabbit reduces gout if carried on the person, and that a bone or paw from the same animal affords protection against stomachache (chapter 28). Rings were made from elk hooves because they granted protection against epilepsy, called "Saint Valentine's disease" (chapter 23); those made from the black callus of a buffalo's hooves or horns prevented cramps if worn on a finger or toe and, to increase their effectiveness, some people wrapped them in wires made from four different metals: gold, silver, copper, and iron (chapter 10). The dried tongue of a fox bound to the right arm and worn continuously protected one from afflictions affecting the eyes and face (chapter 5), and wolf scat sealed inside a small clay pot worn at the neck removed pain. Herr specifies that the scat must be white and must never have touched the ground, which is possible if it remained hanging in a bush. The string used to hang it around the neck had to be made from the wool of sheep that had been killed by wolves (chapter 4).

We find survivals of such practices—or amazing correspondences

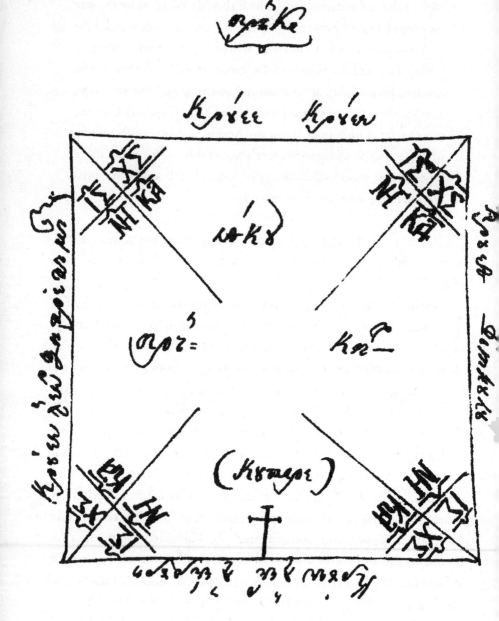

Fig. 4.1. Romanian amulet against erysipelas; the writing around it says,
"Cross, cross / the Lord's cross / cross in heaven / cross in heaven and on earth."
In the center: "remedy against erysipelas / (insert name)."

with Herr's observations—in the information provided by Paul Sébillot in his study *Le folklore de France*. For example, it was believed in the Vosges region that a ring made from the white callus taken from a donkey's hoof is excellent against epilepsy.[13]

Jean-Baptiste Thiers was very much aware of similar therapies and mentions them in partial form in his *Treatise on Superstitions*. He provides truncated versions of the spells so that no one can use them:

Heal farcin* by taking three small pieces of virgin wax that must be put inside a piece of . . . bind them with three knots with a hemp rope, & say five times at each knot a Pater & Ave Maria, Christus + Christus vincit + Christus + Christus abicit + Amalor + Alcinor + Descendat + In nomine, and so on.

Heal the daily fever by writing with a certain ink on an olive leaf culled before sunrise & by wearing these words, Ca Roy a, at the neck.

Heal rabies by bearing these words at the neck, Berfer Careau, reducat, and so on.

Wear at one's neck the word ABPACAΔABPA as follows:

ABPACAΔABPA
ABPACAΔABP
ABPACAΔAB
ABPACAΔA
ABPACAΔ
ABPACA
ABPAC
ABP
AB
A

The instructions for using the last are indicated by verses 944–949 from *De medicina praecepta,* the collection of remedies by Quintus

---

*[Farcin is an animal disease like glanders. —*Trans.*]

Serenus Sammonicus, who says it cures hemitritis or demi-tertian fever:

> *Inscribis chartae quod dicitur ΑΒΡΑϹΑΔΑΒΡΑ*
> *Saepius & subter repetis: sed detrahe summae*
> *Vt magis atque magis desint elementa figuris:*
> *Singula qua semper rapies & cetera figes,*
> *Donec in Augustum redigatur litra conum.*
> *His lino nexis collum redimire memento.*[14]

The illness retreats with the removal of each letter until it finally vanishes. According to some, this magic word represents the three figures of the Trinity.[15] A fourteenth-century Middle Dutch manuscript recommends this against quartan fever:

> Write in a brevet that you will place around the patient's neck: †
> aladabra † ladabra † adabra † dabra † abra † ra † a † abraca, and
> the name of the person.[16]

COSTA BEN LUCA'S TREATISE
ON PHYSICAL LIGATURES

The *De physicis ligaturis*[17]—which was widespread during the Middle Ages under the name of Costa ben Luca (Qustâ ibn Lûqâ, tenth century), whom medieval authors sometimes called Constabulence (!)—was translated into Latin by Constantine the African. It is presented as a compilation of works by different authors—the Arabic Aristotle, Galen, Dioscorides, Avicenna—and reproduces a series of amulets recommended for medicinal purposes. Costa takes the trouble to tell us, "I have drawn all this from old books so that your mind shall no longer oppose incantations, adjurations, and suspensions [of amulets] around the neck."

Costa takes five stones from the Arabic Aristotle and describes their therapeutic and/or apotropaic virtues. All must be worn around the neck or on the finger. This is how emerald can protect against epilepsy, hyacinth against pestilences, and sard against nightmares. Carnelian soothes wrath and halts hemorrhaging and menstrual flows, while onyx increases saliva in children but causes nightmares.

From Galen, Costa takes the following remedies: wolf scat hung around the neck on a wool string ease stomach pains; bones eaten by the same animal have a similar effect, but they need to be attached with a stag hide lanyard; to prevent stomach pains, a piece of coral can be placed on the belly or hung around the individual's neck.

Costa takes some strange amulets from Dioscorides: When attached to the arm, teeth from a rabid dog are effective against epilepsy, and greater celandine, bound with calf hide before it has touched the ground, has the same effect and cures this affliction. For protection against fever, hang from your arm the tightly woven web of a white spider. Against scrofula, hang a piece of sorrel or plaintain root around your neck. When attached to the neck or hand, crocus seeds or laurel root are effective against scorpion bites; a hare's foot worn on the left arm will keep dogs from barking. This information includes phylacteries that would no longer fit that definition according to modern criteria. First, we have two contraceptives: elephant excrement blended with honey and placed on a woman's vagina, and henbane dissolved in mare's milk and then put in buckskin and worn around the woman's neck. We are then informed of a way to increase sexual desire: stag's eyes added to elderberry root in the garden, which is watered in the evening with red bull urine and then ripped from the ground with the eyes and attached to the arm! Finally, a method to be recommended to anyone who needs a tooth pulled: a dried asparagus root attached to the teeth allows them to be extracted painlessly.

Among the three prescriptions taken from Avicenna, we should note that peony root protects children from epilepsy; pyrethrum root does the same when hung with hairs from a black dog; and the right foot of the turtle heals the right foot of a man, while the left heals the left, and so on.

ASTROLOGICAL MEDICINE

In the theory of the humors established by Claudius Galen (129–199), Marcus Aurelius's doctor, the four triads of the zodiac (Aries, Leo, Sagittarius; Taurus, Virgo, Capricorn; Gemini, Libra, Aquarius; and Cancer, Scorpio, Pisces) are connected to the elements. In respective order they are fire, earth, air, and water. They act on the four humors based on their qualities. The first triad is hot and dry, the second cold and dry, the third hot and moist, and the last cold and moist. In the same order, they rule over yellow bile, melancholia or black bile, blood, and phlegm or spleen. Diseases and fevers arise from the alteration or disturbance of said humors; one then turns to the corresponding sign of the zodiac to make a remedy, which takes the form of phylacteries and amulets, like those medals collected by René of Anjou in huge quantity, according to his inventories.

Another example of the same thinking can be found in the *Sacred Book of Hermes to Asclepius*. Here, preceding a list of thirty-six amulets, we read:

> Every sign of the zodiac rules over the part of the body that belongs to it and causes a disease in the surrounding ones. So, if you do not wish to be affected by this, you must carve on a stone the representations and characters (or the essence) of its decans, and add to them their plant. Once this has been done, you can wear the stone like an amulet and you will possess a strong and beneficial remedy for the body.[18]

This theory is called melothesia.[19] Melothesia can be based on the planets or on the signs of the zodiac (as in the text cited above). The *Sacred Book of the Decans* recommends this for making phylacteries to thwart the effects of cosmic disorders:

> Engrave upon the stones the forms and figures of the decans themselves and, after having placed beneath it the plant of each decan

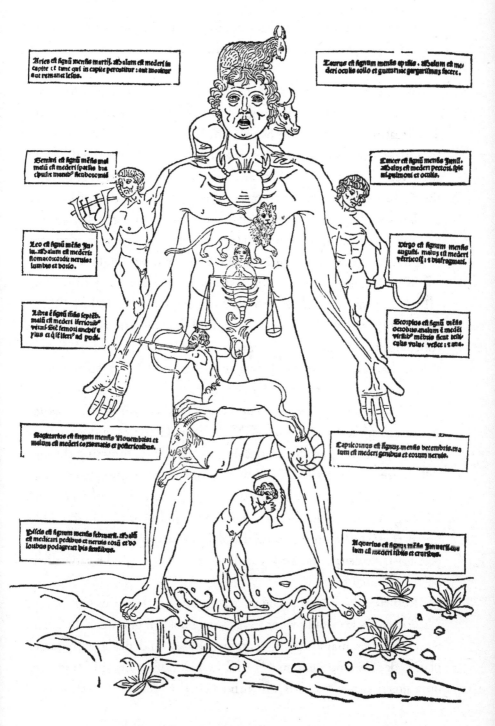

Fig. 4.2. *Figure from the* Book of Medicine, *Venice (1495)*

and also its form, and thereby crafting yourself a phylactery, wear it as a powerfully beneficial aid to the body.[20]

Whatever form they take, healing or prophylactic amulets were worn on the person, on clothing, on hats, on belts, and even in purses. The treatise *De sigillis* (On Seals), which medieval scholars attributed to Arnaldus de Villa Nova, states that a person can wear several, mainly the twelve seals of the zodiac, at one time, but that the seal of Aries should be on the head, woven on or into the hair, and that of Leo over the kidneys.[21] Seals were also used as infusions in potions, herbal teas, and other beverages, or even to mark medicines: the imprint of the seal on a remedy conferred upon it the power to catalyze astral forces.

When engraved on a metal, astrological seals were used to craft medals and rings. Arnaldus de Villa Nova employed one in July 1301 to treat Pope Boniface VIII, who was suffering from attacks of nephritic colic, and by chance or providence, he cured him. Toward 1426, Jean Piscis, chancellor of the University of Medicine of Montpellier, saved a Tuscan clergyman by virtue of a Leo medal.

There is nothing new about the use of these kinds of remedies. A text from the first century AD tells how Thessalos, a doctor from Tralles, went to Egypt for initiation into astrology. Browsing through the libraries, he discovered "a book of Nechepso containing twenty-four ways of treating the whole body and every disease in accordance with each sign of the zodiac by means of stones and plants."[22] It should be noted that Nechepso was a mythical Egyptian sovereign whose high priest was Petosiris, and all kinds of more or less magical treatises have been attributed to him.

Refuting Nechepso, Galen wrote in his treatise *On Simple Medicines,* "Who would want to take the books of grammar* by a man who describes magic spells, metamorphoses, and deals with sacred plants, decans, and demons?"[23] And he mentions a decanic engraving on a green jasper stone to which medicinal virtues were attributed.[24]

---

*In other words, grimoires.

However, zodiacal medicine continued to be employed throughout the entire Middle Ages. The ancient healers and surgeons used the *Sacred Book of Hermes to Asclepius,* which essentially maintained that each sign of the zodiac is the master of the part of the body under its jurisdiction and causes illness in its surrounding areas. If someone wishes to avoid being touched by its effects, it is necessary to take the figures and essence of the sign's decan, engrave them on their stones, and then add their plants. Once that has been done it can be worn as an amulet and the individual will have a powerful and salutary remedy for the body. Traces of these opinions can frequently be found in the lapidaries. In the lapidary of Socrates and Dionysius, the greatest phylactery of the body is a sard engraved with a ram and Athena holding a heart, while an onyx carved with the coils of a serpent and the forequarters or head of a dog, or the head of a lion and rays, will prevent stomach pains and facilitate digestion. It so happens that this cynocephalic serpent is none other than Sopdet, the first decan of Cancer in ancient Egypt, and the lion-headed serpent is Chnoubis, decan of Cancer or Leo.[25] These "hybrids" give a good idea of the layering of traditions that trace back to ancient civilizations.

One of the great practitioners of the Middle Ages, Guy de Chauliac, doctor to popes Clement VI, Innocent VI, and Urban V, believed in the efficacy of similar remedies. In his *Inventorium* (written in 1343), in the section dealing with kidney stones and other stones, he did not shy away from referring to the authority of Hermes, Arnaldus de Villa Nova, and Pietro d'Abano when he stated "that the image of a Lion, and the Moon moving away from Saturn's influence," heals them if one wears this image in a baldric made from sea calf skin or a belt made from leonine leather.[26]

Obviously the ecclesiastical authorities took a dim view of such medications because they brought into play too many magical or superstitious elements, like unknown names and *characters,* and the use of phylacteries was widespread in medical and Jewish milieus. The Spanish rabbi Moshe ben Nahman Girondi (1194–1300), called Nachmanides and nicknamed "the Prince of the Kabbalah," healed the afflictions of the kidneys by virtue of a seal depicting Leo;[27] in 1303, Abba Mari ben Eligdor wondered about the lawfulness of a "superstition" like this. Among the users of zodiacal seals, we find celebrities like Solomon ben Aderet (1235–1310), rabbi of Barcelona, and Isaac ben Judah Lattes.[28]

In 1389, the theological college of Paris condemned these practices, and Jean Gerson, former chancellor of the university, inserted his decision in his booklet, *Les Erreurs de l'art magique:*

> It is an error opposed to faith, natural philosophy, and the true astrology to believe that images of copper, lead, gold, white or red wax, or any other material, baptized, exorcised, and consecrated— or rather, abominated—according to the magic arts, on predetermined days, possess the marvelous virtues that are taught in books.[29]

Museums possess countless examples of zodiacal medals. The obverse of a medal for Aries, for example, shows a ram surrounded by "ARABEL TRIBUS JUDA: V and VII." The reverse shows Alpha and Omega encircled by "Sanctus Petrus: VERBUM CARO FACTUM EST, ET HABITAVIT IN NOBIS," words taken from the Gospel of John (19:30). If we examine the writings of Arnaldus de Villa Nova, however, it would seem this inscription is not exactly correct. In his treatise on seals, *De sigillis,* he gives a precise description of how this medal is made:

> Take very pure gold and melt it down when the sun enters into Aries, the fifteenth day of the calends of April, then make a round seal from it while saying: "Come Jesus, light of the world, true lamb of God who removes the sins of the world, and casts light into our darkness"; recite the psalm "Lord, our Lord, etc." . . . Next, when the Moon is in Aries or in Leo, engrave a ram on one side when the Sun is in Aries and, around it, "ARAHEL TRIBUS JUDA. V ET VII"; on the other side, carve these most sacred words: "The word made itself flesh and came down among

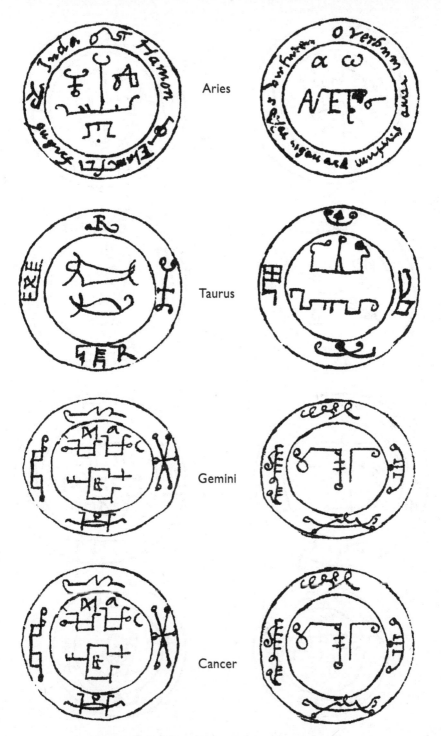

Fig. 4.3. Zodiacal signs, Ghent Manuscript:
Aries, Taurus, Gemini, Cancer

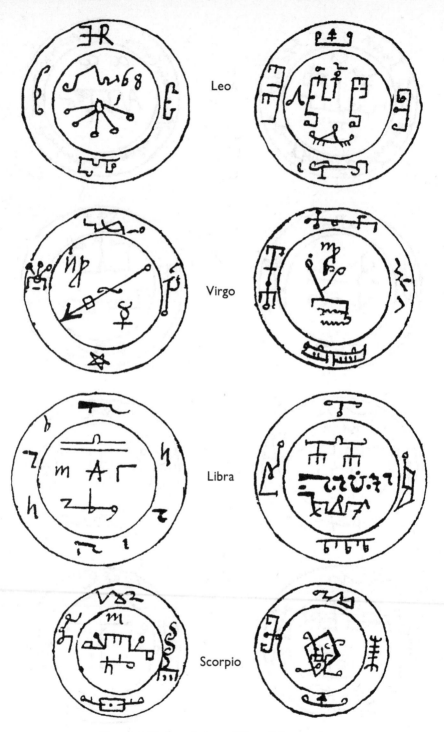

Leo

Virgo

Libra

Scorpio

Fig. 4.4. Zodiacal signs, Ghent Manuscript:
Leo, Virgo, Libra, Scorpio

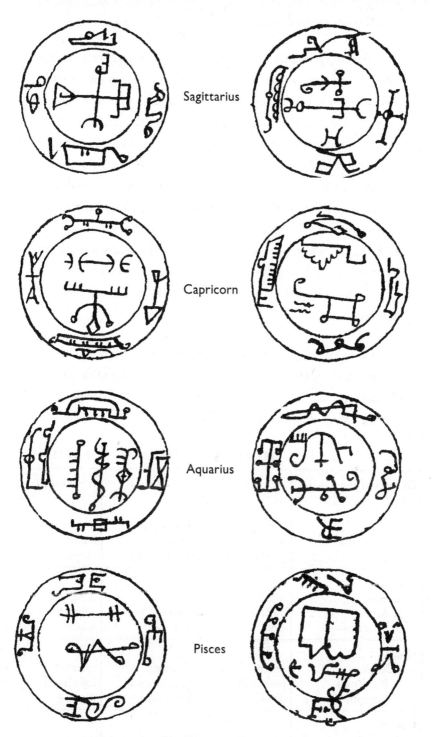

Sagittarius

Capricorn

Aquarius

Pisces

Fig. 4.5. Zodiacal signs, Ghent Manuscript:
Sagittarius, Capricorn, Aquarius, Pisces

us," with, in the center, "Alpha et Omega et Sanctus Petrus." This valuable seal works against all the principal demons and enemies, evil spells, is good for commerce and obtaining favor, it protects from all dangers, lightning, storms, inundations, and the attacks of wind and pestilences. The dwellers of a house in which it has been placed shall have nothing to fear. It heals the demon-possessed, the frenzied, the maniacs, and angina, as well as all afflictions of the head and eyes, and those that cause the catarrh to descend from the head. And, as I say in summary, it drives away all evil and procures good things. May he who wears it make sure to avoid, as much as possible, all filth and lust as well as the other mortal sins. He shall wear this seal over the head with reverence and honor.[30]

To use astrological remedies, it is necessary to know the receptacles of the force of the zodiacal signs. The following table shows what two important works, the *Sacred Book of Hermes to Asclepius* and the *Lapidary of King Alfonso* (Alfonso X), say.

	HERMES	**HERMES**	**LAPIDARY**
Decans of the Zodiac	**Plants**	**Stones**	**Stones**
Aries 1. Chenladori 2. Chontaret 3. Siket	isophrys nastort great plantain	babylonian siderite bostrochyte	hematite bizedi alaquec
Taurus 1. Soou 2. Aron 3. Rhomenos	sphairitis dictame goult	selenite Venus stone hyacinth	dehenich zumbedic zebech
Gemini 1. Xocha 2. Panchrous 3. Pepisoth	orchis potentilla libane	diamond panchrous heliotrope	emerald lapis lazuli diamond
Cancer 1. Sotheir 2. Ouphisit 3. Chnouphos	mugwort peony sphairitis	dryite green jasper euchaite	crystal alaquec yacoth

| | HERMES | HERMES | LAPIDARY |
Decans of the Zodiac	Plants	Stones	Stones
Virgo 1. Athoum 2. Brysous 3. Amphatham	cisalpine bouduc couchel catanance	corallite dendrite enthlizon	aliaza coral zavarget
Libra 1. Sphoukou 2. Nephthimes 3. Phou	polium geranium citronella	jasper-agate sard emerald	crystal magnet emery
Scorpio 1. Bos 2. Oustikos 3. Aphebis	mercurial scorpiure peony	hematite pyrite sardonyx	carnelian topaz aliaza
Sagittarius 1. Sebos 2. Teuchmos 3. Chthisar	sage andradactylon centaurea	phrygite amethyst aerizon	carnelian hematite amariella
Capricorn 1. Tair 2. Epitek 3. Epichnaus	delphinium anemone carline	serpentine chalcedony anankite	magnet coral emerald
Aquarius 1. Isy 2. Sosomno 3. Chonomous	asarabacca scarlet pimpernel thyrsus	knetite magnetite mede	turquoise emery coral
Pisces 1. Tetimo 2. Sopphi 3. Syro	verbena libane chamomile	beryl perileukion hyacinth	red hyacinth yellow hyacinth coral

It would be a great error to assume that this type of correspondence became lost over the centuries. A 2001 *Catalog for the Modern Man* carries an advertisement for a "chest of a dozen magical stones," sold for the equivalent of $50 and described as follows:

Aventurine, carnelian, agate, jasper, tiger's eye. . . . Like the zodiacal signs to which they correspond, they are twelve fine stones, twelve magical stones to be worn as a necklace in order to profit from the beneficial virtues that have been granted to them since the dawn of time. In this way, the rose quartz, the stone of Taurus, is reputed to strengthen the heart, soothing and calming it. Once considered a precious stone, transparent as pure water, the mountain crystal is the stone of Leo. It is reputed to relieve eyestrain and soothe headaches, while bringing light into the body. Mounted as pendants, these stones come in their own chest accompanied by a gold chain. Wear each of them like a talisman intended to protect your well-being during the corresponding period of the zodiac; you will thereby gain the best benefits of its—magical—virtues.

And in June 2000, the health food shop Laboratoire des Puits tournants in Querrieu (in the Somme region of France) praised "resonance stones":

Minerals are able to establish resonance with the individual who carries them, and to transmit vital potential over a specific wavelength. It is up to each individual to know which stone best serves their needs, and to choose the stone from the appropriate scale that is most adaptable to this exchange. . . . The minerals chosen have been ranked in accordance with their differentiated effects on the body, the mind, as well as on their resonance with energetic centers and structures. It is up to the individual to select them in accordance with their affinities.

The four-page brochure offers several examples, from which I quote the following:

Tourmaline: a rough stone that strengthens the lymphatic system. A protector of places: computer, television set, telephones.

Psyche: dispels negative influences. Accompanies the automobile driver.

This says quite a lot about the "static" evolution of mentalities and mind-sets in certain domains. We should note, however, the adaptation to technological progress, since now our common electrical appliances can also be protected—alas, the brochure does not specify from what.

THE TREATISE *ON SEALS*
BY THE PSEUDO–ARNALDUS DE VILLA NOVA

Mistakenly attributed to Arnaldus de Villa Nova in the late Middle Ages and Renaissance, *De sigillis* provides a list of the twelve metallic seals that correspond to each sign of the zodiac. Its author indicates which metal should be used in each instance; the astral configuration necessary at the time of manufacture; the astral configuration of the engraving and what should be depicted on the front and back; and finally, the prayers that should be spoken during these operations. These prayers are essentially psalms.[31]

The therapeutic aims cover a vast range, from the healing of the frenzied and demon-possessed (Aries) to feet swollen by gout (Pisces), as well as all kinds of diseases, anginas, and tumors (Taurus), cancer, hand pains, genital warts, and barber's itch (Gemini), stomach pains (Leo), and so forth.[32] An analysis of the text shows that these seals are halfway between amulets and talismans. Ten out of twelve seals have an apotropaic and/or healing virtue, and only two possess additional powers. Aries protects from demons, enemies, evil spells, lightning, storms, floods, violent winds, and pestilences, and it is good for commerce, acquiring favors, and thwarting peril. Aquarius, meanwhile, provides protection against all that crawls; such entities can neither approach nor harm someone carrying this sigil.

These magical therapies did not die out with the Renaissance. In his study entitled *Discoverie of Witchcraft* published in 1584, Reginald Scott mentions a famous doctor of his time, Argerius Ferrarius, who notes, "Physicians use ligatures, the hanging of amulets [*periapts*], phylacteries, charms, characters, and so forth, presumed to do good."[33]

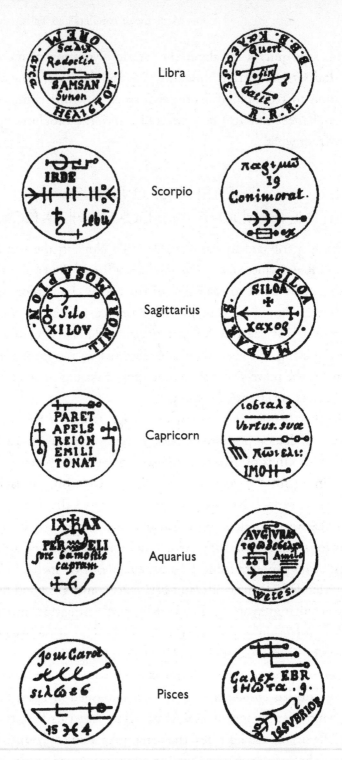

Fig. 4.6. *Zodiacal seals based on the Pseudo-Paracelsus*

The trial of Francesco de Nobilibus, an alleged sorcerer condemned in Grenoble in 1604, specifically admonishes this man "for healing diseases by means of brevets hung around the neck of the patient or applied to the afflicted area."[34]

The reader should now have an overview of the ideas and representations, as well the knowledge and theories, that people had regarding amulets and talismans in previous centuries—in short, everything that underlies the history of the subject. This overview is necessary

Fig. 4.7. Talismans
(*Reichelt,* Exercitatio de amuletis)

to understand the next half of the book and allows us to enter the domain of "learned" or "high magic." This will have the subsequent benefit of demystifying—or more precisely, demythicizing—a subject about which so much foolishness has been written by commercial charlatans or the disciples of this or that self-proclaimed prophet. So let us now learn how to craft a talisman!

Fig. 4.8. Talismans
(Reichelt, Exercitatio de amuletis)

PART TWO

The Use of Amulets and the Making of Talismans

CURIOSUS
AMULETORUM
SCRUTATOR

In quo

De natura & attributis illorum, uti &
plurimis illis, quæ paſſim in uſum tam

inthcoria quàm praxi vocari ſveyerunt,

ac in ſpecie

DE

ZENECHTIS,

Vel quæ peſti opponuntur, agitur;

Superſtitioſa atque illicita notantur,

rejiciuntur, & utilia illuſtrantur

Theologis, Juris-Conſultis, Medicis, Physicis,

Philoſophis ac quibuicunq, in ſpecie

CURIOSIS

apprimè inſerviens accommodatus & ad normam

Academ. Leopoldino-Imper. Curioſ.

adornatus

JACOBO WOLFF. Philoſ. & Medicin.
Dôt. Prof. Publ. Jenenſ.

Cui acceſſit

JULII REICHELTI

Exercitatio,

DE

AMVLETIS,

Liber utiliſſimus, æneisque figuris inſtructus.

FRANCOFVRTI & LIPSIÆ,

Fig. 5.1. *The title page of* Curiosus amuletorum scrutator
by Jacob Wolff (Frankfurt and Leipzig: Groshuff, 1692)

5

AMULETS

Allegedly invented by Zoroaster, amulets allow us to protect ourselves. They are very numerous; I have collected several hundred from ancient texts. These display myriad facets and reflect the mind-sets of our remote ancestors. It is certainly not possible to present them all, but the description of a few select examples based on their diversity or their humorous nature will allow the reader to get a good sense of this unusual world. It should be noted that amulets preserve the body as well as the mind, the concrete and the abstract alike. Once an overview of them is gained, several major subjects of concern become apparent, for example, illnesses, demons, and evil spells.

This is terrain that has been made uneven through the layering of elements that trace back to all the civilizations of antiquity. The earlier elements were grasped to a greater or lesser extent, ceaselessly recopied, and then were Christianized to a certain degree in the herbals and lapidaries of the medieval West. Amulets therefore form a major chapter in the history of humanity. We can divide them into three major categories: botanical, zoological, and mineralogical, although there is an uneven distribution of phylacteries into these three domains.

In decreasing order, we find stones, then plants, and lastly the animals of the three kingdoms: earth, sea, and air. Metals remain rare; they are primarily used as support settings for gems. This imbalance may be the result of vagaries in the transmission of the material, or it may reflect those in the constitution of our corpus. The medical treatises, such as those of Galen (129–199),[1] Dioscorides (first century),[2] Marcellus Empiricus of Bordeaux (fourth to fifth century), and Alexander of Tralles (sixth century), whose work provides the richest evidence and who introduced amulets into popular medicine,[3] and the herbals, such as those of Pseudo-Apuleus (which dates from the fifth century), Platearius (ca. twelfth century), and Hildegard von Bingen (1098–1179), provide us with a meager number of examples. The same is true of the thirteenth-century Encyclopedists. On the rare occasions when they do mention amulets, they refer to Pliny the Elder, Galen, or the *Kyranides*. What we find in Pliny's *Natural History* clearly indicates the provenance for such information. When Pliny mentions the amulet-related use of a particular plant or animal part, he often says, "If we believe the magicians."[4] In fact, it is entirely necessary to scrutinize magic books in order to find the relevant material to analyze, for these books are what fed the other scholarly texts. The corpus of Greek magical papyri provides us with a wealth of information.[5] The *Kyranides,* translated in 1169 from a Greek original,[6] can be regarded as the most important treatise on amulets and it has the merit of showing us how the gradual shift from amulets to talismans came about.

A great disparity can be perceived with regard to animals: some— for example, the wolf, bear, seal, and hyena—are described as the source of countless phylacteries, while other animals figure in only one. An animal was selected for such use on account of its personal mythology. It is well known today that each animal has its own etiology,[7] in other words, a story that explains its origin, certains details of its morphology, or even the sound of its cry. What we have here is a body of knowledge that was built up over time based on observation. This knowledge was given structure by specific visions of the world whose common denominator is the idea that there is an explanation for everything: finding that explanation is key to mastering one's environment.

Numerous animal amulets consist of an organ such as the heart or a body part. The most common parts mentioned are the teeth, the hide, the fur, the eye, the hooves (or claws), the tongue, and the brain. In the case of birds, it was especially the head, the beak, a claw, and the wingtip. These parts act alone or in combination with other elements, and making a concrete identification of the latter is just one of the difficulties we are presented with. The reader of these ancient texts constantly stumbles against words not to be found in the dictionaries and belonging to the three major domains mentioned above (mineralogical, botanical, and zoological). This is why, in my translations, there is often no choice but to retain the original terminology. As a result, certain amulets still retain some of their mystery.

For an introduction to this discombobulated world, we can take Pliny the Elder as our guide. His *Natural History* conveys the bulk of the knowledge of classical antiquity. Pliny's advantage is to show us, for example, that the word "amulet" appears rarely among scholars. As for "talisman," this word only appeared with the meaning given to it in fourth-century Greece.

The cynocephalic plant protects against all sorcery (XXX, 18); the lambrucha (wild grape) is used as an amulet, Pliny tells us with no further elucidation (XXIII, 20). Placed inside a house, great burdock protects against all evil spells, which is why "they call it an amulet" (XXV, 115).

Next come animals or animal parts. Carried three times around a house, then nailed beneath the window, the bat gives protection against malevolent spells (XXIX, 83); the blood of the basilisk has the same property (XXIX, 66); a wolf's tooth worn as an amulet dispels childhood fears and teething problems (XXVIII, 257); small hard objects like sand can be found in the horns of snails, and attached to the child (*adalligatae*) they facilitate teething (XXX, 136). The dried head of a bat worn as an amulet (*adalligatum*) drives off sleep (XXX, 140), while one of a hyena's large teeth attached to a string (*alligatus*) protects one from night terrors and fear of shadows (XXVIII, 98). If a person attaches the front right foot of a chameleon to his arm with hyena skin, he will be protected against robbery and night terrors (XXVIII, 115), while the back marrow of a hyena used as an amulet (*adalligata*) is effective against hallucinations (XXVIII, 103). The notched feelers of beetles can be used as amulets for children (XXX, 138). The hairs from a child's first haircut, worn as amulets (*circumligatus*), are said to heal the onset of gout (XXVIII, 41).

Bones play an important role: when worn, those of the stag strengthen loose teeth (XXVIII, 188), and those found in wolf excrement, if they have not touched the ground—that is, those from wolf scat found hanging in bushes—can heal the colon when attached to the arm (XXVIII, 211). Sometimes we find a combination of elements. For example, for quartan fever magicians prescribe the wearing of an amulet of cat feces with an owl's claw; in order to avoid any relapses, it should not be taken off until the end of the seventh day (XXVIII, 228). To heal quartan fevers, individuals hang around the patient's neck a fragment of a nail pulled from a cross and wrapped in wool (*involutum lana collo subnectunt*), or a piece of rope also from a cross. Once the patient is cured, these objects should be hidden inside a cave where the sun never shines (XXVIII, 46).

Manufactured objects also serve as protective devices and here it is hard to know if we are dealing with an amulet or a talisman. Servilius Nonianus placed a piece of paper wrapped in linen around the neck marked (*chartam inscriptam*) with the two Greek letters rho and alpha, believing it offered protection against ophthalmia. The consul Muncianus wore a living fly in a white linen bag on his person; both claimed that these amulets (*his remediis*) were sure proof against eye inflammation (XXVIII, 29).

Stones in general make good amulets and this belief was extremely widespread in ancient times. Little stones swallowed by hinds when they realize they are pregnant, and found in their excrement and worn as an amulet, protected from abortion (XXVIII, 246); amber served as an amulet for young children and protected everyone from madness (XXXVII, 50). Amber was used as an amulet throughout the East (XXXVII, 118).

In order to clarify things a bit in this profuse and little-known domain, I will show the distinction between simple amulets and compound amulets, by gradually introducing all their facets, the primary being whether they were engraved by natural or human agency. We can start by looking at a representative sample of simple amulets, which, incidentally, could easily serve as advertising for jewelers, commercial gardeners, and other trades.

SIMPLE AMULETS

Simple amulets act through the intrinsic virtue attributed to them by tradition. Depending on its origin—Egypt, Chaldea, Greece, and so on—the same element is capable of being effective in a variety of domains that, over the course of time, came to be considered as a single category. This tendency became increasingly pronounced over the period from antiquity through the Middle Ages.

Simple amulets consist of a single element—an animal body part, a plant, or a stone—to which numerous powers are generally attributed. When examined more closely, however, these powers often possess a common denominator. For example, the association between illnesses, evil spells, and demons is logically explicable;[8] we are dealing with a single complex here. In certain cases we can ask, which is more important, the animal part or the animal itself? In fact, we sometimes see that the beaks of various birds or the hides of different animals have the same power. Clearly we are being confronted with numerous variations on several themes, a little like we might find in the world of music.

In the corpus I have assembled, which is drawn from several hundred different sources of evidence, ligatures or healing amulets make up the majority of the items. Since they do not strictly correspond to the definition of the amulet as a protective device, and because they deserve their own detailed study, I will not give them special attention in this investigation. They will turn up occasionally, however, among the other phylacteries.

Amulets Derived from Animals

If you nail the hide of a seal to the prow or mast of a ship, lightning shall never strike it; if you hang its heart from the mast, it shall never sink. (*Kyranides,* 84–85)

The tongue of the weever worn by children drives evil spells and illnesses away from them. (*Kyranides*, 35)

Bear hide placed where fleas are to be found will cause them to flee. (*Kyranides*, 137)

Worn secretly under one's clothes, the right eye of a wolf . . . sends all kinds of ghosts fleeing from its wearer as well as all tame or wild animals, [and] it permits one to pass through their enemies without being seen and also dispels all fevers that are accompanied by shivering. (*Kyranides*, 116)

When worn, the fox's heart gives shelter from all evil spells. (*Kyranides*, 140)

If you tear out the eye of a living hyena and you wear it on your arm in a piece of purple cloth, you shall drive away all night terrors and the witch [*striga*] that strangles infants and prevents couplings and births, and every devil will be sent fleeing. (*Kyranides*, 132)

Hung in front of doors [*ante portam suspensa*], hyena skin will prevent all betrayal. (*Kyranides*, 133)

When worn around a man's neck, the claw of the owl is a good luck charm [*ungula fortunate est*] and phylactery. (*Kyranides*, 152)

The heart of a vulture wrapped in its own skin . . . sends demons, brigands, and wild beasts fleeing. (*Kyranides*, 153)

Worn, the teeth of the *ioulos* [an unknown fish] drive demons and curses [*daemones et fascinationes*] away. (*Kyranides*, 189)

If someone wears the paw of the sun lizard in a golden tube attached to their left arm, and engraved on this tube is AULU SAURE, he will avoid all serious illness and never suffer any impairment while he wears it. (*Kyranides*, 108)

The bear deserves special attention because it provides several excellent amulets for human beings by virtue of the belief that it is a close relative of man. A Greek text states the following: "The bear is a wild animal, very hairy, lazy, and similar in all respects to man; it is intelligent and spontaneously walks upright. Each of its limbs were made in imitation of the limbs of man." Therefore, the bones from its head could cure headaches; the claws from its right paw, when worn, would deter all fever, and its heart makes one friendly, lucky, and a source of awe; its eyes dispel all eye afflictions and they attract affection; gout in the hands and feet are cured when people wear the tendons from its paws.[9]

The renowned physician Arnaldus de Villa Nova provides the following recipe in a chapter devoted to methods for combating evil spells:

> Hung inside the house, the wolf's tail prevents its invasion by wolves. If you place a goatskin in your house, all demons will flee the premises. When carried on the person, the vulture's heart causes all demons as well as all animals to flee its owner's presence.[10]

In Ireland, prehistoric flint arrowheads mounted on silver offer protection against elfshot and inoculate the individual against diseases and/or spells. In seventeenth-century Scotland, the adder stone was used to repel evil spirits; to prevent the fairies from stealing the stone, it would be kept in an iron box.[11]

Amulets Taken from Plants

In addition to observations like "attached, the plantain works wonders against scorpions," or again, "worn around the neck, verbena is effective," the herbal of Pseudo-Apuleus (*De herbarum virtutibus*)[12] offers a good glimpse of the use of plants as phylacteries. Its information also sometimes matches that provided by Pliny the Elder. Here are a few examples:

> Whoever carries verbena with its root and leaves is protected from snakebite. (Pseudo-Apuleus, 3, 7)

> Birthwort sends demons fleeing. (Pseudo-Apuleus, 1, 19)

Worn on or carried in the hand, mugwort prevents travel fatigue; it causes demons to flee and, when placed inside the home, forbids poisons and deters the evil eye. (Pseudo-Apuleus, 1, 10)

In the category of ligatures, we find these examples:

Attached to the leg, henbane causes inguinal inflammations and pains to vanish. (Pseudo-Apuleus, 1, 4)

Attached to the body, water germander heals tertian and day fevers. (Pseudo-Apuleus, 76, 3)

Mandrake wrapped in clean linen and placed around the neck of children will protect them from evil spells. (Pseudo-Apuleus, 131, 5)

When worn around the head or on the belt, bryony protects from ill health and woes. (Pseudo-Apuleus, 67, 1)

As a further example, the following comes from the French translation of the *Kyranides:*

He who wears the root of the eryngo shall have no cause to fear demons or their temptations. (*Secrez,* 325)

From time to time, we encounter an astrological detail similar to those we have also found in lapidaries:

To heal a lunatic, it is necessary at the waning of the moon, when Taurus or Scorpio is in its first decan, to wrap a buttercup in clean linen and hang it around the afflicted individual's neck. (Pseudo-Apuleus, 1, 9)

Arnaldus de Villa Nova mentions several highly useful plants:

Hung either over the threshold or put beneath the threshold of the house, mugwort prevents evil spells from harming any of its inhabitants. St. John's wort in the house causes demons to flee. An entire spring squill hung above the doorsill removes all evil spells [*tollit maleficium*]. If you carry bryony root on your person, you cannot be cursed.[13]

Amulets Derived from Minerals

Amulets made from minerals are by far the most numerous type. Such an amulet is capable of providing protection against a multitude of dangers and attacks; it need only be worn or carried. Here are a few that can be found in the most important lapidaries, such as the lapidary of Damigeron-Evax[14]—which directly descends from the widespread traditions of classical antiquity and is still quite pagan—and that of Marbode,[15] who was born in Angers around 1035, was named bishop of Rennes in 1096, and died in Saint-Aubin around 1123. He Christianized the material and selected the texts he preferred from the multitude at his disposal. Marbode obviously knew the lapidary of Damigeron-Evax, but he reused only a portion of it or was inspired by other sources. When comparison of the sources is illustrative of how the material evolved, both accounts will be provided alongside one another.

> **Anthropocrine:** Worn around the neck on a multicolored string, the anthropocrine stone provides deliverance from the magical and malefic art. (Evax, 53)

> **Carnelian:** Worn on the finger or around the neck, carnelian calms anger. (Marbode, XXII)

> **Ceraunia:** Lightning shall not strike whoever wears a ceraunia with an attitude of respect, nor will it strike a house or properties in which this stone has been placed. Anyone traveling by boat on a river or the sea shall not be drowned by storm or struck by lightning. (Marbode, XXVIII)

> **Chrysolite:** When held in or worn on the hand of the plaintiff, chrysolite is valuable in a trial. (Evax, 39)

Fig. 5.2. Gnostic gems

It is said that chrysolite, when mounted in gold, creates a phylactery. It offers robust protection against night terrors. If it is bored through and threaded on the hairs from the foal of an ass, it will terrorize demons and, as some believe, cause them torment. When it is set this way, it should be worn on the right wrist. (Marbode, XI)

Coral: Coral is a phylactery that deters all afflictions and provides rescue from the threat of robbers. If you hold it in your hand in war and battle, it will be an invincible phylactery—effective, dreaded, and fearless. (Socrates and Dionysius, 20)

Coral is used to craft amulets [*gestamina*] that are useful in many ways; it has been shown that it is salutary for those who wear it. . . . It deters lightning, gusts, and storms far from the ship, house, or field where one is wearing it; . . . it averts the dangerous darts of hail from the harvest. . . . It drives away the demonic shades and witches (or ghosts) of Thessaly [*Thessala monstra*], and provides easy beginnings and favorable outcomes. (Marbode, XX)

Diamond: Diamond repels all fear, the visions of questionable dreams, specters of the shadows, poisons, and trials. You shall craft a bracelet of gold, silver, iron, and copper that will be twisted together, and wear it upon your left arm. (Evax, 3)

Diamond makes its wearer invincible, drives away apparitions and deceitful dreams, sends dark poisons fleeing, calms quarrels and trials, and repels relentless enemies. This stone must be mounted in silver or gold and worn on the left wrist. (Marbode, I)

Emerald: Emerald worn around the neck sends the demi-tertian fever fleeing, heals those who have lost their reason . . . restores vigor to fatigued eyes, and can, or so it is believed, divert storms. (Marbode, VII)

Galactite: Galactite resists the evil eye and curses; whoever wears it shall never be bewitched. (Evax, 34)

Hephaistite: Whoever wears a hephaistite around his left arm can scorn all hardships and troubles. (Evax, 15)

Hephaistite drives grasshopper swarms, sterile clouds, and harmful hailstorms far from the fruits of the earth . . . ; it gives its bearer safety whenever he is imperiled. These stones should be worn [esse gerondas] on the chest, at heart level. (Marbode, XXXI)

Pyrite: In a ligature, pyrite acts against evil spells. (Evax, 56)

Rhinoceros: The stone found in the nose or horn of the rhinoceros drives demons away if one wears it. (*Kyranides,* 125)

Sard: Whoever wears around his neck or on his finger a sard the weight of twenty barley grains shall see nothing terrible or frightening in his dreams and shall have no dread of curses or evil spells. (Marbode, prose 4)

Syrtites: Who possesses syrtite can resist all evil spells and the hazards of other stones. (Evax, 22)

Topaz: Topaz removes all evil spells from the home. (Evax, 54)

The object in the following example has a twofold origin: it is made of iron, but not just any iron. Iron itself is already, sui generis, a powerful phylactery that causes demons and fevers to flee. The hide of an ass is also a phylactery: "He who sleeps or rests on the hide of an ass shall dread neither Gello nor Gillus, that is witches, nor nocturnal encounters," states the *Kyranides* (123), which could then justify the following detail:

Iron: Whoever, without fire, makes an iron ring from the bit of a donkey and wears it, shall drive off demons and fevers. (*Kyranides,* 123)

Gems are combined with metals to make rings and other jewelry. Medieval manuscripts provide us with countless recipes for manufacturing talismanic rings. In addition to the major treatises I have already mentioned, which speak, for example, of the rings of the seven planets, we can find valuable evidence in the lapidaries. Here are two very revealing statements:

If, on an aphroselenite stone or a crystal, you find a man carved, mounted on an eagle and holding a rod in his hand, mount it in a ring of brass that is blended with an equal amount of aurichalcite or copper. He who slips this ring [on his finger] on Sunday before sunrise shall vanquish all his enemies and subjugate them; if it is on a Thursday and during a war, all men will happily obey him. It is necessary for its wearer to dress entirely in white clothing and abstain completely from meat.

If, on a crystal or any one of twelve stones, you find a man carved with the face of a lion and the claws of an eagle with, beneath them, a two-headed dragon with his tail uncoiled, mount it in a ring of aurichalcite and place musk and amber beneath the stone; when you wear it, men, women, and all spirits will look on you favorably and obey you; it will multiply your abilities and increase your wealth.[16]

COMPOUND AMULETS

Compound amulets are made from two elements of the same nature, such as two stones, or two things of a different nature, for example an animal hide and a stone. The magician's purpose is to obtain maximum effectiveness by combining the virtues of several ingredients or materials, which is generally done by working with a virtue common to both stones, or working with a stone and its sympathetic metal. We can find this information in the vast orphic corpus, that is, in the texts deriving from the *Lithika* by the Pseudo-Orpheus[17] (the *Nautical Lapidary,* the lapidary of Socrates and Dionysius, the lapidary of Evax,[18] and so on) and in the *Kyranides,* as well as in the latter's adaptation in Old French, the *Livre des secrez de nature.*[19] Finally, Camillo Leonardi's compilation printed in 1502 contains a very rich selection drawn from myriad sources.[20]

Here is an illustrative example:

If one places the hide of a seal in a house or a ship, or if one wears it, no misfortune shall befall its bearer because it turns aside thunder, dangers, curses, ferocious beasts, demons, brigands, and nighttime encounters. It helps to have the sea stone known as coral with it. (*Kyranides*, 201)

By themselves, coral and seal skin are good arresters of lightning; by combining them, one obtains a very nice lightning rod! Here are some more examples of minerals or animal parts combined together:

The carbuncle and chalcedony worn since infancy prevent one from drowning if shipwrecked. (*Nautical Lapidary*, 1)

The beak and tongue of a vulture carried on one's person are good for traveling at night because they keep demons, wild beasts, snakes, and misfortune at bay. (*Kyranides*, 154)

An eagle's heart wrapped in fine silk and worn on one's person protects one from all illness. (*Secrez*, 298)

Placed over iron filings, the chrysolite is a phylactery against night terrors. (Evax, 47)

References to "night terrors" crop up very frequently in the texts. This term designates demons, and most specifically, nightmares. "In Greece, the pagan and Christian orphic hymns dreaded spirits and devils by whatever name they were called . . . as shown by this pandemonium of amulets and papyruses," Louis Robert notes,[21] and his study shows that these nocturnal terrors went hand in hand with the "ill-omened meeting," an encounter with a wicked spirit who only appears at night. An echo of this can be found in Psalm 90 of the Septuagint, whose fifth and sixth verses provide protective formulas:

Thou shall not be afraid of terror at night; nor of the arrow flying by day; nor of the evil thing that walks in darkness, nor of calamity, and the demon of noon.

I should not forget to point out one of the most marvelous amulets with powers that each of us would love to have at our disposal:

If one carries on their person the heart and head of the plover, one will be protected throughout their entire life from diseases and all suffering [*illaesum et inocuum ab omni infirmitate*]. (*Kyranides,* 175)

SIMPLE AND COMPOUND PROCURING AMULETS

We call the simple or complex magical objects that supply any kind of blessing or advantage "procuring amulets." It is not uncommon for an amulet to have more than one property, even when it only consists of a single element, and for its other effects to procure some blessing for its owner.

Jasper: Worn piously, jasper drives hydropsy and fevers away . . . , blessed, it bestows grace and potency, and it is even believed to drive off dangerous delusions. (Marbode, IV)

Hyacinth: It protects [*facit tutum*] travelers and roads. It is a good amulet [*tutamen*] against pestilences, serpents, and poisons. It makes him who wears it pleasing to God and men alike.[22]

As we see in the preceding, the protective aspect is not the sole function; it is compounded with a procuring function. In the following case, all that survives are the benefits it provides:

Agate: Worn, the agate makes one eloquent, powerful, charming, persuasive, robust, and of good mien, and it makes one pleasing to God and man. (Evax, 17)

While gems are all-powerful, other materials need to be combined in order to have an effect. Here we move from the simple procuring amulets, like those mentioned above, to the compound amulets, such as "Brain and heart of the peacock procures grace and love for its wearer"

(*Secrez,* 302). Beyond this are the complex amulets, three examples of which are provided below to give a glimpse of the benefits that can be gained by wearing these phylacteries.

> Take the hairs that grow between a seal's nostrils and mouth [its mustache!], a green jasper, and the liver of a hoopoe, a small root of Gorgonian eryngo [?], a peony root, a verbena seed, the cosmic blood of the chrysanthemum, that is to say the plumary herb [?], the tip of a seal's heart, and then the crest from the hoopoe's head; if you have all this, it will be better. When you have wrapped them all together with a little musk around the four perfumes, place it all in the skin of a mongoose, seal, or stag, or vulture, and wear it in a state of purity. . . . This phylactery deters all evils and procures all blessings. (*Kyranides,* 50)

> **Evanthus:** In order to be loved, gracious, known by all and a figure of awe to everyone, take the stone called evanthus, engrave upon it the belly and fur of a sea urchin, its tail and head [!] as if everything was attached; place beneath it arugula root and a nightingale's tongue, mount the entire thing in gold or silver, and wear it. You shall be loved and known by all, and given a warm welcome, but only by men; devils shall flee you. (*Secrez,* 324)

> **Aethite:** The two stones of the eagle are quite marvelous. He who shall bear in a wolfskin that which is above the right eyebrow shall fear no evil thing, nor spirit, nor demon. No woman can form any obstacle to his designs. The stone procures honors and good things in all cases. (*Secrez,* 298)

These procuring amulets are already quite close to talismans; the only thing missing is the element of ritual.

By virtue of the engravings or natural imprints on precious stones, the individual can obtain the same result as from a complex combination:

Topaz: The topaz should be carved with a falcon; it shall procure grace, benevolence, and love, and give nobility to a man. (*Secrez,* 310)

Diamond: An image of an armed man carved on a diamond has the power to fight enchantments and to bring its owner victory in war. (Ragiel, 22)[23]

The names of deities—and that of God, since we are in the very Christian Middle Ages—hold great power:

Ceraunia: If you find the names of God carved in a ceraunia [thunderstone, thunderbolt], they can protect the premises on which they are located from storms, and they give their owners power and victory over their enemies. (Ragiel, 20)

We even have a Gnostic god, Abraxas, whose presence is attested on medals and cameos in museums all over the world:

A man depicted in a jasper, with a shield in his left hand and an idol in his right, or some kind of weapon, with vipers in the place of feet, a rooster's or a lion's head, and a breastplate: a stone carved this way makes it possible to fight one's enemies, brings victory to its owner, and protects him from poison. It also stems the blood from whatever area it is spilling. (Thetel, 2)

Other very pagan engravings refer to astrology rather than zoology, as we can assume with a reading like the following, which has no other point of comparison:

Ruby: If you find the beautiful and terrifying figure of the Dragon either in the ruby or in another stone of the same nature and of the same power, know that its power is to increase worldly goods; it also brings its owner joy and health. (Leonardi, XIV, 1)

The Dragon (Draco) is a constellation of the Northern Hemisphere, and it recurs regularly in the nomenclatures, especially those of Eastern origin that distinguish between the Head and the Tail of the Dragon, and the ascending and descending nodes of the moon, whose role in magic cannot be overemphasized.

In the following example, we find the juxtaposition of two domains, the astral and the mineral:

> A man with a sword in his hand carved into coral has the power to protect the place it is located from lightning and storm, and to protect its owner from vices and enchantments. (Ragiel, 15)

The man represents the planet Mars, whose connection with lightning and meteors is unknown, although all the lapidaries tirelessly repeat that coral provides protection against them. We thus see the convergence of two traditions here, as shown by the following text:

> Amulets [*gestamina*] useful for many things can be crafted from coral; it has been shown to be salutary for those who wear it. . . . It wards off lightning, wind gusts, and storms from the ship, house, or field where one is holding it . . . ; it deters the dangers of hail stones from harvests . . . , it drives away demonic shades and Thessalian witches [*Thessala monstra*; the latter word could also mean "ghosts"], and gives easy beginnings and favorable outcomes. (Marbode, XX)

COMPLEX AMULETS

Complex amulets are the subject of one of the most interesting but most intensive chapters of my research. I have distinguished six basic types within the corpus. They follow below with examples.

The first type consists of amulets made with elements of the same provenance:

> If someone seals within the hide of a stag or a seal the heart of the seal, the tip of its tongue, the whiskers of its nose, its right eye, and

its rennet, and wears it, he shall vanquish all his enemies both on sea and land, and all diseases, sufferings, and woes; demons and wild beasts shall avoid him; in fact he will be happy, lucky, rich, and desired. (*Kyranides,* 134)

Who bears the heart of an eagle, the skin of its head, and its wing-tips sewn within its own skin and placed in a golden tube shall not be wounded if he marches into the midst of battle, and shall suffer no harm from lightning or storm. (*Kyranides,* 145)

The second type consists of amulets formed from elements of varying origin:

If, on hephaistite, which is also called pyrite, you carve a flamingo with a scorpion near its feet, and you place a bit of eryngo root beneath the stone, you shall have an amulet against all venomous animals; it will also ward off nocturnal apparitions . . . as well as repel all glamors. (*Kyranides,* 44)

Or another example:

The scorpion's sting added to a basil tip still holding the seed, and a hummingbird's heart, worn around the neck in a buckskin will heal lunatics of their madness. This phylactery [*periapta*] drives away demons. (*Kyranides,* 94)

The third type consists of amulets that are simply a stone carved with one or more animals, or one motif:

If someone carves a lobster on an agate and carries that stone in a ring, he will never be bitten by a scorpion. (*Kyranides,* 191)

A bull and a ram on a stone procure facility with words and protection against hydropsy. (Thetel, 16)

It is said that a green jasper with the engraving of a cross[24] can prevent its owner from being swallowed by the waves. (Thetel, 3)

The fourth type of amulet is characterized by the combination of a carved gem, plants, and animals:

> Carve a harpy on an emerald and beneath its claws a moray eel: seal beneath this stone some smilax root and carry it against delirious visions, terrors, and all that affects lunatics. . . . It is a divine phylactery. (*Kyranides,* 43)

> Take an aetite, carve an eagle on it, then, beneath the stone, put a grape seed with an eagle's wingtip, and if you don't have one, that of the sparrow hawk, then once it has been mounted, wear it. It will ward off every disease that has ever been heard of. (*Kyranides,* 30)

The fifth type of phylactery can be distinguished from the previous example by its engravings. We have letters or a figure with *characters,* plus an animal and/or a plant:

> Carve on a thyrsites stone a sparrow hawk and Dionysius holding the bird, then seal a piece of greater sage root beneath this stone . . . with it, one is safe from danger and invincible in court. In fact, the name of Dionysos is EVIRA SUB SICHI CHEIV EX III OIOO ACUL. (*Kyranides,* 53–54)

The encrypted name of Dionysos clearly seems to accompany the depiction; otherwise there would be no reason to include it in the description. Thanks to the evidence below, we learn what such an engraving is used for:

> Worn in a ring, the agate makes its bearer a skilled orator, sociable, persuasive, powerful, amiable in all matters, vigorous and with good countenance. It is consecrated this way: take a bronze needle, engrave IACHÔ [= Iahveh] on the stone, mount the stone in the ring, and wear it after making its imprint. (Socrates and Dionysius, 39)

The name written on a gem is sometimes very hard to decipher because, without outrightly stating so, the copyist of a particular manuscript has used the Greek alphabet. The following text provides an excellent illustration of this phenomenon:

> If a green jasper is topped by a head and shoulders, set it in a gold or silver ring, wear it on your person, and you shall escape every manner of death. Write the following letters on the ring: B.B.P.P.N.E.N.A., and your body shall be spared all illness, especially fever and hydropsy, and the stone will be of great aid in bird hunting. And you will be reasonable and friendly in all things, both in times of war and peace, [and] this stone will help women conceive and give birth. It brings peace, harmony, and several other blessings to those who wear it; these latter must be just and honorable in their conduct. (Solomon, 15)

In an Old English charm from the tenth century, the letter sequence BEPPNNIKNETTANI can be read. This has been deciphered to show that it includes the name of Saint Veronica in Greek letters followed by an obscure noun—GVTTANI—that can be found on medieval objects, rings, and broaches in this form: THEBAL GVT GVTTANI. What the lapidary of Solomon presents, therefore, is only a fragment of the original engraving.

The sixth type of amulet exhibits the greatest level of complexity. This is attained when the engraving depicts a person (whole or partially), a god, a couple, and one or more animals, combined with elements from the plant and animal kingdoms:

> If a stone is topped with the image of a bearded man, with a long face and curved eyebrows, seated on a plow between two bulls, holding a knife in one hand and wearing the head of a man and the head of a fox around his neck, this stone will be useful for plantings and for all crops, for finding treasure, and for fighting: it will transform enemies into allies and heal many diseases. It also

helps epileptics. And if a child wears it around his neck, the stone will ward off all fears, and protect him from the torments of evil spirits, and if a sick person wears it, he will recover his health; in order for the stone to have even greater power, it should be set in an iron ring that is twice its weight. (Solomon, 36)

Astrological considerations can be an aspect to this type of amulet, which is evidence of the transition from amulet to talisman. This is because, among other things, the amulet must be created at a precise moment: the time when the configuration of the sky is favorable for that undertaking.

Engrave on the nemecite stone the form of a maiden whose feet are resting on a fixed wheel, and who is holding a rule in her left hand and a rod in her right, and with one of her feet is mounting an ox. Beneath the stone place some necya and pilot fish, and set it all in a gold or silver ring when the sun is in the sign of Scorpio. Know that this ring has marvelous virtues: whoever gives it to one possessed by the demon, that individual will confess his incontinence and the demon shall flee, and the man will remain sensible and virtuous. It is good against the dreams and fantasies to which the demon-possessed are prey, and against the fears of small children, and against all evil things that occur at night. He who wears this ring can tell how old everyone is and how many years they will live and what their age will be when they die. It is necessary for this individual to abstain from sin. (*Secrez,* 328)

This is not a unique example. Here is a second description that also points up an issue regarding vocabulary: what exactly does the author mean by ring (*annulus*)? Taking into consideration the present context as well as other accounts, the word simply means "talisman," which solidly corroborates the hybrid nature of this type of amulet and documents the transition from the amulet to the talisman.

Take the festinus stone, also called Vulcan [= hephaistite], carve on it a flamingo with a scorpion at its feet, add some eryngo root, and set it all in silver or gold when the sun is in the sign of Scorpio, and guard this ring [talisman] for it is the most valuable jewel that exists against venom for whoever wears it. It is good against all enchantments, witchcraft, and the evil visions that come at night when one is either sleeping or awake. It is good against the gravel that causes one to piss blood, and against kidney and bladder diseases. This ring must be made when the sun is in the sign of Scorpio, and it should be kept for it is quite precious. (*Secrez,* 326)

Complex amulets reveal how the manufacturing of an amulet became increasingly complicated, but also, with the introduction of astrological considerations, how the gradual shift to talismans took place. We shall revisit this point.

THE SUPPORT MATERIALS

Support materials come into play as soon as there is an engraving or inscription.[25] A vast array of stones, many of which are unknown today, were used. Gems represent practically the entirety of support materials, the remaining support materials are founded in the fact that a name or phrase provides the amulet's effectiveness. Around 400, the physician Marcellus Empiricus tells us, for example, that to heal eye problems, it is necessary to write "OUBAIK on a piece of virgin parchment attached to the chain from a weaver's loom so it can be worn around the neck."[26] Marcellus also mentions papyrus and tin strips,[27] while the *Kyranides* cites a gold tube[28] and animal hide:

If you place the tip of a fox penis in a bladder or a piece of hide on which you have written TIN BIB ILITHI with Smyrna ink, and attach it to your person, you can copulate without danger. (*Kyranides,* 139)

The information remains partial, however, unless we take the early Middle Ages into consideration. The evidence from this era attests to the general wearing of amulets, and it provides some clarifications about them. In the eighth century, for example, Saint Boniface complained to Pope Zachariah (died 752) about the fact that people were publicly selling and wearing amulets in Rome.[29]

During this same period, the *Homily on Sacrileges* said: "Whosoever not only enchants but writes letters, attaches angelic or solomonic characters or a snake's tongue around men's necks . . . is a pagan and not a Christian," and later adds that these are made on strips of bronze, iron, or lead, or on parchment.[30] In 813, the Council of Tours spoke of bones and herbs, and the Council of London in 1047 mentioned the remains of the dead.[31] Both the clergy and the guardians of public order viewed amulets with suspicion. The Burgundian, Salic, and Visigothic laws classify amulets, at least some of them, as evil spells.[32] In 650, the Council of Rouen toed the same line by labeling amulets as impious or criminal (*nefaria ligamenta*),[33] and the *Life of Saint Eligius,* written in the ninth century, commands:

> No one may hang amulets [*ligamina*] around the necks of men or beasts . . . these are not the remedies of Christ but diabolical poisons.[34]

FROM AMULET TO TALISMAN

Many amulets are distinguishable from others because they are engraved, which is the infallible method, it is said, to increase their power. In the thirteenth century, an individual named Volmar wrote a lapidary in verse in which he explored this subject. In a short introduction at the start of a new chapter in his work, he states:

> The stones are nothing outside of those that have been engraved. I am going to speak to you about their virtues and power as well as their strength and benefits. Once upon a time the pagans knew how to read the future in the stars, whether good or ill, which many among them still do, those who are scholars. More than one knew that precious stones had to be engraved at the right time and they knew how to discover that time. A portion of these stones

remains to us after they were driven from these lands. There are an immense number of them, but I shall only name a few.[35]

And another anonymous author, speaking of "the virtue of stones that are engraved and those that are carved this way by natural means," states:

Much is granted their force above all others.

Engravings appear in two forms, artificial or natural. In the first case, it is the human being that carves the stone according to the instructions provided by the texts. In the second case, it is nature that has impressed a certain figure atop a gem. These stones are called "cameos." Generally speaking, the ancient treatises distinguish the second kind of stone from the first by using the stock phrase "If you find upon a stone . . ." Doubt is permissible when it simply says "such a figure engraved on . . ." or "such a stone decorated by . . ."

Most of the time the carved figures are astrological depictions of constellations or planets. In the case of animals, the reading is simple: the eagle refers to the constellation of the Eagle and so forth. In the other cases, identification is much more haphazard as we shall see later. But all the animals that are depicted on the stones are not necessarily astronomical symbols, as shown by the following recommendation:

To bear a jasper decorated with the image of a hare that does not correspond with a celestial sign protects one from attacks by demons and spirits. (Leonardi, XIX, 2)

Below we have examples of stones with astrological engravings. Three contain representations of constellations (the Eagle [*Aquila*], the Vulture, and the Hare [*Lepus*]), and three show signs from the zodiac [Leo, Taurus, and Sagittarius]:

If an upright eagle is depicted on an eagle stone (aethite) and this stone has been set in a lead ring, he who wears it has the power

Tabula IIII.

Fig. 5.3. Leo and other talismans
(*Reichelt,* Exercitatio de amuletis)

to catch many fish, no wild beast can harm him, and it will be esteemed by men. (Chael, 37)

If one finds the image of a vulture on a chrysolite, its power is to enchain the demons and the winds, to contain them and gather them together, it protects the place where it is located against evil spirits, and against their ravages; and demons shall obey whoever carries it upon their person. (Ragiel, 9)

It should be noted that "the falling Vulture" (*Vultur cadens, Botercadent*) is the name given to Lyra in the hermetic corpus.

An engraving of a hare in a jasper has the power to protect its owner from a demonic shade, which will not be able to harm him. (Chael, 39)

If one finds a well-drawn image of a Lion in a garnet, it will have the power to retain honors and spare its owner from all illness. It also brings honors and protects its owner from the perils of traveling. (Ragiel, 4)

The image of a Bull in a prase counters, it is said, evil spells, and brings recognition to the leader. (Ragiel, 16)

A man armed with a bow and arrow in an iris stone protects its owner and the place it is located from harm. (Ragiel, 11)

Misreadings and scribal errors often obscure an original meaning. In the following text, the Latin *cygnus* (swan), which refers to the constellation of the same name, was read as *agnus* (lamb), thus eliminating the engraving's connection with astrology:

If the image of a lamb is carved in a stone, it will protect its bearer from paralysis and quartan fever. (Thetel, 7)

This kind of error is quite frequent. For example, here we find a turtledove (*turtur* in Latin) where it should be the constellation of the Vulture (*vultur*):

> If you find a turtledove carved upon a parangon,* and you set it in a lead ring, its owner shall never be wounded or affected by illness. And he will be honored by all men, particularly the elders. (Solomon, 22)

Interpretation is further complicated with a certain group of astrological engravings for which it is impossible to say with any certainty whether they are astral, zodiacal, or decanic.[36] These are the paranatellons, coded representations of heavenly figures, which were once extremely popular and appear in countless variations. Wilhelm Gundel has provided an excellent study of them,[37] but he was not able to inventory all the figures because many manuscripts were still unknown during his time.

> If a bird with a leaf in its beak, as well as the head of a man looking at this bird, are depicted in a paragon, and you have mounted this image on gold, you will be rich, wealthy, and have the respect of all. (Chael, 25)

> If someone finds a precious stone of any kind, with the image of a basilisk or a siren on it, which is a creature that is half-woman and half-serpent, it will have the power to send venomous animals fleeing. (Chael, 17)

In order for the reader to get a good sense of the difficulties involved in identifying the celestial bodies engraved in the amulets in a cryptic or symbolic form, here is what Algol (Beta Per) looks like:

> A man's head with a long beard and a little blood around his throat, carved into a diamond, brings, you should know, victory and audacity, and it protects the body from wounds, And it permits the favor of kings and princes to be obtained. (Hermes, 1)

And here is how the tradition depicted Andromeda:

---

*Today this term is used in reference to black marble, whereas it evoked a golden stone in medieval texts.

If one engraves into a hyacinth or a crystal an image of a woman whose hair is flowing over breasts, as well as a man who has just arrived and is showing her some token of love, and one sets this stone in gold, and if this stone contains amber, aloe, and that herb called polium, the owner of this stone will obtain the obedience of all, and if you touch a woman with this stone, she will act in accordance with your will; and if you place it beneath your head when going to sleep, you shall see everything you desire in dream. (Chael, 30)

As for Orion, it is his hunting horn that makes him identifiable:

A man with a hunting horn is good against scabies, itching, and atrocious dreams. (Thetel, 20)

Fortunately, we sometimes have much more precise information at our disposal. In the description below, Mars is named, and thanks to the comparison of several manuscripts, we know that the Virgin is Venus:

A jasper on which an armed Mars is depicted, or a virgin wrapped in a toga, with a laurel branch in her hand, makes its owner powerful and capable of anything, and it protects him from a violent death, drowning, and adversity. (Solomon, 44)

At one time, Mars and Venus each had their own separate amulet, then they were merged into one. The proof is supplied by what survives of the original tradition:

A jasper bearing the image of a virgin with a flowing garment, and a laurel in her hand, protects its owner from drowning. Thanks to this stone, the individual shall not be tormented by the devil, he will be powerful, and he will obtain everything he desires. (Thetel, 10)

And alas, in many cases all the researcher can do is to present a plausible hypothesis. The man with the scythe, described in the lapidary of Solomon, must be Saturn:

If you find engraved on a stone a standing man holding a scythe in his hand above his head, with a crocodile at his feet, mount it upon a lead ring with a small piece of spring squill root beneath the stone. The wearer of this ring will be spared by all enemies; and if he encounters any, none shall have an ill word to say of him. (Solomon, 30)

I should note here that another author, who says exactly the same thing, suggests an additional virtue: the wearer will also be spared "by the thieves on the roads" (Chael, 35). The *Picatrix* offers us a good reference: "According to other sages, the form of Saturn is that of a man standing upon a serpent, with a scythe in his right hand and a spear in his left" (II, 10). In one case we find a snake, in another a crocodile— how are we to tell which of these two traditions is the original one?

On the following amulet, the carved figure is certainly Jupiter, recognizable by his scepter—is he not the king of the gods?—and the presence of the eagle:

A black stone with a man holding a scepter in one hand and a bird with its wings extended in the other, with a crocodile beneath his feet, is good against attacks by the devil, against all enemies, and expels demons from the possessed. It is said that Alexander wore this stone. (Thetel, 11)

However, each planet has numerous engravings. The *Picatrix* tallies an average of four for each planet (II, 10), but Venus has many more,[38] so we would have to assemble the largest possible corpus in order to get our bearings, as in the following example:

If you find a precious stone on which a standing man is engraved with the head of an steer but the feet of an eagle, imprint this image in wax, carry it on your person, and you shall find none to speak ill of you. (Solomon, 19)

A depiction of Venus shows a man with a bird's head and the claws of an eagle for feet, while another of Mercury has a man with a rooster on his head and aquiline feet. But I have yet to come across any example of a man with a steer's head, so the mystery persists.

As for the constellation of Perseus, the vagaries of the tradition have transformed the Gorgon's head into that of a devil:

> A man holding the head of a horned and winged devil on one hand and a snake in the other, with a lion beneath his feet, and the sun and moon hanging above the image—this stone should be set in lead; it then possesses the power to compel demons to answer the questions put to them. (Thetel, 9)

The lion is a symbol for the constellation of the same name; the serpent may be referring to Ophiuchus.

Were it not for the existence of a miniature in the Jagiellonian Library in Krakow,[39] we would be at our wit's end trying to identify the heavenly body concealed behind the following image:

> If, in a diamond, you find the image of a naked man, standing, with a young naked girl standing at his right, with her hair bound around her head, and the man has his right hand resting on the neck of the young girl and his left on her chest, and he is looking at her face while she is looking at the ground, it is necessary to fix this stone to a ring that is its equal in weight, while placing beneath the stone a hoopoe tongue, myrrh, alum, and as much human blood as necessary to equal the weight of a bird's tongue. None who sees this ring can resist its owner, whether in war or in any other context; no thief or wild animal will be able to enter the house in which said stone is placed. An epileptic who drinks the water in which this stone has been steeped will be healed. Imprint this stone in red wax, hang it around the neck of a dog, and so long as this stone remains in that place, he will never be able to bark; every individual who would bear the seal in question in the midst of thieves, dogs, and enemies, shall be spared by these latter. (Solomon, 35)[40]

This is a description of Mars! And the tradition for this glyph is vouched for by Hermes:

> The form of Mars is that of a named man, standing upright, who has on his right before him, a beautiful virgin who is standing up and who is the form of Venus. . . . Mars is resting is right hand on her neck, and the left, which is extended, on her chest, turning his face toward her.[41]

By and large, the use of amulets survived through the Middle Ages. This is what the doctor Laurent Joubert (died 1582) revealed in his treatise *Des erreurs populaires* (On Popular Errors):

> Against the gout cramp: It is necessary to wear on the feet through the entire night, against the ankles, a jazerant, like bracelets, made of virgin lecton [brass].

> Against all fever: Wear a living spider in walnut hung around the neck.

> Against colic: Wear a ring of lecton [brass] on the little finger. It is said this remedy is also good against epilepsy.

> Against seasickness: It is necessary to wear a ring of three wrapped strands: one of silver, one of brass, and the third of iron.[42]

Here is how people sought protection against evil spells circa 1735:

> Attach these words to your person: Habor Ahtloger Æratin in somiso Pstres I: T: S: Amen.[43]

In this last example it is easy to see the Christian expression: "In the name of the Father, the Son, and the Holy Ghost." The support material for the amulet is not specified, which suggests that at this time and henceforth, the spell was more important.

Having taken this documentary tour through the world of amulets, the reader now knows that the most crucial element of the amulet is primarily its support material, whereas for the talisman it is the ritual of crafting the object. The recipes for manufacturing them consist of a series of forceful declarations. It is that simple. Their use is intentional—the man who makes or has made, buys, and wears such an object does so out of conviction based on the authority of the tradition. This authority derives from the tradition's antiquity and the great names attached to it. Furthermore, in the past as well as in the present, when misfortune threatens or strikes, a common reaction is to turn to the supernatural and irrational. In the case of astrological phylacteries, the philosophy of melothesia—which maintained that the heavenly bodies governed a part of the body and thus determined health—was omnipresent. This was certainly the factor that encouraged the evolution of a large number of amulets into talismans.

Another point is worth underscoring. Compared to the examples of amulets I have cited from the past, the modern amulets offered for sale today are but a pale reflection. This is a case of selling a pig in a poke! In October 2003, when I was at large shopping center in east Paris, I came across a small shop selling them. They were being sold for the equivalent of $12 apiece—a real bargain when one considers the unprecedented advantages the customer would gain from owning one! It is amusing to see how these mass-produced items—which simply recycle magical signs that can be found in the *Key of Solomon*—might be misinterpreted by ethnologists whose work is focused only on the present day and who have no knowledge of the past. If they are being manufactured, even on an industrial scale, it is because a clientele exists for them. This is something that speaks volumes about the enduring nature of ancient mind-sets. However, merely inscribing three kabbalistic signs on any kind of support material does not effectively make something into an amulet. In short, these phylacteries have persisted through the centuries without ever becoming obsolete, but they did lose a good part of what supplied them their numerous virtues. The same observation holds true for the talismans, and it is to them that we shall next turn our attention.

Mysterium
Sigillorum, Herbarum & Lapidum

Oder

Vollkommene Cur und Heilung aller Kranck-
heiten Schäden und Leibes-auch Gemüths-Be-
schwerungen durch underschiedliche Mittel ohne
Einnehmung der Artzney.

In 4. Classen ordentlich abgetheilet Alß

I. Erste Cur und Heilung durch die himmlische Influrtz mit Hülff der Kräuter und Wurtzeln.

II. Zweyte Cur und Heilung durch die himmlische Influtrtz aus den Metallen und Sternen mit Hülff der 7. Sigillen.

III. Dritte und zwar Summarische völlige Cur und Heilung durch die Zusammensetzung der 7. Metallen und Sigillen.

IV. Vierdte Cur und Heilung aber Menschlichen Laster und Gebrechen.

Joh. Arzt.

Was können die Sterne darzu daß die Astronomi ihre Influntz und Wirckung nicht besser wissen/ was können die Kräuter darzu / daß die Medici ihre Natur und Krasste nicht besser verstehen?

Matth. am 10.

Es ist nichts be- deckt/das nicht werde entdeckt werden/noch verborgen das man nicht wissen werde.

Mit beygefügten Figuren und Kupfferstücken auch gantzem Grund
dieses Astronomisch-und himlischen Processus.
Durch
**Israel Hiebnern von Schneeberg/ Mathematicum bey der uhralten
Universitat zu Erffurdt.**
In Verlegung Johann Andreas Bechtolers, 1651.

6

THE CRAFTING
OF TALISMANS

In order to manufacture an effective talisman, a knowledge of certain fundamental rules is necessary. In the seventeenth century, there were six such requirements. The latter were clearly presented by various authors, such as Jean Albert Belin in 1658. We shall therefore begin with him, before looking further back into the past to show how many elements were omitted in order to conform with the criteria of "natural (i.e., licit) magic."

It is therefore first necessary to select the support material, a stone or metal because "the stones, the minerals & the metals have received mutually the forms of all Astrals & come closest to the nature of Heaven, being composed of a matter that is stronger & more compact, & more apt to receive & conserve these celestial virtues."[1]

Once the material has been chosen based on its sympathy with a planet, "it is necessary to engrave the characters, seals, images, or figures of the Planets on the Metals corresponding to these same Planets, or to do even better, it is necessary to melt, and cast in a mold or in sand, the melted metal to be imprinted with this seal, figure, image, or character, which consists of two things: The first, so that the metal is excited, either by the engraving or by the fusion. . . . The second, so that the figure is marked on it."[2]

To attract the force of a heavenly body into a talisman by means of the carving obliges the operator to turn to a planet determined by his intention. "It is third necessary that the Planet be in its best disposition," says Belin, who reminds his readers that the planets have enemies that "alter & and infect their natural influences with contrary qualities."[3]

Next, it is essential to respect a precise hour to make the talisman and for "the attraction of the Planet to be drawn at the Planetary hour," and Belin reminds us in passing that the planets govern a specific hour in every day.[4]

The weather conditions should be good, but this is not absolutely mandatory "because although the Astral influences penetrate through everything & that all the most opaque bodies are to them as glass, nevertheless the air & light serve them as vehicle & passage . . . it is more suitable to begin the operation in an airy place & when the weather is calm."[5]

The last condition is quite modern as it asks the "worker" (in other words, the practitioner) to concentrate on his task and not allow "his mind" to drift "into other strange thoughts."[6] Here we can recognize the influence of Arabic magic, in which the practitioners, through the effort of their mind and their imagination, strive to unite their own *spiritus* to the *spiritus mundi* (*coniugi cum ipso mundi spiritu*).[7]

If we compare this information with what other much earlier authors say, we can see that the ritual has been considerably reduced. In fact, seeking to show that the virtues of talismans were natural and that manufacturing them did not, therefore, run afoul of the law, Belin retained only the astrological aspect of their crafting and dispensed with anything that was redolent of magic. Since the tenth century, and even earlier in the East, scholarly treatises have been teaching us that certain prayers, suffumigations, and inks are necessary for these operations— which is to say, in other words, that the "chain of sympathy" far exceeds the simple relationship between a support material and its planet.

I would therefore like to start filling out Belin's subjective précis by reminding the reader of the foundation of medieval talismanic science, namely sympathy. Jacob Wolff notes this trend of thought in the form of a saying: *periapta vel antipathia vel sympathia operari arbitrantur* ("to work, amulets observe either antipathy or sympathy").[8] Wolff considers *periapta* to be ligatures.[9]

CHAINS OF SYMPATHY

In the world of magic, everything is connected by occult correspondences. The celestial bodies govern all things and disperse their energies in minerals, plants, and animals. They also rule over the different parts of the human body. To obtain an effect, the dispersed virtues are gathered back together based on their affinities. The *Treatise of the Fifteen Stars,* attributed to Hermes, provides us with a primary table of certain correspondences.

Stones	Stars	Plants
Agate	Algomeisa* (Procyon)	Solseqium/primrose
Beryl	Alhabor (Sirius)	Savine
Carbuncle/ruby	Aldebaran (Bull's eye)	Anabulla/Titi mallus
Chalcedony	Cauda Capricorni	Maiorana
Chrysolite	Vultur Cadens, Botercadent (Vega)	Satureia
Crystal	Lampada/Alchorya†	Fennel
Diamond	Pleiades	Black hellebore
Emerald	Algol (Medusa's head)	Celandine
Garnet	Cor Leonis (Arexal, Regulus),	Plantain
Jasper	Alchimech Alramech,‡ Saltator	
	Benenays (Ackair)	Chicory
Magnet	Ala Corvi	Lapatium maius
Onyx	Alhaioth (the Goat)	Prasium/marrubiam
Sapphire	Cor Scorpionis/Calbalazeda§	Aristolochia longa
Sard/amethyst	(Antares)	
	Alchimech Alaazel (Spica)	Sage
Topaz	Alfeca (Corona)	Adal/rosemary

*Arabic *alghumîsâ*
†Arabic *al-choraya;* Hebrew *lampada*
‡Arabic *al simak al râhmih*
§Arabic *kalb-elasad*

While the stars are the reference here, the lapidary of Damigeron-Evax provides a short list of correspondences between minerals and planets, and includes what should be engraved upon them based on the social status of the person for whom the talisman is intended.[10]

Planet	Stone	Free Men	Freed Men	Slaves
Saturn	Agate	Ops [goddess] sitting	Fides publica	Sleeping lion
Sun	Heliotrope	Radiant Sun	Head of the Sun	Altar with torch burning above it
Moon	Chrysolite	Moon seated	Cow	Lunar crescent
Mars	Sardonyx	Mars carrying a trophy	Mars bearing arms	Weapons of Mars [lacuna]
Mercury	Hematite	Mercury seated on a stone [lacuna]		
Jupiter	Herbeuse	Jupiter seated on an eagle	Motionless eagle	Eagle holding a crown in his claws
Venus	Egyptilla	Venus victorious	Venus [lacuna]	Dove motionless in the air

The Damigeron-Evax lapidary also contains fragments of a small decanic library that is introduced as follows:

Here are seven stones that men should keep as phylacteries for the sake of protection, for they are healthy and powerful.

Leo	Chrysolite
Cancer	Aphroselenite
Aries	Hematite
Sagittarius	Ceraunia
Taurus	Mede
Virgo	Arabic
Capricorn	Capostracite

The treatise goes on to say, "I have followed all the engravings of each, which are for all the bodies of the phylacteries, that is to say, safeguards." The descriptions are corroborated by archaeological discoveries throughout the ancient Greek world, which can now be seen in the collections of the major museums.

Out of the enormous corpus of documents I have assembled, I have selected five authors, covering a period that spans the time from early antiquity to the sixteenth century, in order to show what is constant and what varies in the attribution of gems to stars and the signs of the zodiac (see table below). Including more than this would hardly prove useful, as with only slight exaggeration I can state that this material is infinitely variable.

I would like to cite the words of a thirteenth-century grimoire because it offers a great synthesis of the notion of sympathy:

> The person who wishes to connect with the spirit of a planet so that it will serve him, shall use all that is subordinate and which adapts to the nature of said planet, everything that is appropriate for its spirit: food and drink, clothing, suffumigations, activities, times of day, dyes, prayers, sacrifices, stones, shapes, talismans, and constellations.[11]

	Hermes[12]	Evax[13]	Notker[14]	Balenis[15]	Agrippa[16]
Sun		Heliotrope		Sapphire Diamond	
Moon		Chrysolite		Crystal	
Saturn		Agate		Turquoise	
Jupiter		Herbeuse		Carnelian	
Mars		Sard		Emerald	
Venus		Egyptilla		Amethyst	
Mercury		Hemathite		Magnet	
Aries		Hemathite	Scythis		Sardonyx
Taurus		Mede	Smargdus		Sard
Gemini			Lychnis		Topaz

	Hermes	Evax	Notker[1]	Balenis	Agrippa
Cancer		Aphroselenite	Astrites		Chalcedony
Leo		Chrysolite	Ceraunos		Jasper
Virgo		Arabic	Eliotropia		Emerald
Libra			Dentrides		Beryl
Scorpio			Iacinctus		Amethyst
Sagittarius		Ceraunia	Cristallus		Hyacinth
Capricorn		Ostracite	Adamas		Chrysoprase
Aquarius			Ydathites Enidros		Crystal
Pisces			Iaspis		Sapphire
Aldebaran	Rubin				
Pleiades	Cristallus				
Algol	Dyamas				
Alhaioth	Saphirus				
Canis Major	Berillus				
Canis Minor	Achates				
Cor Leonis Arexal	Gorgonza Granet				
Ala Corvi	Onichilus				
Alaazel	Esmaracda				
Alrameth	Iaspis				
Benenays	Adamas				
Alpheta	Topazion				
Cor Scorpionis	Amatista				
Botercadent	Crisolitus				
Cauda Capricorni	Calcedonius				

THE REQUISITE KNOWLEDGE

The *Picatrix,* a translation of an Arabic compilation of magical texts, often reiterates the knowledge that the magician who wishes to craft talismans should possess. It even lists the sciences in which mastery is essential: astronomy, mathematics, music, and so forth. Above all else, the magician "should not occupy his soul, his heart, his intelligence, and his will with any other work but this one, for he who crafts a talisman needs all the strength of his thought and the energy of his gaze to bind the pneumatic spirits together" (III, 6). These pneumatic spirits are four in number: "The Archon, spread throughout the world; the pneuma of the instrument by which the spirit is attracted; the pneuma of good sense; and that of manual crafting" (III, 6).

Every talismanic operation consists of compelling the descent of a spirit into an object in order to infuse that object with that spirit's force. To attract the spirit, the practitioner should know the nature of the planet whose spirit he wishes to draw down, and whose strength or virtues he wishes to spread. He should know what color, what taste, and what odor is governed by its nature. It is therefore necessary that his body possesses this color externally, which obliges the wearing of certain garments, and that he is appropriately perfumed. The same holds true internally: the practitioner should ingest certain foods in order to perform this work.[17]

The magician should also know the exact nature of the support material of the talisman he is making and make sure there is nothing incompatible between its nature and that of the spirit descending into the shaped image (IV, 4). He will use the chains of sympathy to select this support material insofar as his working amounts to binding natural effects. This is only possible, the *Picatrix* says (IV, 4), when one knows what effects animals, plants, and minerals possess, and what planets, fixed stars, and signs of the zodiac cover this or that region of the earth. In short, it is necessary to master astronomy and to know the stations of the planets, their exaltation and their debilitation, the longitude and latitude of the houses of the moon, the nature of the earth's regions, their waters, soil, atmospheric precipitations, animals, and their position

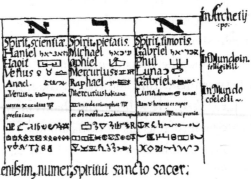

Fig. 6.2. A table of the twelve months of the year showing correspondences between the names of God, the angels, their characters, the months, the gods, the stones, the animals, the sacred birds, the trees, and the plants (after Johannes Trithemius, Calendarium natural magicum perpetuum).

with respect to the equator. Based on his working, the magician should observe when the planet concerned is fully in its place in the zodiac to ensure its effects are not obstructed by those of another celestial body opposed to its nature (III, 5).

Through collecting the clues scattered in the grimoires, we can draw up a list of the astrological requirements, a *vade mecum* of sorts for the practitioner. It is necessary to know:

- the relationships of the planets and constellations;
- the movement of the heavens;
- the signs with oblique or straight risings, the fixed and movable signs, the diurnal and nocturnal signs;
- the favorable and unfavorable planets;
- the talismans adapted to the planets and signs; and
- the words and figures that move the sidereal spirits and the powers.

It is necessary:

- to work at night because the manufacture of the talismans will be better for it;
- to distance the unfavorable planets from the ascendant and its master;
- to place a favorable planet in the house that gives a good aspect to the ascendant and the master;
- to know when the Moon is without opposition—it should not be in conjunction with the Dragon's Tail (the southern point of intersection of the lunar and the ecliptic orbit), nor in a squared aspect with unfavorable planets;
- to avoid times when the moon is in the third, sixth, eighth, or twelfth houses;
- to place the ascendant in accord with the reasons and qualities of what is being requested; and
- to never choose as the master of the ascendant a planet that is in retrograde.

In addition to everything from the category of astronomy and astrology—which were one and the same science during the Middle Ages—various other considerations pertaining to the rite are to be respected. One must have perfect faith in one's undertaking, perform numerous suffumigations, fast often, make many orisons, aspire to what is possible, choose a good place for the operations, and clearly indicate what one wants.[18]

The constraining rules are even collected in the form of aphorisms with intermingled commentary—"The images [talismans] of the fixed stars last longer than those of the planets" (IV, 4); "the power of the talisman is greater when it comes from the seven planets, and more enduring beneath the gaze of a favorable planet" (I, 5)—as well as empirical observations and recommendations, such as "The most solid talisman is made of stone" (IV, 4).

The required bodies of knowledge are detailed, and each planet is assigned a region of the earth (the "climates"), minerals, plants, animals, one or more colors, and inks.

For the workings performed under the aegis of the planets, the sum of knowledge is impressive because the talisman should, among other things, bear a certain number of names that precisely reflect its temporal position (in other words, the astral configuration beneath which it was manufactured). Let us take the example of Mars based on the book dedicated to him (*Libro de Marte*).[19] Mars possesses a heaven, Maon, and an angel, Samahel. Mars's name changes in accordance with its heaven and its climate. When it is in its heaven, the planet is called Dandavitz, and the seven climates over which it extends its influence are called Dacdabotz, Bahandiz, Andahutz, Encaduz, Ardaotz, Antanditantiz, and Maydarz. When Mars is in Aries, its name is Madyn; in Taurus, Soroz; in Gemini, Ariz; in Cancer, Zarir; in Leo, Zaphetume; in Virgo, Szabrir; in Libra, Azrin; in Scorpio, Kapiz; in Sagittarius, Kezzar; in Capricorn, Gadhiroth; in Aquarius, Sobroz; and in Pisces, Szaz.

It is also necessary to know its name in the seven languages used in magic because in principle people should address the gods in their own language. (It is not known exactly where this technique originates.)

Mars is called Setaybon in Chaldean, Madyn in Hebrew, Zezimul in Indian, Camel in Coptic, Marteh in Arabic, Pirtis in Greek, and Mars in Latin. But Mars also has different names depending on the seasons, and the *Libro de Marte* indicates what they are first based on Solomon, and then based on Tymkym,* an Indian astrologer whose name appears frequently in learned treatises:

	Spring	Summer	Autumn	Winter
Solomon	Aarum	Darom	Bearom	Panthaphos
Tymkym	Xarmyn	Oebridel	Oazkhulyl	Camelunch

The necessity of knowing the languages opens up an additional perspective on the world of correspondences and sympathies.[20] In fact, the *Ghâyat al-hakîm* (III, 1) informs us that each of the seven planets governs a language: Saturn for Coptic and Hebrew, Jupiter for Greek, Mars for Persian, the Sun for the Romance languages and part of Greek, Venus for Arabic, and Mercury for Turkish and for Khazarian; the Moon, finally, rules the Slavic tongues and Sabaean. The Latin translation of *Picatrix* replaces Coptic with Chaldean, Khazarian with "the languages of other peoples," and Slavic and Sabaean with German, meaning the Germanic languages.

We should not make the mistake of imagining that the above is sufficient, because the talismanic working must be done at a certain hour of a certain day, and each must be called by its respective name. Furthermore, the name of Mars's day, Tuesday, changes based on the four seasons! Following the sequence of the table above, these names are Saryon, Oaorguernedan, Piranella, and Aglagamusth or Aguaglamuth.

Every planet is finally divided into nine parts over which eight angels or spirits rule. Let's take, for example, those of Mercury. They are arranged as follows: "The name that includes the spirits of Mercury is Merhuyez; that of his upper spirit, Amirez; that of his lower spirit, Hytyz; that of the right, Cehuz; that of the left, Deriz; that of the front,

---

*Also spelled as Timtim, Tymtim, Tumtum, Tintinz, etc.

Maylez; that of the back, Dehedyz; that of his movement in the sky and progression through the signs, Mehendiz," which we can illustrate with the following diagram.

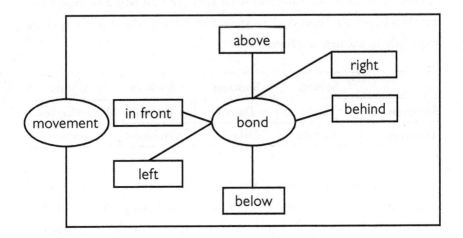

In Mars, the angel's name is Barrostarkas; on the outside, Sascyel; above, Tatael; below, Amalel; on the right, Jlyl; on the left, Rembal; in front, Peroriel; behind, Ganafiel; and around Rerberiel.

ASTROLOGICAL GEOGRAPHY

It is common knowledge that the configuration of the sky changes depending on where you are standing. This point is of major importance for talismanic workings as they call upon the force of the heavenly bodies. Since the time of Ptolemy and probably even before, it has been believed that each geographical region fell under the jurisdiction of a sign of the zodiac. The scholars of ancient times perfected the results of their observations and specified that each decan of a sign ruled over a part of the world. It so happens that each decan has a master or lord—an angel or demon—that must be invoked in the working. The table on page 169 establishes what Hermes[21] had to say on this topic.

Sign	Decan 1	Decan 2	Decan 3	Decanic Angels
Aries	Ocean region	Bactria	Lydia	1. Aulathamas 2. Sabaoth 3. Disornafais
Taurus	Medea	Land of the Amazons	Babylonia	1. Jaus 2. Sarnatas 3. Erchumbris
Gemini	Troadea	Persia	Parthia	1. Manuchos 2. Samurois 3. Asuel
Cancer	Syria	Assyria	Ethiopia	1. Seneptois 2. Somathalmais 3. Charmine
Leo	India	unknown	unknown	1. Zaloias 2. Zachor 3. Frich
Virgo	Arabia	Armenia	Meroe and Elephantine	1. Zamendres 2. Magois 3. Michulais
Libra	Egypt	Trachonitria	Libya	1. Psineus 2. Chnusthisis 3. Psannators
Scorpio	Phoenicia	Cilicia	Cappadocia/ Galatia/ Phrygia	1. Nebenos 2. Churmantes 3. Psermes
Sagittarius	Pamphylia/ Achaia	Nickere Sea	Africa	1. Clinothois 2. Thursois 3. Renethis
Capricorn	Mauritania	Pannonia	Galatia	1.Rempsois 2. Manethois 3. Marxois
Aquarius	Syria	Germany	Sarmatia	1. Ularis 2. Luxois 3. Crauxes
Pisces	Britain	Dacia	Tuscany/ Italy/ Campania	1. Fambrais 2. Flugmois 3. Piathris

THE MOON

The heavenly body that plays the largest role is the Moon, and the *Picatrix* notes:

> One should never undertake any working as long as the Moon is not placed in a degree that is favorable to it, because the Moon exercises manifest and not hidden effects. (I, 4)

And a little farther:

> The Moon has priority over the other planets with respect to its rule over the world of birth and death. It is the intermediary because it receives the effects of the planets and transmits them to said world. (II, 3)

The Moon travels through twenty-eight stations (in other words, it has twenty-eight houses or mansions), and each of them is beneficial, malefic, or both simultaneously, depending in part on the position of the other sidereal bodies. Each station specializes in a specific domain, even if there are intersections and overlappings. The talisman crafter "must absolutely know the circuitous and fixed signs, the fixed and movable signs, those that have a body [i.e., Gemini, Virgo, Libra, Sagittarius, and Aquarius], the diurnal and nocturnal signs, and the fortunate and ill-omened planets. He should, in addition, know when the Moon is sheltered from the accidents that can befall it, and what star and what zodiacal sign are appropriate for the talismanic working. Finally, he must know when the lunar eclipses take place: take great pains to avoid them when performing beneficial workings! . . . Make sure, as well, that the Moon is not waning."

Let's look at several examples. The first station is called Alnath and it is under her that talismans are made for travelers, for parting spouses and friends by inspiring enmity, and so a slave can escape. To discover buried treasure, the second station, Albotain, is necessary. If you wish to draw misfortune upon your enemies and tighten the shackles of prisoners, it will be necessary to work under Algebha, the tenth station;

and to sink a ship or destroy a man's possessions, it will be under the twelfth station, Acarfa.

Each station is suitable for an entire set of magical measures and these vary from one author to the next, as does the amount of detail conveyed. The working includes the choice of a support material—metal, stone, and so forth—an engraving, a perfume, and a prayer or a curse. Here is what we find pertaining to the fifth house:

> In the fifth, to win the favor of princes and persons cloaked in dignity, and to be welcome, they engrave a man's head on silver and suffumigate it with sandalwood.

El Zodiologon de Kancaf el Indio (The Zodiac of Kancaf the Indian), translated from Arabic in thirteenth-century Spain, offers us a fairly complete nomenclature of the sympathies and one characteristic of the lunar houses. With the help of this text, I am able to draw up the following table.[22]

Mansion	Nature	Metal	Lord	Perfume
Alnaht	Igneous, malefic	Brass	Roya	Laudanum
Albutaynn	Warm, moist, malefic	Gold	Arbeyl	Ginger
Zoraya	Average beneficial	Chinese copper	Mugib	Camphor/musk
Aldebaran	Dry, malefic	Iron	Abahra	Plant tar
Alhacia	Hot, dry, malefic	Brass	Hazlu	Black hellebore
Hannaa/ Tahya	Virtuous, dry, beneficial	Gold	Reulan	Opopanax
Aldirah	Moist, average beneficial	Silver	Zahnahyl	Hoopoe feather
Alnatia	Cold, malefic	Tin	Haberaliz	White incense
Tarf	Aqueous, malefic	Tin	Hayhalemah	Feather of an eagle and a fledgling
Gebha	Cold, moist, half beneficial, half malefic	Silver	Iadar	White incense

It is obvious that if one wants to carry out a beneficial talismanic working, the first preference would be the Moon's sixth house. Thus, if the magician ignores the information I have provided here, he risks ending up with a result contrary to the one that he intended.

If the magician wishes to make a talisman for harmony and benevolence, for example, he should use tin, silver, or white wax, wait for the Moon to enter Cancer, address himself to the angel Gabriel, who is then attended by Michael and Samiel, as well as to the winds Hebetel and Halmitab, and their assistants, Bylol, Milalu, and Abuzoba, and finally conjure them by Camoha, Ramoha, Heyehyl, Cefaha, Safaha, Cassal, Naca, and Nadaa.

If the aim is a love talisman, the magician takes silver or white wax, and when the Moon is in Cancer in July, or in Pisces in May, he addresses Abdala and his servitors Barphul, Mayalulu, and Ebuzoba and conjures them by Namoz, Heyel, Caffaa, Bassal, Nacha, and Cana (Calta) Cahala.

When one wishes to undertake a working beneath the Moon, the choice of place is of the utmost importance and changes in accordance with the sign of the zodiac in which this dead planet finds itself.[23] I have detected a clear predominance of places close to water. If the Moon is in Aries or Taurus, one must select a site near a river or other running water; if it is in Libra, it is necessary to choose the east bank of a river; if it is in Sagittarius, the magician must go to the banks of a swift stream with clear waters; when it is in Scorpio, it is necessary to work in a place thickly planted with trees where there is a lot of water.

Next come the high places. When the moon is in Cancer, the magician should find a site on a height overlooking the fields, and when it is in Gemini he should find a hill where the winds are blowing. Things are less specific for the other signs. If the Moon is in Leo, one should work in a wilderness area; in Aquarius, it should be a field at night; and in Capricorn, in a house where only two people are present! The text says nothing about Virgo.

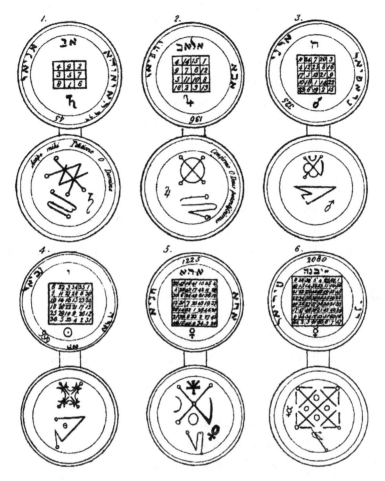

Fig. 6.3. Seals and numerical squares of the planets

COLORS, DYES, AND INKS

Each planet is associated with a color that is dependent on the objective one is pursuing: red is good for talismans crafted at the request of those in need of assistance; white for friendship and love; black for illness, bonds, wounds, and executions; yellow to attract or repel animals and for malefic workings. The individual should therefore address the body on which the color is a dependent. It so happens that each heavenly body rules over three each, and the practitioner should know which.

Saturn: black, white, pale
Jupiter: yellow, white, tin color
Mars: red, yellow, pink
Sun: yellow, pink, red
Venus: red, yellow, gold
Mercury: yellow, ash, pink
Moon: white, red, gray

The practitioner should also wear a garment whose color will be in sympathy with his working. For example, red clothes would be necessary when addressing Mars. For Saturn, the practitioner would wear a cape and black shoes; for Jupiter, yellow and white cloth; and so forth.

In order for the requests to be granted, the practitioner should clothe himself in accordance with the planet, the constellation, or the zodiacal sign. I would like to point out some divergences from the previous list in the following one, which also specifies the type of colored cloth to wear.

Saturn: black and woolly
Jupiter: green and silky
Mars: fire color and silky
Sun: golden yellow and silky
Venus: pink and silky
Mercury: multicolored and silky
Moon: luminous white and silky

Each decan of the zodiac has its own dye. That of the first decan of Taurus, for example, is ash gray; it is made with the help of soot and gum. The second decan of Sagittarius is yellow, and the dye is made with golden yellow pigment, lead oxide, and gum. One comment allows us to deduce that "dye" also means "ink" because, in the case of Sagittarius, the author of *Picatrix* remarks, "And write with it!" (III, 3).

THE SUPPORT MATERIALS

The planets rule over metals and stones, which shall be chosen in accordance with the objective one wishes to achieve. It is upon these support materials that the magical figures, which allow the force to come down into them, will be carved. There are marked divergences between the different texts, so I have settled on the *Picatrix* (II, 10) for our reference, but by making judicious selections to avoid boring the reader.

Saturn rules over iron, diamond, galena, onyx, magnetite, and, more generally speaking, red stones: golden marcasite and hematite are partially subject to him. Jupiter rules over lead, emerald, crystal, chrysolite, and, more generally, brilliant white and yellow stones. Mars governs the sulfurs, red and spotted stones, and red bronze and partially rules marcasite, galena, and alaquech. Venus has power over red metals and partially over silver. Coral, lapis lazuli, and malachite also fall under her jurisdiction, and she partly governs magnetite and almehe (*mahâ*, a white stone). Mercury's dominion includes quicksilver, of course, as well as tin and emerald and partially ceruse. The Moon rules over silver, white marcasite, small pearls, crystal, onyx, and, partly, almehe. Red copper, lapis lazuli, pearl, coral malachite, and partly silver, beryl, and magnesium, are subjects of Venus. The Sun's sphere, meanwhile, contains all clear, brilliant stones, and it partly rules azumbedich, ruby, and golden marcasite.

We can see in this simple list that some stones are subject to the influence of several planets. If someone wishes to put them to good use and attract their virtues, it is necessary that the heavens do not present any conflicts between them, which is to say they have to be in good aspect.

This does not resolve all the problems concerning the choice of support material because the stones also fall under the jurisdiction of the thirty-six decans of the zodiac and the constellations. Some authors maintain that a plant should also be added to ensure maximum effectiveness. In fact, "stones, plants, animals, and other things are not governed by a single heavenly body," says the *Picatrix*. "All the stars have their own natures, attributes, and conditions" (I, 32). Two thirteenth-century Anglo-Norman lapidaries permit us to draw the following correspondences from their headings.

Ruby:	Capricorn	Red jasper:	Mars
White hyacinth:	Jupiter	Aphroselenite:	Mars
Chrysolite:	Sun	Crystal:	Mars
Jasper:	the Hare	Turquoise:	Aquarius
Carnelian:	Venus	Jasper:	Hunting Dogs

The *Sacred Book of Hermes to Asclepius* has the merit of offering us a fairly complete panorama of everything concerning the decans. In it, we find the name and field of activity for each one, the names of the stone and plant necessary to craft the talisman, and the carving that should be accomplished. As an example, let us examine the decans of Aries. The first, whose name is Chenladori, has the face of a well-dressed small boy who is carrying a scepter and has his hands raised; if he is carved like this on a Babylonian stone and some isophryse is placed beneath it, and the entire thing is sealed within an iron ring, one will win the favors of each and all. The second is Chontaret or Kay. He has a dog's head and carries a scepter in his right hand and a discus in his left, and he is clothed. He rules over the temples, the nose, and all that afflicts them. If one carves him on a siderite and then adds some iberis to it before mounting it upon a gold ring, one will be protected from all afflictions of the head and nose. However, this individual should abstain from eating stork, fish, or seabird. The third is Siket. He resembles a woman wearing a knee-length garment, holding a scepter in his right hand and a pitcher in his left. This decan rules over hearing, the uvula, and the teeth. This decan should be engraved upon a bostrochyte, with the addition of some large plantain. This combination should then be sealed in whatever one wishes, and the wearer should abstain from eating the tripe of a ram.

PHYSICAL PREPARATION

Before launching into an operation that always includes some danger, it is necessary to purify oneself. "If you wish to pray to a planet or ask it something, start by placing your faith in God, purge your heart of evil thoughts, rid your clothing of all stain, purify and clarify your soul," says the *Picatrix* (III, 7). All the texts are in agreement in recommending sexual abstinence (for two to seven days), a bath, a change of clothes, and a fast or a specific diet. Here, too, it is appropriate to avoid alienating the planets by neglecting their requirements. The *Picatrix* (IV, 2) recommends a seven-day fast that ends on the day dedicated to the planet. Let's look at some examples. For Jupiter, one would fast from Friday to Wednesday; for the Moon, from Tuesday to Monday; and for the Sun, from Monday to Sunday. The aim here is to attract the good graces of the planetary angel.

Thanks to the Spanish *Libro de Luna* (Book of the Moon), we know that the duration of the fast is different depending on whether a planetary or zodiacal talisman is being crafted. "He who wishes to manufacture a zodiacal talisman," the grimoire says, "should fast for three days preceding the working and begin it on the fourth day."[24]

After having fasted for the requisite time period, the practitioner eats the liver of the animal that he sacrificed to the planetary angel or spirit. A black crow is sacrificed to Anzil (Ashbîl), the spirit or angel of Saturn; a sheep to Roquiel (Rûfijâ'îl), that of Jupiter; a spotted cat to Zemeyel (Rûbijâ'îl), that of Mars; a calf to Yebil (Ba'îl), that of the Sun; a wood pigeon to Anbetayl (Bîtâ'îl), that of Venus; a black rooster to Arquil (Harqîl), that of Mercury; and a sheep to Cahîl (Saljâ'îl), that of the Moon.*

I have not found similar prescriptions for the spirits of the decans of the zodiac, but this does not mean they do not exist. An enormous number of manuscripts remain to be scrutinized and only a small fraction of them have been published. I will therefore leave the work of completing this investigation to others.

The purpose of purification is to procure for the practitioner's body the nature of the planet whose spirit he wishes to move in order to obtain the desired effects. He should therefore eat foods

---

*In parentheses I have provided the written forms from *Ghâyat al-hakîm,* IV, 2.

corresponding to this planet, sometimes in accordance with a restrictive ritual. Sages "abstain for forty days from consuming meats and feed on the fruits of the earth, grains and plants. Each day they reduce the amount of food they eat until the fortieth day, so on that day they eat only one-fortieth of what they had eaten on the first day. . . . They practice abstinence and take remedies that cause them to lose their desire for food and drink."[25]

INGREDIENTS AND ACCESSORIES

The magician should supply himself with all kinds of ingredients and certain objects. One early recipe says that to craft a love talisman, he will use a she-wolf's vulva, a hare's penis, eyes from a white cat and fat from a white dog, incense, galbanum, camphor, white sandalwood, and aloe. Another recipe asserts that this item requires the marrow of a gazelle, mutton fat, camphor, the brain of a hare, white wax, white sugar, a white cloth, a silver needle, a silk thread, and a pot of dirt. It is easy to see the concurrence of certain components (vulva, penis) and the desired result. The specification for things that are white in color is easily explained as it is the color of Venus/Aphrodite, the goddess of love.

When the talisman is intended to work a curse, the ingredients can be alarming in nature. One recipe recommends the practitioner take a decapitated man's head, his spleen, his heart, and his liver, plus animal heads, oil, fire, and henbane.[26] Here the magician becomes synonymous with the sorcerer.

When the magician is working by means of the planets, he must imperatively follow the rules of sympathy. If he is working through Saturn, he must have fire, a cow or calf, and the ingredients for the suffumigation ad hoc.[27] If he is working through Jupiter, it is a bit more complicated. The operation requires a table, a tripod, an iron incense burner, musk, camphor, aloe, various perfumes, chives, a candle, four baskets filled with pomegranates, the cooked roasted meat of ram, chicken, and dove, plates of cabbage, four pitchers of wine, four transparent vases, and myrtle branches.[28] The practitioner must also wear a white cape and a crystal ring adorned by a cross. Once in possession of all this—and having respected the rules concerning time, place, celestial configuration, and so forth—the magician following the ritual will proceed with the suffumigations.

THE SUFFUMIGATIONS

In the East, aromatic substances have always been used in ceremonies of consecration, mainly as offerings, and the Bible provides us with a clear example:

> And the Lord said unto Moses, "Take unto thee sweet spices, stacte, and onycha, and galbanum; these sweet spices with pure frankincense: of each shall there be a like weight. And thou shalt make it a perfume, a confection after the art of the apothecary, tempered together, pure and holy. And thou shalt beat some of it very small, and put of it before the testimony in the tabernacle of the congregation, where I will meet with thee." (Exodus 30:34–36)

The Catholic and Orthodox churches have clearly retained these rites; however, they have been reduced to the suffumigation of incense.

To consecrate the talisman, suffumigations are necessary and the ingredients taken into account are meticulously listed. Here we will examine some examples in the *Picatrix*.

For lunar talismans, it is necessary to collect laurel leaves, cinnamon, sesame, cumin, the fat of a white snake, dried rabbit brain, and that of a white cat, along with fox blood that has also been dried. For talismans of Jupiter, one needs dried myrtle and marjoram flowers, dried walnuts and hazelnuts, the dried brains of a rooster, duck, and wood pigeon, dried peacock and camel blood, camphor, and musk. And for talismans of Saturn, one needs the fruits of the mandrake and dried olive leaves, the fruits of the castor oil plant, black Bengal nuts, and dried chickpeas.

The second stage consists of crushing and filtering the blend and mixing it with honey in order to make wafers that can then be dried in the sun. While this preparation is taking place, the talisman maker should address the spirit of the planet of the desired talisman, and do so "in the six directions."

While collecting these products was not too difficult in the Middle East, this was certainly not the case in western Europe during the Middle Ages, but we have to believe that the highly exotic nature of the ingredients reinforced the mystery surrounding the crafting ritual. There is another difficulty that should not be lightly dismissed: the question of the proportions. A comparison of the *Ghâyat al-hakîm* with the various manuscripts of its Latin translation (the *Picatrix*) reveals how any attempts of experimentation by the amateur will be a futile endeavor! In fact, the units of measure employed are not the same in the East and West, and the adaptation of the systems is only an approximation. Furthermore, the copyists of the manuscripts used codes for the weights and measures and they have not always been clearly deciphered.

Here are the ingredients for the suffumigations of the Sun and Mercury based on the *Picatrix* and the *Ghâyat al-hakîm*.*

	Picatrix (IV, 6)	Ghâyat al-hakîm (IV, 6)
Sun	flower of nard, yellow and red sandalwood, 10 drams of each	Indian nard, 5 mitqâls
	truncheon, thyme, rose laurel wood, 6 drams of each	yellow and red sandalwood, 3 mitqâls of each
	costus, 2 drams	truncheon, bark of red cinnamon, 3 mitqâls of each
	eagle brain and blood, cat brain and blood, 20 drams of each	costus, 2 mitqâls
		brain and blood of a sparrow, brain and blood of a vulture, 10 mitqâls of each—blood and brain should be of equal quantity

*The dram represents close to one-eighth of an ounce; the mitqâl, around 4.64 grams.

	Picatrix (IV, 6)	Ghâyat al-hakîm (IV, 6)
Mercury	henbane flower, wild nard, 20 drams of each	flower of bulrush, malobathrum, asaret, 10 mitqâls of each
	amber and toad testicles, 4 drams of each	amber and castoreum, 2 mitqâls of each
	red turnip, 2 drams	
	dried crow and black cat brain, 20 drams of each	blue bdellium, 1 mitqâl
		magpie, hoopoe, and tortoise brain, 10 mitqâls of each
	blood of a fox, 40 drams	
		blood of a domestic ass, 30 mitqâls

With only slight exaggeration, I can say that every operation by the planets required a suffumigation. The instructions provided in the various grimoires parallel and complete one another. The *Libro de Marte* (Book of Mars) indicates that for Mars, red and yellow sandalwood was used along with incense and bdellium. The *Oraciones en los Signos* (Orations on the Signs) informs us that when Mercury is in Aries or Gemini, it is necessary to take gray amber and aloe; when it is in Taurus, flowers and quince; in Libra, Indian saffron root and celandine, a poppy; and so forth.

For the workings by the Moon, there is one suffumigation per house. The *Zodiologon de Plinio* (Zodiac of Pliny) provides a complete list of ingredients, which offers some remarkable details.[29] For the apprentice magician, I will provide them here. The number of the house is indicated in parentheses. For "simple" suffumigations, one takes perfumes (7, 16, 26)—nothing more precise is stated—of sulfur (8); pine resin (9); aloe (2); sandalwood (5); gray amber (10); storax (1, 19); stag's horn, in other words, plantain (18); tree flowers (25); shavings of horn, which is a plant (24); ape skin (17); fox skin (20); skin of a saltwater fish (28); and cat or dog skin (14). For "compound" suffumigations, combined are red myrrh and storax (4); aloe and gray amber (6, 13); liquid storax and asafetida (27); sulfur and scarab (21); incense and nutmeg (15); and lion hide and asafetida (12). The *Plinio* collection does not indicate anything for the eleventh, twenty-second, and twenty-third houses.

PRAYERS, INVOCATIONS, AND CONJURATIONS

Prayers and invocations form part of the consecration ritual of the talisman. Thanks to them, the power of the selected astral body spirit descends into the crafted object. While the smoke is rising from the burner, the practitioner must address the demon, spirit (intelligence), or angel of the body chosen, based on the objective that is being sought. The *Picatrix* (III, 7) recommends this:

> If you wish to pray to a planet or ask something of it, start by placing your faith in God, purge your heart of all evil thoughts, your clothing of all stains, and clarify and purify your soul. Furthermore, you should know which of the seven planets you need to address for this matter and the nature of the planet under whose jurisdiction it falls. Then turn toward that planet whose nature corresponds to your design, wear its clothing, make suffumigations with its ingredients, and invoke it with its invocation.

Here is a detailed ritual to address Jupiter as given in the *Ghâyat al-hakîm* (III, 9). The author of the treatise recommends the following for the practitioner:

> Prepare yourself on a Thursday when the Sun has entered Sagittarius or Pisces, and when the Moon is in the Head of the Ram, the exaltation of the Sun. Construct a room and decorate it as nicely as possible. Enter it alone; this is the sanctuary. Take various foods, sweet, dry, and moist: honey, butter, nut oil, and sugar; make thin wafers with flour, butter, milk, sugar, and saffron, as many as you can. Place a large table platter on a solid pedestal in a corner of the room in front of an oven with the ingredients, and place on the platter musk, camphor, and aloe wood, the triple perfume, galia, and a handful of mastic. Then make piles of the wafers without breaking them and place dry and moist sweets on the platter with a lit candle in the middle and, next to it, four baskets

filled with pastries, cold meats, roasted and boiled, of ram, hen, and chicken, and a variety of vegetables. Near each basket place a pitcher of wine and a clean goblet and, between two, some aromatic flowers. Suffumigate one corner of the platter with mastic and another with aloe, then, when you are alone, recite this prayer:

"DAHAMUS, ARMAS, HITIS, MAGAS, ADRIS, TANIRS, FARUS, DAHIDAS, AFRAWAS, KI'AQIRAS! Approach all together as one, breathe these perfumes and eat these foods!"

You will repeat this prayer seven times and then you will leave the room and wait quietly for a period of some time. Then go back for the sixth time and make your request. The spirits shall then appear to you, handsome and well dressed, and you may request of them what you wish.

The invocations are almost always constructed along the same lines: the practitioner praises the heavenly body, recalls its characteristics, and asks it to grant his prayer. "O high lord, you who possess a great name and live in the highest heaven," says the *Picatrix* (III, 7), for example, and an invocation preceding a conjuration of Jupiter opens with these words "May God keep you safe! Lord bless you who are supreme fortune, who is hot and moist, equal in all works." The conjurer then says:

"I conjure you, first by the name of God most high who has given you power and spirit, and by your good wishes and your splendid effects, by your precious and noble nature, to do this for me." Then say what you request!

The practitioner continues his praise and finishes his speech with "Grant all the requests that are made for the good!" This done, he must humbly prostrate himself with submission and servility, reverence and slowness, and sometimes repeat the prayer and invocation several times. It is helpful to select the hour and the day of the planet invoked because this contributes to the smooth functioning of the operation.

A comparison of these prayers with older accounts strongly suggests that they became codified both in spirit and in their mode of expression. The Greek magical papyri provide several prayers to planetary spirits of this sort. I will cite two to show the difference between Hellenic magical traditions and Middle Eastern ones. The first is addressed to Zeus (Jupiter); the second to Ares (Mars).[30]

> Lord god, all-powerful father, creator of all things visible and invisible, king of the rulers and dominator of the dominant, grant us the strength of your grace so that Zeus may submit to us, because all is possible for you, lord. Zeus, I conjure your wisdom, your knowledge, your healing energy, your celestial path, over which you walk by the names herein: ANOPH, ORSITA, ATNOX, ONIVEGI, ATZINIEL, ANKANITEI, TYNEOS, GENIER, KANIPTZA, so that you may pour your grace upon me in this task I am accomplishing.

> Terrible god, unspeakable god, invisible god whom no human being has seen or can see, god who caused the abysses to shudder when they saw him and who reduced the living to the state of dead men, grant us your grace so that we may subject the god Ares to our will. Ares of fire, I conjure the god who created the intelligible substances and the entire army of fire: I conjure your energies, your path, and your brilliance by the names herein: OUTAT, NOUET, CHOREZE, TINAE, DACHLI, AMBIRA, NOLIEM, SIET, ADICHAEL, TZANAS, PLESYM, so that you may bestow your grace upon me for the task I am accomplishing.

However, unsympathetic commentators like the seventeenth-century scholar and astrologer Jacques Gaffarel felt that the words served no purpose:

> Thus, with regard to our discourse, let us state that in the manufacture of these figures all words are indifferent, & they are only good for amusing the most simple, as when Albinus said for healing the tertian and quartan fevers, pains of the nerves, ventricles, and the

shameful parts, it is necessary to engrave the image of a scorpion on gold or silver, when the Sun is in its own house, & the Moon in Capricorn, & and when engraving this, it is necessary to say, *Exurge, Domine, Gloria mea, exurge psalterium & cithara, exurgam diluculo,* & recite again the Psalm: *Miserere mei Deus, miserere mei, quia in te confidit anima mea.* This has given birth to a thousand superstitions & people have begun seeking to cure illnesses with simple words without any regard for the stars nor for anything else.[31]

The maker of talismans must be master of uncommon knowledge, restrictive rituals, and countless ingredients—in other words, such a person must be a magician, a sage, and a scholar. One may wonder about the reason why the grimoires provide their meticulous enumerations with lists of everything that must be respected in order to move the sidereal spirits and procure their forces for oneself, but these books supply the answer: every magical working that puts you in contact with the spirits is dangerous. This is so self-evident it is not even mentioned most of the time, or else it is alluded to indirectly, such as when the recommendation is made to draw a circle equipped with every possible safeguard (sacred names, symbols, *characters*) in the center of which the practitioner will stand. As the *Picatrix* informs us:

> When the rules are not bound to the operations, the spirit and the body run a very great danger [*spiritus et corporis maximum generatur periculum*]; those who do not know how to execute the workings properly run extreme risks and terrible accidents befall them [*accident pericula expavescenda maxima*]. . . .
>
> If he is not wise and versed in the nature of spiritual beings and stars, he who works through these names and these words* will be slain by the power of the spirit that descends. . . .
>
> If you do not do as you have been told, your working will fail and know well that misfortune shall befall the agent [*scias quod damnum accidet operatori*].[32]

---

*In other words, the practitioner who compels the spirits to come down to earth.

LA SVPERSTITION DV TEMPS,

Reconnuë aux Talifmans , figures Aftrales, & ftatuës fatales.

Contre vn Livre Anonyme intitulé

LES TALISMANS

IVSTIFIEZ.

AVEC LA POVDRE

DE SYMPATHIE

foupçonnée de Magie.

Par le R. P. F. FRANÇOIS PLACET,
Religieux de l'Ordre de Premonftré,
& Prieur de Bellozanne.

A PARIS,

Chez la Veufve GERVAIS ALLIOT, & GILLES ALLIOT, Libraire Iuré, rue S. Iacques, à l'Image S. Nortbert, proche S. Yves.

M. DC. LXVIII.
Avec Approbation & Permiffion.

Fig. 7.1. *The cover of Father François Placet's book*
La Superstition du temps, *1668*

7

THE USE
OF AMULETS
AND TALISMANS

Amulets and talismans have not only been used for individual protection. They also serve to protect groups of people, for example in the family home or in cities.[1] They can likewise provide protection to the means of life, most often the fields. At the beginning of the Common Era, Syrian Christians wrote on their homes "Flee, flee Abizon, because here live Sisinios and Sisinia and the voracious dog." Others inscribed the first verse of Psalm 79 and 98, or even Psalm 90, which was very widespread as a domestic amulet.[2] During the Middle Ages, Jews attached an amulet to the doors of their homes called a mezuzah, which was intended to ward off demons; it contained an extract from the Torah (the Pentateuch or Law of Moses). For the same purpose, the great reformer Martin Luther wrote a verse from Genesis on the walls and openings of his house.

The magical object that appears in tales and legends is often simply called a "talisman." It can be found at the entryway to a town or castle. We will not discuss these examples further, however, since by and large these texts date from more recently than the Middle Ages. Nevertheless, they quite often contain extremely ancient themes and motifs.

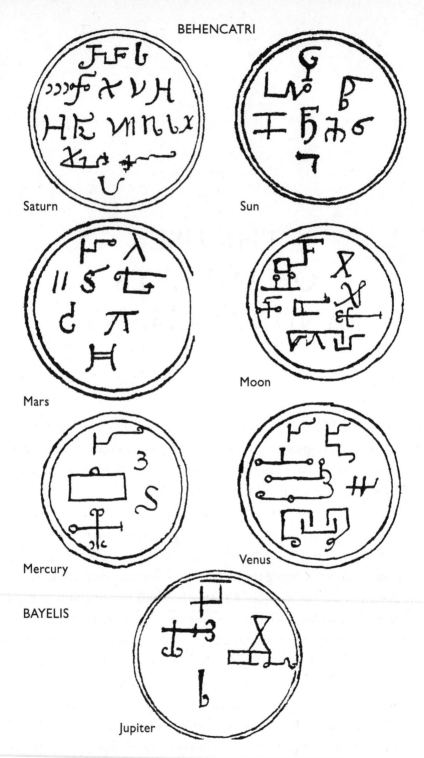

Fig. 7.2. *Planetary seals of Behencatri, from the Ghent Manuscript*

WHERE AND HOW TO WEAR AN AMULET

The ancient texts seem to provide a complete panoply of the ways in which amulets were worn or carried. These descriptions range from the utterly vague (simply stating that the amulet must be somehow "attached," *adalligatum*) to the extremely precise. Below we will look at several examples regarding bezoars, animal concretions considered to be stones, which were worn hung around the neck or elsewhere on the body.

According to the *Kyranides,* the heart of a victorious stork should be attached to the arm, while the eyes of a tarantula should be attached to the left arm, and the right foot of the "solar lizard" to the same place.[3] The stones found in the bellies of fledgling swallows go on the right arm. The skin and head of the vulture, and the heart of the salamander, are attached to the elbow.

An engraved jasper and the stone taken from the head of the rainbow wrasse (a fish) are worn on the chest, while the back feet of a frog are attached to the feet, as are the skin and bone from the thigh of a white-tailed eagle.

A hyena's tongue should be placed in one's shoe. One wears a belt made of sealskin, and one hides the right eye of a wolf beneath one's clothes to ward off ghosts and wild beasts, and to dispel fevers and shivering.

The Pseudo-Apuleius herbal indicates that mugwort should be carried in the hand if you wish to avoid travel fatigue, but more it states that it is necessary to have the plant on your person or with you. Thus, for example, someone who has a peony on his person is protected from lunacy, or bryony can be worn around the neck or at the belt if one seeks protection from afflictions. Clearly there is not always an obvious relationship between the place where the amulet is fastened and the affliction one is seeking to ward off or cure. The main thing is to have the amulet on your person.

When the amulet is intended to protect a place, it is simply set down there. When placed in a house, for example, mugwort wards off the evil eye and thwarts poisons.

Often it is necessary to place the amulet in a container such as a tube, a capsule, or a box made of gold or iron, or in a gold leaf, a rag, a piece of a rock snail, or an animal hide. Buckskin recurs frequently in the recipes, whereas the skin of an eagle, vulture, and mule each only appear once, respectively.

> The right eye of a seal carried in buckskin brings love and success to its bearer.[4]
>
> After successfully hunting an eagle, the one who wears its heart, the skin from its head, its eyes, and the tips of its great wings will be amorous and cherished. And he who bears it in a phylactery will be made peaceful thereby and well as loved and loving, and if he marches into the midst of battle, he shall not be wounded, he will no longer suffer the damage caused by storm or lightning, but in all things will be looked on well and tranquilly. But he must wear it sewn into its own skin and placed in a gold tube.[5]

THE TALISMANS OF PLACE

The Cities

The Byzantine anthology *Patria* informs us that Apollonius of Tyana erected numerous magical barriers around Constantinople[6] and that these talismans forbade access to the city by harmful animals, both crawling and poisonous beasts, but also insects like mosquitoes and flies.[7] An Arabic collection of magical spells known as the *Tabula Smaragdina* or *Emerald Tablet* goes into detail in this regard. Here Apollonius bears the name of Balinas:[8]

> The talisman of scorpions. It holds them at a distance from the town and cancels their effect inside it. This is the talisman that Balinas crafted for the inhabitants of Emese* and it still exists today.
>
> Observe the entrance of Saturn into Scorpio when the Moon is there, and consider the rising of the sign of Scorpio. Then begin preparing this image when the end of the first part of Scorpio is rising so that you shall have completed it when the entire sign of Scorpio

---

*[This is the Syrian city now known as Homs. —*Trans.*]

is visible. The upper half of the image depicts a man and the bottom half a scorpion. Place it on an iron column and fasten it there with an appropriate solid nail. Its erection and the crafting of the nail must be done at Scorpio's rising, and the same is true for the preparation of the column. If it is not finished, one must stop once Scorpio's rising has been achieved; the work shall be completed at the next period of Scorpio rising. You shall raise the column between two solid walls, and surround it by a building that you shall cover so that the talisman will be protected at the middle of the locality. All the scorpions present in the city shall flee or die, none will see the light of day again.

This book therefore provides us with a means of manufacturing that is strictly connected with the celestial bodies. This talismanic protection, which is called apotelesmatics, is confirmed by other passages. I would like to cite two of them because they form part of largely unknown texts that deserve to see the light of day. The first comes from the indispensable Balinas; the second is from Hermes Trismegistus:

The talisman of serpents. This is the one the sage Balinas affixed to the walls of Epiphania. He carved it upon a stone that he inserted in those used to build the castle, and it has remained there until today. Serpents flee it wherever it may be found, and if a viper bites someone and this person hastens to this image and gazes at it, he will be delivered from his affliction and cured.

One should observe the moment when the Moon enters the last half of Sagittarius in which the ascendant is located . . . and immediately engrave the following figure on a stone [the manuscript shows a large horned serpent sticking out its forked tongue]. If one carves this on a steel or iron bracelet, it gives its wearer a charm against vipers. Someone bitten by a viper shall be healed if he looks at the snake carved on the bracelet.

Description of the talisman that Hermes crafted against violent winds for the purpose of calming them. If one takes its imprint in wax and carries it onto a ship going to sea, one will be protected from tempestuous winds. The wind is favorable and blows at an average strength. This talisman is the same that the sage Balinas placed in the Syrian city of Emese when its inhabitants complained to him about the violence of the winds blowing there, whereupon the winds calmed down.

If you wish to make one, observe if Jupiter is in Libra or Aquarius, and that the previous part of the opposition or conjunction is located in a windy sign and if the Moon and Jupiter are in said sign, without any aspect to Saturn. Then carve into a hard yellow stone the image of a man standing squarely on his feet, on a stool, holding something in his hand that looks like a large shield with which he is protecting his face and chest, and a stone sword in the other hand, but in an entire block. Next carve the following signs on his forehead and these on his chest—these are magic *characters* [italics added]—then the following figure on the rim of the shield. Once this is done, have a tall building erected in the center of the city or region and place this image at its highest point. If the image if large and solid, and has no reason to dread the cold and rain, it does not need to be protected. If it is small, give it shelter by building something over it. Thanks to the higher will of God, the winds of this region will be regular.

In the Arab world, Ibrahim Ibn Wasif Shah's *Summary of Wonders* provides numerous examples of these urban talismans.[9] Memphis "was defended by formidable talismans" (II, 6); the city of Outirâtis "was surrounded by talismans in the shape of idols whose bodies were those of men and whose heads were those of monkeys. Each had the power to repulse certain afflictions and produce certain blessings" (II, 1 and 4). When El-Welid sought to rebuild Alexandria, "animals came out of the walls every night and overturned the construction. He had gold and copper statues made depicting them, which were placed in the city's foundations, knowing that they would send the monsters fleeing" (II, 8). Adim built a lighthouse on the bank of the Orient Sea, on top of which was placed an idol turned toward the east with its two arms extended to mark the boundary over which the sands and monsters should not cross (II, 3).

Ibrahim notes that the Egyptians made famous talismans and they knew which were capable of deterring the enemies of their land. Nekraus II "set talismans of every varying shape over the gate of each city to protect its entrance" (II, 2). The magician Adjinas is renowned for those he made for King Afraous, but after being vexed by his successor, "with the resources of his art, he gradually canceled the virtue of the talismans of Egypt because there are, in the face of each talisman, powers capable of destroying its force and other talismans that can fight it" (II, 2). Ibrahim finally mentions the tombs of kings like Misraim and Koftarim, whose treasure chambers were filled with powerful talismans. Regarding Nekraus I, he says, "Fixed [upon his tomb] were talismans to repel reptiles and harmful beasts from the building, and whoever wanted to rifle through it, man or genie" (II, 2). Other Arab authors mention numerous talismans such as the lion of Hamadhân in Persia, which protects the city from cold and snow, the statues of Fustat that prevent floods, the stone bulls buried in Lorca, and the copper leeches of Huecas. We would be mistaken, however, to look upon such practices as only those of another civilization. In his *Historia Francorum* (History of the Franks), Gregory of Tours (538–594) describes the burning of Paris and notes:

> However the churches and the houses belonging to them were not burned. It used to be said that this town of Paris was, as it were, hallowed from antiquity, so that no fire could overwhelm it, and no snake or rat appear there. Only a short time before, when a drain by the bridge was being cleaned out and the mud which blocked it was being taken away, they discovered a snake and a rat made of bronze. They removed them both and from this time onwards an inordinate number of rats and snakes made their appearance. Subsequently the city began to be plagued with fires.[10]

Gregory clearly established a cause-and-effect relationship between the disappearance (or change of location) of the bronze figures and the eruption of calamities, and this passage has been frequently cited by more recent authors, such as Jean-Baptiste Thiers in the seventeenth century.

Virgil, who was regarded as a sorcerer in the Middle Ages, remained a renowned figure because of his urban talismans. He erected a bronze man facing Vesuvius with his arbalest held out; as long as no one broke the unspoken ban on touching the string of the weapon, the fire was contained and imprisoned inside the volcano.[11] In his *Imperial Diversions,* which he completed around 1214, Gervasius of Tilbury stated:

> We know that in Campania, in the city of Naples, Virgil erected a bronze fly by magic: it was of such proven effectiveness that as long as it remained intact at the site where he placed it, not a fly entered the city, no matter how long and wide.[12]

According to Cecco d'Ascoli (1257–1327), astrologer to the duke of Calabria, this fly would have been a stone on which an astrological sign could be seen. In this same city, Gervasius goes on to note, "was a meat market in whose wall, it is said, Virgil placed a piece of meat of such power that as long as it remained sealed within this spot, no meat, no matter how old, inside the walls of this market, would offend the nose of he who smelled it, nor the sight of those who looked at it, nor the taste of those who ate it." Jean-Baptiste Thiers knew most of the medieval Western legends concerning talismans (which he often confused with amulets) and he drew up a brief list:

> Such was the Palladium of Troy; the Roman Shields; the fatal Statues of Constantinople; the Statue of Memnon in Egypt that moved and pronounced oracles as soon as the Sun went overhead; the Statue of Fortune of Sejan, which inspired respect & brought good fortune to all those who possessed it; the bronze Fly & the gold Leech of Virgil, by which means he prevented flies from entering Naples & and caused the leeches in a well to die.[13]

In his 1673 text entitled *Galgen-Männlin* (Mandrake), the great German novelist H. J. C. von Grimmelshausen (ca. 1620–1676) notes: "I have been told a great many things about talismans [*von Talismanibus**] or about these figures which, under certain constellations, are engraved upon precious stones or metal. What amazing powers they have!"[14] He also recalls several famous talismans of his time: the statue of Venus in the Cypriot city of Paphos, the Palladium of Troy, the Amyles of Rome, the statue of Fortune in Selan, as well as the two creations of the enchanter Virgil—the bronze fly and hedgehog—and three by the magician Apollonius: a stork in Constantinople that sent its fellow storks fleeing, a talisman against flies in Antioch, and one against scorpions in Tripoli and Arabia. Grimmelshausen pokes fun at the belief while telling the story of a woman who, on acquiring a talisman, discovers that it is a thief's thumb, and he adds that magicians and other sorcerors scavenged any item they could from hanged men: "Three years ago," he says, "a hanged thief was seen stripped of everything."

In his *Démonomanie* (I, 3), Jean Bodin mentions several talismans that enjoyed a legendary reputation and turn up repeatedly in many of his writings:

> It is said that there was not a fly to be found in the palace of Venice & in the palace of Toledo there was but one. But we have to think, if this is the case in Venice & Toledo, that some idol is buried beneath the doorsill of the palace as was discovered several years past in a city of Egypt, where crocodiles were never to be seen, as was the case in other towns along the Nile that had a lead crocodile buried beneath the doorsill of the temple, which Mehmet Ben-Thaulon had destroyed. The inhabitants complained about this, saying that since then crocodiles have been plaguing them.

Antoine Mizaud (died 1576) gives three recipes in his 1574 treatise devoted to superstitious beliefs:

---

*The word "talisman" was introduced into German by the poet and translator Georg Philipp Harsdörffer in his *Frauengesprächsspiele* (1641–1649).

He who seeks to drive the flies from a place and make them vanish should carve a fly in the stone of a ring or on a copper or tin strip when the second face, that is the median degrees of the eleventh to the twentieth degree of Pisces, is rising over the horizon. One carves the image of a fly, spider, or snake depending on what one wishes to drive away. While carving, it is necessary to say: "Here is the image that will send flies fleeing for eternity." Next, it should be buried in the center of the house or hung from somewhere inside.

However, if one owns four of these images and buries them at the four corners of the house, or hangs them, or hides them in the walls in such a way that no one can make off with them, this will be even better. But this burial, or hanging, should be carried out when the first face of Taurus is rising. Henceforth, no fly will be able to enter the house or stay there. . . .

Whoever wishes to banish and drive thieves from his home should make an image of a man in bronze when the first face of Aries is rising and the moon is in that spot. Once this is done, he should say: "By this image, I banish and expel all thieves and murderers for eternity." He should then wrap the image in black linen and bury it at the center of the house.[15]

Other Places

We are fairly well informed about the talismans used by our ancestors to ward off certain calamities from their fields or their homes. In the seventeenth century, a wolf's head attached to the door of the house was good against sorcerers, and two hundred years later, in the Limoges region, a paw from the same animal, hung above the door to the sheepfold, was considered lucky. Even into modern times, Christ's monogram or Solomon's seal was carved on door lintels of houses.[16] In the Germanic regions, the following conjuration was inscribed over doors:

May the blood of Jesus Christ purify us of all sin and free us from all visible and invisible evil spirits †††️ Amen.

Planted on the roof of a dwelling, Jove's beard (houseleek) provides protection against evil spirits (Maine region, France) and lightning (Auvergne). In Berry, it was once a good luck charm, but in the Tarn region it warded off illnesses and its stems were placed in the shape of a cross over the stable door. In Bearn, on the morning of Saint John's and at sunrise, the peasants gathered several feet of stonecrop (sedum), which they then hung from the ceilings of their dwellings or their barns while speaking six verses. For the protection to be effective, the plant had to wilt for exactly a year, to the same date. "Arbre de Sainte Barbe," a type of seaweed, protects houses from lightning in the Tréguier region. The *Grand Albert,* a well-known grimoire whose sources go far back into the past, gives us a recipe "to prevent the birds from spoiling the sowing by eating the seed":

> You should take the largest toad you can find and imprison it inside a new earthen pot with a bat, and you shall write on the inside of the cover "Achizech" with crow's blood and bury this pot in the middle of the sown field. You should have no fear that birds will come anywhere near; once the seeds begin to ripen, you must take away this pot and throw it far from the field, into a trash dump.[17]

Concern for harvests and livestock compelled people to perform singular practices. Three centuries ago, people would write the name of Saint Basil on a note that would be then attached to a staff or crook in order to protect lambs from the attacks of wolves. More recently, in the Côtes-d'Armor region, a pole with a "Holy Ghost" (the image of a dove) hung from the top would be stuck in potato fields to prevent wild boars from devouring them.

Jacob Sprenger and Heinrich Kramer, who were in charge of the Rhineland Inquisition during the fifteenth century, noted that some Swabian peasant women would leave their homes on May 1st, before sunrise, to cull willow leaves and those from other trees, which they used to make crowns to hang at the stable entrance in the belief they protected their animals from any evil spell.[18]

Leopold Kompert (1822–1886), born and raised in the Prague ghetto, recorded the use of a talisman to protect the room of a young woman who had just delivered a baby. This is what he writes in his book *Aus dem Ghetto* (Scenes from the Ghetto):

> Snatchers [*benemmerinnen*] are what people call some midwives who are bound to evil spirits and kidnap the newborns from women in their birth beds. Once a woman like this appears, the child dies or becomes crippled. Sometimes too they cast the children of incubi into the room; they also give the mothers a lactate fever, strike them with dementia, and even death. In those places where they are not given direct admission they slip inside by means of keyholes. They have also been seen in the form of cats with sparkling green eyes and if when seen in this guise they are not driven away with vigorous swats from a broom, misfortune will strike the house.
>
> For protection against these snatchers, at the time when the woman is in the pain of labor, someone immediately goes to a rabbi and obtains a kind of talisman. These are several pieces of paper covered with letters representing the shield of David and accompanied by several kabbalistic formulas, whose initials are supposed to provide excellent protection against evil spirits. These pages are hung in the chamber of the birth mother and are left there for as long as the mother keeps to her bed. If the infant is of the male sex, on the eve of his circumcision, the knife that will incorporate him to Israel is placed beneath his head.[19]

Basing his information on a treatise by the canon lawyer and compiler Simone Majoli (1520–1599), the seventeenth-century author Jean-Baptiste Thiers speaks of another talisman used on this occasion:

> Some Jews . . . make a circle with chalk or charcoal around the chamber inside of which there is a woman in labor; next they write on its walls: Adam, Havah, Chutz, Lilith, and on the inside of the door the name of three angels, or rather three devils, *Senoi, Sansenoi, Samangeloph,* as they learned them from the famous witch Lilith, when attempting to drown her in the sea.[20]

AMULETS AND TALISMANS:
AN ANSWER FOR EVERYTHING

There is one sure observation that emerges from the strange world with which the reader has now become acquainted: those extraordinary objects known as amulets or talismans supply an answer to everything—or nearly everything! Whatever situation may arise, whatever sort of illness or peril, and whatever the individual's mental state, fears, or desires, a means exists to address it, mitigate it, realize it, and grant it. The phylacteries crafted over the last three thousand years, from the civilizations of the Indus into medieval and even modern times, are countless in number. There is one for every degree of the zodiac, several for each decan, and so on; they exist for each planet and each constellation. And beyond the sphere of astrology, it would only be a slight exaggeration to say that there were as many of these objects as there were plants and animals known to our ancestors. With respect to minerals, a recent inventory has shown more than six hundred, functioning alone or in combination with other elements, or even as the medium for an engraving. To this almost endless number, we can add the amulets and talismans made from a written charm, a spell inscribed on vellum, or on another support material.

In the Spanish manuscript *Libro de las formas & ymagines* from the second half of the thirteenth century,[21] which only exists as the table of contents for a now-lost work that included texts by ten different authors,* we can count some 1,363 amulets and talismans.

This manuscript from the Escorial offers us a veritable panorama on the human psyche and what galvanizes it. In it we find prescriptions addressed to various professions such as sailor, merchant, fisherman, livestock breeder, arborist, or beekeeper. I have come up with a list of the following domains:

---

*These ten texts are ascribed to Abolays, Timtim the Indian, Pitagoras, Yluz and Nelyenus, Plinio and Hermuz, Utarid (who could be Utarid the Scribe, i.e., Hermes, or 'Utarîd the Babylonian), Pliny, Ragiel, Yacot (= Jâqût), and Aly. By comparing the *Libro de las formas & ymagines* to other manuscripts, it has been possible to verify the correspondences between chapter headings and content.

- Defense of the body and health against the attack of illness, animals, men, spirits, demons, evil spirits, and evil spells. Thanks to certain talismans, quartan fever can be healed, as well as snakebite, abcesses, jaundice, epilepsy, melancholia, and dropsy. Toothaches can be prevented. Protection can be granted to horses against all dangers, and safety can be assured when traveling by either land or sea.

- Protection and development of one's property. By following the suggested recipes, one can cause thieves, mice, flies, pigeons, leeches, reptiles, and grasshoppers to flee; cause the growth of trees and the increase of their fruits; attract bees when they are wanted; discover hidden treasures; or put out a fire.

- Causing harm to others, their livestock, and their property. The manuscript cited gives recipes for "corrupting the air and making people ill wherever you like"; inspiring enmity; triggering an epidemic; paralyzing or killing whomever one wants (mainly one's enemies); causing sudden death or impotence; causing earthquakes; prompting the death of horses; preventing trees from bearing fruit; and blocking or sinking a ship.

- Reading the future or other things, such as thoughts: knowing if what someone is telling you is true; knowing if food or drink has been poisoned; and revealing those who are envious.

- Practicing magic successfully: mastering necromancy; bending the spirits of darkness to your will or, to put it another way, holding sway over demons; banishing evil spells; causing a man to rise in the air; or transforming wine into water.

- Granting wishes that are not always commendable: making oneself invisible; seeing equally well by day or night; acquiring eloquence; having a strong memory, many sons, or a good reputation; being honored; being feared by men and demons; being obeyed and loved by one's spouse; or obtaining a good wind for sailing. There are talismans that permit a person to be a good craftsman, a fearless hermit, or an excellent carpenter. The traveler will learn how to cross a river or an arm of the sea without getting wet because the water will part "to the right and the left" and he will cross with his feet dry. And on the less decent side of things, there are talismans that allow a person to be shamelessly extravagant and lustful, to transform women into prostitutes, and so forth.

Amulets and talismans come into play in the capital moments of human life. The *Libro de las formas & ymagines* repeats some recipes, which is normal in a compilation including several authors speaking on the same subject, but it also informs us that numerous talismanic objects had their opposite. For example, while one will allow you to get out of prison, another one will keep you in; one will give you the most desirable wind, another will bring a dead calm; and so forth. So, in the final analysis, they do offer an answer for everything.

Amulet and talisman both, an entire series of crafted items or natural products were intended to provide protection from weapons, and we can also cite the evidence from other accounts in this regard. We know that the soldiers of the different nations of Europe wore these items up through the nineteenth century and beyond. Tolstoy mentions them, for example, in *The Road to Calvary,* the plot of which takes place during the Russian Revolution. The list is quite long and extremely varied, so only a brief glimpse of it can be offered here.[22]

There are of course various stones and herbs, of which mandrake is the most famous, and also including a piece of umbilical cord, the amniotic membrane (caul), a piece of skin with menstrual blood, or the moss that grew on the skull of a hanged man. Protection was found by wearing the heart of a black cat that had been boiled in the milk of a black cow, or else the beard of a goat and the eye of a rooster placed in a pouch made of black cat skin. Bullets could be deflected by various written spells carried in a pouch. Among other things, a sword brevet prevented bladed weapons from harming its owner. People carried pieces of bat on their person, or the bell scrapings taken between the first and twelfth stroke of midnight on the night of the Nativity, and here we enter a domain in which Christianity takes on the appearances of magic. The wearing of relics prevents you from injury by weapons, and an amulet of the Gospel of Saint John in a walnut has a similar effect. The same holds true for numerous charms, for example that of Tobias, the Himmelsbrief, and the prayers of Saint George, Saint Coloman, Saint Christopher, and even the Measure of Christ.

Does it come as any surprise to note that the sought-after effects reflect an absolute materialism? Rooted firmly in the activities of daily life, these recipes for crafting amulets and talismans all aim to satisfy the fundamental concerns of every human being: life, death, love, health, prosperity. In rare instances we find something indicative of higher purpose, for example when someone is seeking to obtain understanding of foreign languages—a talisman that most students would dearly love to own!—or to practice magic without risk. But nevertheless, the gems I came across in the course of my research including ones such as these: "To not snore while sleeping," or else naive hopes like "To live a long life in good health," and even "To cause the wheel of a mill to turn without water."

An inseparable part of human history, amulets and talismans carry a message of hope and reflect a great desire: that the trust and faith placed in magic will not be disappointed. Those who manufacture them, and those who resort to these magical objects, believe they can change the course of natural law by means of the arcane sciences.

These objects that "protect and provide" have enjoyed a resurgence over the last thirty years, and it could be helpful to study them in correlation with recent economic and social crises. Who knows what the sociologists and ethnologists might uncover, but undoubtedly it would be similar to the oft-noted "recrudescence of the marvelous" that occurred at certain periods of the Middle Ages. When everything is deteriorating and falling apart, human beings seek refuge in the irrational and entrust their own care and their fate to invisible and supernatural forces.

All in all, amulets and talismans would allow the realization of the impossible. In this sense, they are revealing of the irrepressible penchant of humans for the irrational—a method that is probably better than any other for mitigating the grayness and vicissitudes of daily life, and for dealing with the blows of fate. They reflect dreams and desires of all sorts, and sometimes even the revenge of the poor and powerless, who imagine that the power of a talisman will grant them access to honors and titles. Amulets and talismans have existed in every time and place, and they will endure as long as there are human beings on the earth.

Fig. 7.3. Title page of one of the great collections of talismans and amulets, by Peter Friedrich Arpe

THE SEALS
REPRESENTING
THE PLANETS

*The coding of the depictions of the celestial bodies (paranatellons) so
they could be carved on stones or metal was quite varied and diverse
traditions were incorporated into it. This makes identification of
some engravings a tricky matter, when they are described and the
writer does not identify the planet or sign involved, or any other
revealing aspect. Here is a clear list, attributed to Solomon, whose
first traces we see at the end of the twelfth century.* I will follow it
with representations from other traditions.*

The image of Saturn that is sculpted onto the stones is the following: an
old man with a curved scythe in his hand and a scraggly beard. If this
engraving is found on a stone, it is then a stone of Saturnal nature; its
power will be to render its owner powerful, and to continually increase
his power.

The image of Jupiter is that of a man seated on leaves or on a four-
legged throne, with a wand in one hand and a globe in the other. I have

---

*The Latin text can be found in Camillo Leonardi, *Les Pierres talismaniques* (*Speculum
lapidum* III), 76–79.

also found one that bears an idol, a Cancer or a fish, with an eagle at its feet, but the magicians depict it otherwise; in fact they carve the body of a man with a ram's head, with rough claws and an elongated torso. If you find this figure sculpted onto a stone, in particular a *gagathe,* know that

Fig. A1.1. Sympathies: the human body, the signs of the zodiac, and their gems. From the Almanach auf das Jahr 1481 *printed by Johann Blaubirer in Augsburg.*

it brings its owner love and fortune, and that thanks to it he will easily obtain all that he desires. Furthermore, it raises men to honor and titles.

Mars is depicted several ways on stones, sometimes with a standard in his hand, sometimes with a spear or other weapon, but he is always found armed and sometimes on horseback. A stone carved this way has the power to render its owner victorious, audacious, and valiant and to grant him victory in all conflicts; this is especially true when this image is found on a stone that possesses a similar power.

The Sun is depicted in accordance with different styles, sometimes like a sun surrounded by rays, sometimes appearing in the form of a man seated on leaves, hair disheveled and wearing a rich vestment; it is also depicted on a chariot, and when it is carried by a quadriga, sometimes the signs of the zodiac are found around the chariot. The power of this image, if it is found carved on a stone, is to bring its owner dominance and empires as well as a taste for the hunt; it will also ensure that he acquires good fortune.

There are different images of Venus, as the magicians say; however, here are those that can be found carved on stones: for example, a woman clad in a grand dress and garment holding a laurel branch in her hand. She has the power to bestow a light touch to everything one does and bring all things to their desired end; she removes fear of drowning and brings power.

Mercury is depicted in the form of a man with an elongated chest and a handsome beard, though sometimes without. He wears winged sandals and holds a caduceus, and he often has a rooster at his feet or a snake beneath them. His power is to amass knowledge and make one a good speaker. He also gives merchants much help by enriching them.

The images of the Moon are varied: it is sometimes depicted with the features belonging to the moon, with its horns as if reduced at each end. Sometimes it appears as a nymph equipped with a quiver, and with dogs pursuing a stag. The power of this image is to supply means to diplomatic missions, and in this way to win fortune and honors; it is also said to render all actions quick and easy and to bring all things to their desired ends.

THE TALISMANS OF DOM JEAN ALBERT BELIN

On pages 109–118 of his *Traité des talismans ou figures astrales* (Treatise on Talismans or Astral Figures), published in Paris by P. de Bresche in 1658, Dom Belin (died 1677), named bishop of Belley in 1666, collected the most traditionally common talismans, thereby passing them down to posterity. Here they are, in all their naïveté.

FOR HEALING HEADACHE

Engrave the figure of Aries with that of Mars, who is a man armed with a spear, & Saturn, who is an old man holding a scythe in his hand, both being direct, & Jupiter not being in Aries, nor Mercury in Taurus.

One simply marks Aries and the Sun being there.

FOR AFFLICTIONS OF THE THROAT AND NECK

Engrave the figure of Taurus in the third face, the Sun being over the earth.

FOR KIDNEY AILMENTS AND COLIC

Engrave the figure of Leo in the first face.

FOR JOY, BEAUTY,
AND STRENGTH OF BODY

Engrave the image of Venus, who is a Lady holding apples in her hand, in the first face of Libra, Pisces, or Taurus.

TO HEAL GOUT

Engrave the figure of Pisces, which is two fish, one having the head on one side & the other on the other, on gold or silver, or on gold mingled with silver, when the Sun is in Pisces free of ill fortune & when Jupiter, lord of this sign, is also in good aspect.

TO EASILY ACQUIRE HONORS,
GRANDEUR, AND TITLES

Have engraved an image of Jupiter, who is a man with the head of a Ram, on tin or silver, or on a white stone, on the day & the hour of Jupiter when he is in his house, as in Sagittarius or Pisces, or in his exaltations, as in Cancer, & is free of all hindrance: primarily the evil aspects of Saturn or Mars, that he is visited and not burnt by the Sun; in a word, that he is fortunate in all aspects, as the learned Astrologer can know. Bear this image on you made as described above & with all the said conditions & you shall see something that exceeds your belief.

TO GAIN FORTUNE
FROM MERCHANDISE AND GAMES

Engrave the image of Mercury on silver or tin, or a metal composed of silver, tin & Mercury, on the day & on the hour of Mercury, wear it upon your person, or place it in the Shop of a Merchant; he will prosper in a very short time in an incredible fashion.

TO BE COURAGEOUS AND VICTORIOUS

Engrave the image of Mars in the first face of Scorpio.

TO WIN THE FAVOR OF KINGS, PRINCES,
AND THE GREAT & THE SAME
FOR HEALING ILLNESSES

Engrave the image of the Sun, who is a King seated in his throne with a lion at his side, on very pure and highly refined gold during the first face of Leo, & he shall be strong and know good fortune.

TO HAVE A MORE SUBTLE MIND
AND A BETTER MEMORY

Engrave the image of Mercury, who is a young man, sitting down and holding a Caduceus in one hand & his head covered by a hat in the first face of Gemini or Virgo, on a metal as described above.

TO ACQUIRE RICHES &
EVEN TO CURE THE COLD DISEASES

Engrave the figure of the Shrimp at the hour of Saturn, with Cancer in midheaven, & Saturn in the second face, on refined lead, or on silver or gold.

APPENDIX III

SEALS OF THE PLANETS AND THE PARANATELLONS

Intra circulum primò heptagonum deſcribunt, & intra heptagonum figuram quadrati Veneris; intra ſegmenta circuli charaſteres gymnoſophiſticos deſcribunt, ſigni Zodiaci indices, quibus operatio oportunè inſtituenda; in primo, ſecundo, tertio, & quarto ſegmento ponuntur charaſteres Magici, ſigni ♎ Libræ indices; charaſter in quinto ♓ Piſces indicat; in ſexto, & ſeptimo ponunt ♉ Taurum, ſignum exaltationis Veneris. intra heptagonum verò nomina Angelorum Venereorum collocant, qui ſunt *Requiel, Saquiel, Anahel, Hamahel, Kalaſtin*; quos ſtolidè aſſerunt, ad gratas coniunſtiones, voluptates, & amores propenſiſſimos. Nomen *Iebion* indicat primum diem & horam primam Veneris, ſub qua fanatica praxis auſpicanda. A tergo verò Sigillum ponunt, quod ſuprà citatus Author dicit magnum arcanum, non niſi phantaſticis Philoſophis notum: eius ſignificationem ait eſſe idem, ac *Sator* dulcis, prouocator coiunſtionis, lætitiæ, amoris, & veræ dileſtionis; ſi Dîs placet credere.

Fig. A3.1. Seal of Venus with explanations by Athanasius Kircher,
Œdipus Ægyptiacus *(1652–1654)*

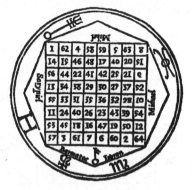

Fig. A3.2. Seal of Mercury with explanations by Athanasius Kircher, Œdipus Ægyptiacus

Primò infcribunt in circulo octogonum lateris, feu radicis quadrati Mercurij numerici, quod intra octogonum defcribunt: deinde octogono circumponunt characteres magicos, qui fignificant operationem in ♊ Geminis & ♍ Virgine, quæ funt domus Mercurij, inftituendam: poftea intra octogonum quatuor Angelorum Mercurialium nomina, quorum naturam benignam, ingeniofam, libenter alijs condefcendentem putant, vt vides, ponunt. *Iebion* primum diem & horam operis faciendi indicat. huic à tergo aliud adiungunt magnarum, vt ipfi fibi imaginantur, virtutum, quorum characterum fenfus hic eft: Euocator, vox rationalis, & fapientis, acutus, & cuncta prophetizans.

Fig. A3.3. Seal of Saturn with explanations by Athanasius Kircher, Œdipus Ægyptiacus

Sed explicemus figuram. Ad Sigillum maioribus myfterijs infigniendum, intra circulum trigonum depingunt æquilaterum, ad radicem quadrati ternariam indicandam. In fegmentis, figuræ fpectantur exoticæ. Characteres in primo fegmento A B fignificant fignum ♎, quæ eft domus Saturni, funtque characteres ex magica Gymnofophiftarum fchola profecti, vt fuo loco docebitur. In fecundo fegmento EDC collocati characteres fignificant ♑ Capricorni fignum. In tertio fegmento F G H pofiti characteres indicant ♒ Aquarij fignum. Intra trigonum ponuntur quatuor principalia fpirituum Saturninorum nomina, *Beel, Cafziel, Micha- then, Datquiel*; quorum naturam dicunt effe maleuolam & odiofam; reliqua nomina *Pechnochan* indicant diem Sabbati, *Ieboin* horam 1. Saturni. Vides myfteria ftolida, quibus naturalia numerorum myfteria obuelare conantur Magi, vt & nugamenta maiorem venerationem apud rerum imperitos nancifcantur. Si quis itaque huius farinæ Sigillum à quopiam portari viderit, is charitate Chriftianâ monere eum tenebitur, de latente fub eo Satanicæ machinationis fraude ad animæ perniciem inftitutæ; quare velis remifque fugiendum, imò mox igni tradendum: quod & de fecuturis Sigillis fentire debent omnes timoratæ confcientiæ homines. Sed procedamus ad fecundi Sigilli vfum.

Fig. A3.4. Seal of the Sun with explanations by Athanasius Kircher, Œdipus Ægyptiacus

Hoc Sigillum Solis ita conficiunt. In circulo defcribunt primò hexagonum, & intra hexagonum (quod lateris feu radicis quadrati Solis index eſt) quadratum numericum ; in fegmentis verò circuli ponunt characteres fignorum fub quibus operatio inftituenda eſt ; in primo, fecundo, & tertio fegmento characteres indicant ♈ ; in quarto, quinto, & fexto fegmento characteres ♌ Leonis ponuntur: intra verò angulos ponuntur nomina Angelorum Solarium *Eaphahel*, *Thardihel*, *Hegeagſigete* , *Raphaël* ; quos putant ad omnem humanitatem, mutuumque amorem eſſe propenſiſſimos : nomina Iebion indicant diem & horam Solis, quâ conficienda eſt lamina. Atque hæ funt vanitates in hoc Sigillo obſeruandæ , igni quàm luci Solari aptiores.

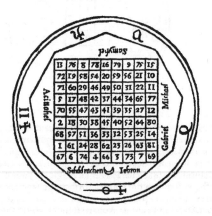

Fig. A3.5. Seal of the Moon with explanations by Athanasius Kircher, Œdipus Ægyptiacus

In circulo ponunt enneagonum, indicem lateris quadrati Lunæ , quod & intra enneagonum ponitur ; in ambitu enneagoni magicos ponunt characteres, qui indicant figna Zodiaci, vel domus Lunæ, in qua, vt valorem ſuum fanaticum machinamentum obtineat, exiſtat, neceſſe eſt. Intra enneagoni latera ponunt Angelorum Lunarium nomina, vt vides ; & *Iebion*, quæ vox ſemper indicat diem & horam Lunæ, quâ operatio perficienda. A tergo ponunt aliud Sigillum magnæ, vt arbitrantur, virtutis, cuius characteres hæc verba referunt : *Dominatorem* , *benignum* , *defenſorem* , *& cuſtodem*.

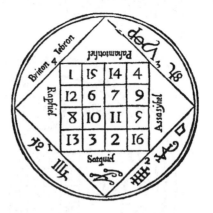

Fig. A3.6. Seal
of Jupiter with
explanations by
Athanasius Kircher,
Œdipus Ægyptiacus

Sed explicemus figuram, cui præfens Sigillum inclufum cernitur, quadra-
to circulo infcripto ; in cuius fegmentis characteres gymnofophiftici indicant figna Zodiaci fiue domus Iouis : in primo fegmento pofiti characteres indicant fignum ♋ ; in fecundo ♐ Sagittarij ; in tertio ♓ Pifcium ;
in quarto habentur illa duo nomina, quæ indicant diem & horam Iouis, in
qua amuletum conficiendum eft: intra quadrati Sigillum ambientis fe-
gmenta ponuntur quatuor Angelorum Iouiorum nomina, quæ funt *Sat-
quiel, Raphiel, Pahamtotihel, Affafyhel,* quos dicunt ad gaudium, hilaritatem,
familiaritatem, & omnem beneuolentiam propendere ; quæ omnia nomina corruptifsima funt, & partim ex Hebræo, partim ex Arabico à male-
feriatis hominibus, nec non fupinâ ignorantiâ fœdatis extracta funt. Et
vt maiorem hoc Sigillum vim obtineat, in tergo amuleti apponunt aliud
characterifticum, vt in figura apparet ; de quo fic Abenmorgum : *Atque
hæc figura magnum fecretum innuit, & interpretantur eam his verbis ; Porta-
tor felix, benignus, honorandus, iuftus, clemens, caftus, pius, pax.* Sed relictis
alijs innumeris vanitatibus, ad tertium Sigillum properemus.

Fig. A3.7. Seal
of Mars with
explanations by
Athanasius Kircher,
Œdipus Ægyptiacus

Figuram Sigilli Martis fic adornant: In circulo defcribunt pentagonum,
ad latus quadrati Martis, quod 5 eft, indicandum ; & intra pentagonum,
quadratum Martis 2 5, numeris fuis digeftum. In fegmentis characteres fignorum continentur, fub quibus lamina incidenda. Primi fegmenti characteres indicant ♄ Capricornum ; fecundi ♏ Scorpionem ; tertij iterum
♏ Scorpionem ; quarti & quinti ♈ Arietis fignum notant : in angulis
verò pentagoni nomina Angelorum Martialium, quæ funt *Panaflor, Ytnar-
chiel, Sampbel, Annabil* ; nomina ex pacto conflata. Character in medio
Panaflor & *Iebion* Martis eft ; *Iebion* primam diem & horam Martis indicat.

Luna crefcente, dicendo : O tu Jupiter planetarum maior , fortuna
dulcis & mitis, ô damaffes , mahadis, Camas, Jadas, Dichidos, Offi-
didos, Canores , conjuro te per eum qui te creavit , ordinavit & po-
fuit , ubi fuæ placuit voluntati , ut fis mihi in hoc opere adjutor , quò
virtute iftius laminæ omnia maleficia folvantur, geftanti conferat lu-
crum, gratiam & amorem , pacem & concordiam hominum, Oomi-
tetoro Zedelay Troppines Zozin Agare Bitelbault, Vitelvault Yton,
per eum, qui venturus èft judicare vivos & mortuos , & feculum per
ignem, Amen. His ter dictis, fuffumigatur lamina maftiche, olibano
& ligno aloes, & cuftoditur in panno ferico citrini coloris, vel porta-
tur. Cum per hanc quis operari volet & maleficia folvere, lamina hæc
in igne ponitur, dicendo: O vos fpiritus Jovis, amoris & dilectionis,
me facite amabilem & complacabilem ad placendum omnibus , ye-
feraye date poteftatem, ut ficut hæc lamina calefit igne, ita etiam, & c.
inde extrahitur Lamina , & in vino extinguitur, dicendo : Sicut hæc
lamina extinguitur in vino, ita extinguatur omne maleficium, & c. ubi
hoc guftaverit & biberit, Joth, he, vau, het, fiat fiat fiat amen. Apertius
fingula explicare nolui, ob curiofos ejufmodi impietatum imitatores,
quibus omnem errorum viam præcludere malui.   Galeno noftrohîc
fidem demus, dicenti : Subftantia eft, quæ fufpenditur, non voces bar-
baræ , ut quidam præftigiatorum facere affolent.

*Fig. A3.8. Seal of Jupiter with the prayer to recite and the instructions
for the suffumigation and for the magical operations, specifically
for destroying an evil spell. From Johann Weyer's* De praestigiis
daemonum, *first published 1563.*

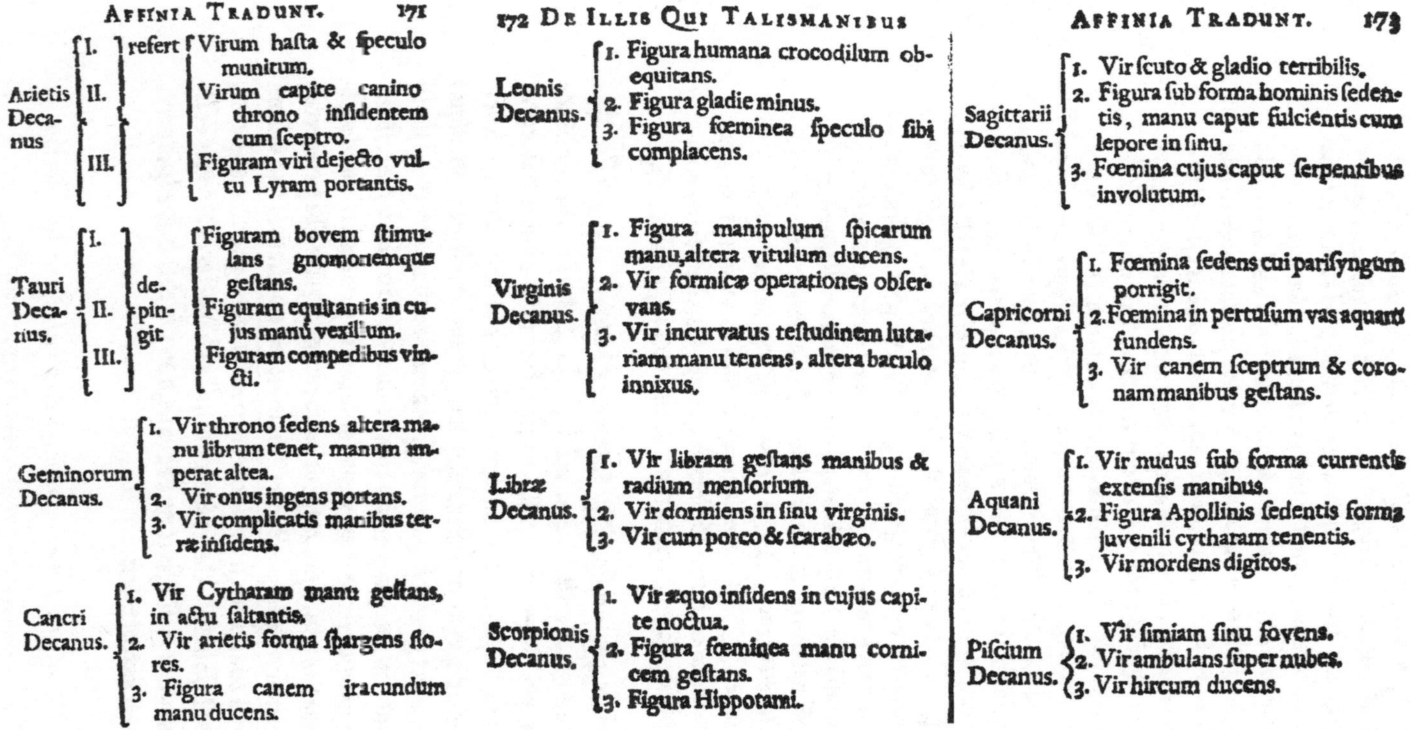

AFFINIA TRADUNT. 171

Arietis Decanus
- I. refert Virum hasta & speculo munitum.
- II. Virum capite canino throno insidentem cum sceptro.
- III. Figuram viri dejecto vultu Lyram portantis.

Tauri Decanus. depingit
- I. Figuram bovem stimulans gnomonemque gestans.
- II. Figuram equitantis in cujus manu vexillum.
- III. Figuram compedibus vincti.

Geminorum Decanus.
1. Vir throno sedens altera manu librum tenet, manum imperat altea.
2. Vir onus ingens portans.
3. Vir complicatis manibus terræ insidens.

Cancri Decanus.
1. Vir Cytharam manu gestans, in actu saltantis.
2. Vir arietis forma spargens flores.
3. Figura canem iracundum manu ducens.

172 DE ILLIS QUI TALISMANIBUS

Leonis Decanus.
1. Figura humana crocodilum obequitans.
2. Figura gladie minus.
3. Figura fœminea speculo sibi complacens.

Virginis Decanus.
1. Figura manipulum spicarum manu, altera vitulum ducens.
2. Vir formicæ operationes observans.
3. Vir incurvatus testudinem lutariam manu tenens, altera baculo innixus.

Libræ Decanus.
1. Vir libram gestans manibus & radium mensorium.
2. Vir dormiens in sinu virginis.
3. Vir cum porco & scarabæo.

Scorpionis Decanus.
1. Vir æquo insidens in cujus capite noctua.
2. Figura fœminea manu cornicem gestans.
3. Figura Hippotami.

AFFINIA TRADUNT. 173

Sagittarii Decanus.
1. Vir scuto & gladio terribilis.
2. Figura sub forma hominis sedentis, manu caput fulcientis cum lepore in sinu.
3. Fœmina cujus caput serpentibus involutum.

Capricorni Decanus.
1. Fœmina sedens cui parisyngum porrigit.
2. Fœmina in pertusum vas aquam fundens.
3. Vir canem sceptrum & coronam manibus gestans.

Aquani Decanus.
1. Vir nudus sub forma currentis extensis manibus.
2. Figura Apollinis sedentis forma juvenili cytharam tenentis.
3. Vir mordens digitos.

Piscium Decanus.
1. Vir simiam sinu fovens.
2. Vir ambulans super nubes.
3. Vir hircum ducens.

Fig. A3.9. Description of the decans of the zodiac. These paranatellons are meant to be carved on amulets and talismans in order to cloak them with the virtues of the god or spirit of the decan.

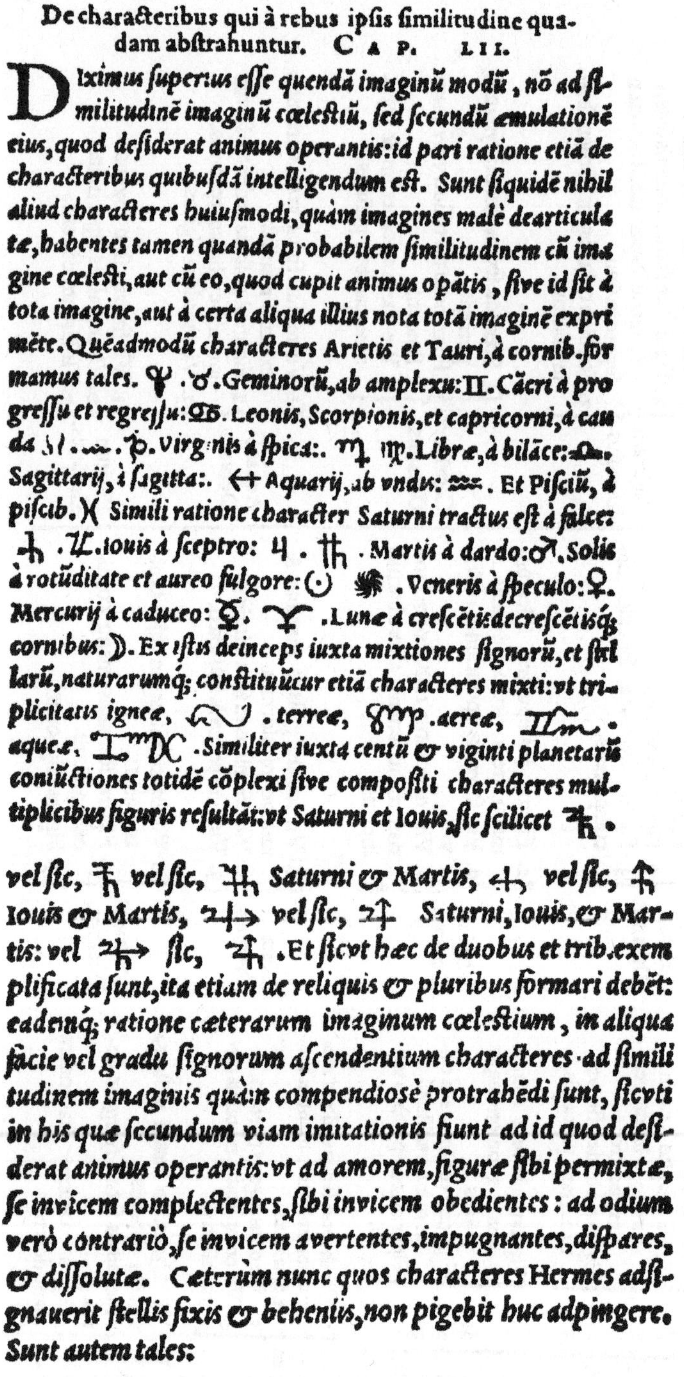

De characteribus qui à rebus ipsis similitudine quadam abstrahuntur. C A P. L I I.

Dximus superius esse quendam imaginũ modũ, nõ ad similitudinẽ imaginũ cœlestiũ, sed secundũ æmulationẽ eius, quod desiderat animus operantis: id pari ratione etiã de characteribus quibusdã intelligendum est. Sunt siquidẽ nihil aliud characteres huiusmodi, quàm imagines malè dearticulatæ, habentes tamen quandã probabilem similitudinem cũ imagine cœlesti, aut cũ eo, quod cupit animus opãtis, sive id sit à tota imagine, aut à certa aliqua illius nota totã imaginẽ exprimẽte. Quẽadmodũ characteres Arietis et Tauri, à cornib. formamus tales. ♈ · ♉. Geminorũ, ab amplexu: Ⅱ. Cãcri à progressu et regressu: ♋. Leonis, Scorpionis, et capricorni, à cauda ♌ · ♏ · ♑. Virginis à spica: ♍. Libræ, à bilãce: ♎. Sagittarij, à sagitta: ♐. Aquarij, ab vndis: ♒. Et Piscũ, à piscib. ♓ Simili ratione character Saturni tractus est à falce: ♄. ♃. Iouis à sceptro: ♃. ♂. Martis à dardo: ♂. Solis à rotũditate et aureo fulgore: ☉. Veneris à speculo: ♀. Mercurij à caduceo: ☿. ♈. Lune à crescẽtiẽdecrescẽtisãq cornibus: ☽. Ex istis deinceps iuxta mixtiones signorũ, et stellarũ, naturarumãq constituũtur etiã characteres mixti: vt triplicitatis igneæ, ♌. terræ, ♍. aereæ, Ⅱ. aquæ. Ⅰ♏♓. Similiter iuxta centũ et viginti planetarũ coniũctiones totidẽ cõplexi sive compositi characteres multiplicibus figuris resultãt: vt Saturni et Iouis, sic scilicet ♄.

vel sic, ♄ vel sic, ♄ Saturni et Martis, ♄ vel sic, ♄ Iouis et Martis, ♃ vel sic, ♃ Saturni, Iouis, et Martis: vel ♃ sic, ♃. Et sicvt hæc de duobus et trib. exemplificata sunt, ita etiam de reliquis et pluribus formari debẽt: eademãq ratione cæterarum imaginum cœlestium, in aliqua facie vel gradu signorum ascendentium characteres ad similitudinem imaginis quãm compendiosè protrahẽdi sunt, sicvti in his quæ secundum viam imitationis fiunt ad id quod desiderat animus operantis: vt ad amorem, figuræ sibi permixtæ, se invicem complectentes, sibi invicem obedientes: ad odium verò contrariò, se invicem avertentes, impugnantes, dispares, et dissolutæ. Cæterùm nunc quos characteres Hermes adsignauerit stellis fixis et beheniis, non pigebit huc adpingere. Sunt autem tales:

Fig. A4.1. *Magical characters from Heinrich Cornelius Agrippa von Nettesheim's* De occulta philosophia

CREATING AND CONSECRATING MAGICAL OBJECTS

If you consulted the dictionary, you would see the definition of "talisman":

Object upon which consecrated signs are engraved and to which magical properties are attributed. It holds an exceptional magical power most commonly used for protection. The most effective form of talisman is the pentacle.

According to this definition, a talisman could be a pentacle, an amulet, or some other object.

TALISMAN NO. I: A PRECIOUS STONE

This could be an agate, moonstone, and so on. This ritual can be used each time you need a stone for a ritual. For example, if you take an amethyst for a magic potion intended to increase your psychic powers, it will have moderate strength over your third eye. If you perform this next ritual before making the potion, it will have great force over your third eye,

So you will need two white candles and one blue one, the stone in question, frankincense, rice flour, sea salt, powdered rose petals, and powdered rosemary.

Place the candles on the altar, the two white above and the blue one below, so that they form a triangle. Place your stone in the center and light the candles. Then, say:

To all the winds of the north, south, east, and west, I offer this incense. May its smoke majestically ascend to you.

Sprinkle a pinch of rosemary over the flame of one of the white candles. Let rice flour fall over the other. Then sprinkle the crushed rose petals over the blue candle and say:

To you, wild and purifying fire, I offer these herbs to feed your infinite power.

Place a pinch of salt on the stone while saying:

To you, water, source of life, I offer this child torn from your bed. To you, nurturing earth, I offer this stone of peerless beauty so that you may keep me safe in your heart like your beloved child.

Now, while spreading out your arms, say:

To you, elements of life and death, I humbly give homage with these modest gifts. Protect me from the wickedness of men and the pangs of your torment, as long as I am wearing this talisman. I will be eternally grateful to you for this.

Let the candles burn all the way down. Between rituals you will keep your stone hidden from prying eyes.

TALISMAN NO. 2:
A PRECIOUS STONE

You can also use a precious stone for its magical properties. For example, to relieve stress, choose a diamond. (See the correspondences to know which stone to pick.)

Then consecrate the stone as you should with your tools, after performing the ritual just above for talisman no. 1. You should wear this stone around your neck whenever you feel the need.

TALISMAN NO. 3:
THE MAGIC POUCH

Make yourself a pouch from white cloth, and get a pinch of protection powder (this can be found in occult shops), a pinch of sea salt, and a pinch of sage.

Blend the herbs and salt together and recite the following incantation:

I consecrate this amulet to protect me from negative spirits, whether they come from the visible or the invisible world.

Place the blend in the small cloth pouch and carry it on your person at all times.

TALISMANS AND AMULETS,
MAGICAL OBJECTS

I must confess that I have never used talismans. Furthermore, I have never been able to keep any object as a talisman; I always lose them. So I have done without talismans or even a simple object that could be a good luck charm or amulet.

The difference between a good luck charm and a magical object resides in the energy and the way in which this energy was awakened. A good luck charm starts off as a simple object, but the owner's belief confers energy on it that gradually activates it and awakens inside it. For example, if you carry an object that you are sure contains beneficial properties, you are going to unconsciously transfer your energy into it and this energy will become permeated by the wish you believe the object is capable of granting.

This is just psychology, you say? Yes, it is, and psychology forms part of magic, as magic works in the domain of the mind. In magic, you are calling on the forces of your mind like you call on the forces of your muscles when performing a sport.

But is a talisman then an object that merely affects its wearer on a psychological level? Not quite. The talisman will be crafted with the intent of creating a magical object. In the beginning, you know full well that it is only a simple object. You are going to give it life and make it magical. You are going to awaken or transmit an energy into it that will be permeated by your will, and this energy will be concentrated in the talisman. At the moment you render the talisman active, that is to say at the time of its consecration, you will, pure and simple, have a magical object that began as a mere object.

What you really need to realize, and this is true for gris-gris, wish boxes, and any other magical object, is that you are performing a magical action that permits the astral energy of the object to be transformed. The astral energy moves from a passive state and becomes active. Physically the object remains the same; astrally the object has been changed.

WARNING

The talismans that can be bought in the marketplace are just mere objects. It is up to you to consecrate them and make them active.

If the seller in an occult shop tells you the talisman is already consecrated and active, do not buy it, because it is you who should consecrate the object. If you are unable to, then a magician (a real one!) can do it for you, as he will really know the right approaches to take to make the talisman active. Furthermore, you will be in contact with the magician and can specify exactly what you want, which is not the case in a shop where the object has already been consecrated.

For me, it is a matter of taking precautions, because you do not really know how the vendor was able to consecrate the object. But if you do decide to buy the talisman, choose one whose effect is fairly general and not specific (examples: attract love, money, and so forth).

CREATING AN AMULET OR TALISMAN AND CONSECRATING IT

There are symbols from Hebrew and other traditions that have been used in the crafting of talismans. Depending on your purpose, you should consult the correspondences in order to choose the ideal planetary days and hours for the realization (successful, preferably) of a talisman.

I still don't have any images of talismans, but as soon as I do, I will show them to you. If you have bought a talisman at a store, you need to prepare and consecrate it. Because it has been handled, different people will have left their energies on it. To remove all of these energies, the first thing to do is purify the talisman.

THE PURIFICATION OF A TALISMAN

Start by washing the talisman in cold water. Next pass it through a purifying incense like frankincense (there are others just as good).

Pick up the talisman in your hand and place your middle and index fingers two centimeters above it. Visualize a blue ray coming out of your fingers to purify the talisman. To end this cleansing, steep the talisman all night in a bowl of spring water in which sea salt has been diluted. Your talisman is now perfectly clean!

CHARGING A TALISMAN

Now, we are going to charge it. This consists simply of magnetizing it while keeping in mind that function your talisman should perform (protection, love, money, powers, and so on). Place your hand above the talisman and perform an energy transfer. Visualize the talisman's aura for as long as you are performing this energy transfer, while keeping in mind the function it will fulfill. Do this for at least fifteen to twenty minutes a day for a week, preferably while the moon is waxing. Each day, your talisman will become more charged.

CONSECRATING A TALISMAN

Here is the last step for making your talisman fully active. Open your circle and invoke the guardians. Pass your talisman through the incense and say:

> I consecrate you by air. May the breath of life awaken your power so you may be the talisman for [name its function; for example, "the talisman of protection"]. Awake!

Fig. A4.2. The only two authorized characters from the Catholic church. From the title page of the dissertation of J. Koblich.

Bring it close to the candle and say:

I consecrate you by fire. May the divine fire awaken your power so you may be the talisman for [name its function]. Awake!

Swish it through the water or sprinkle it with a couple of drops and say:

I consecrate you by water. The purifying water awakens your power so that you may be the talisman for [name its function]. Awake!

Sprinkle it with a several grains of salt or a little dirt and say:

I consecrate you by earth. May our mother earth awaken your power so that you may be the talisman for [name the function]. Awake!

Place the talisman above the pentacle and join your hands above it. Visualize the energy of the talisman and visualize it awakening, and say:

May the breath of Mana give you life, so that you may serve me and fulfill your function. Now you have a life; you are the talisman for [name the function]. By the power of the four elements, by the power of the One, you are awakened.

Visualize your talisman as active. Close the circle and henceforth carry the talisman on your person.

NOTES

INTRODUCTION.
TO GUARD AGAINST ADVERSITY,
MISFORTUNE, ILLNESS, AND DEATH

1. Massé, *Croyances et Coutumes persanes,* vol. 1, 326–27.
2. Baïkov, *Dans les collines de Mandchourie,* 253.
3. Montelle and Kieffer, *L'Ondine de la Nied et autres contes,* note on the Kutscherplatz.
4. Pineau, *Le Folklore du Poitou,* 500.
5. Abbé Noguès, "Pratiques empiriques."
6. For more on the ancient Turks and Bulgarians, see Ivanov, *Livres et Légendes bogomiles (aux sources du catharisme),* 322ff.
7. *Rituels, Magie et Sorcellerie,* special issue, August 2000, 2.
8. Ibid.
9. Robert, "Amulettes grecques."
10. Wolters, "Faden und Knoten als Amulett"; Bissing, "Ägyptische Knotenamulette."
11. Arnold van Gennep, cited in Seignolle, *Contes, Récits et Légendes des pays de France,* vol. 3, 69–71.
12. Düwel, "Buchstabenmagie und Alphabetzauber."
13. Lecouteux, *Le Livre des Grimoires de la magie au Moyen Âge;* English edition: Lecouteux, *The Book of Grimoires: The Secret Grammar of Magic.*
14. Lecouteux, *Charmes, Conjurations, et Bénédictions,* 14.
15. Demonsablon, "Note sur deux vêtements talismaniques"; Hamès and Epelboin, "Trois vêtements talismaniques provenant du Sénégal."
16. For a short list of these grimoires, see the introduction in Lecouteux, *The Book of Grimoires.*

17. Kieckhefer, *Magic in the Middle Ages,* 75–80.

18. I am using here Joan Evans's fine study, *Magical Jewels of the Middle Ages and the Renaissance Particularly in England.*

CHAPTER ONE.
ON THE WORDS "TALISMAN" AND "AMULET" AND SOME DEFINITIONS

1. Froehner, "Sur une amulette basilidienne inédite du musée Napoléon III," 224.

2. Marquès-Rivière, *Amulettes, talismans et pantacles dans les traditions orientales et occidentales.*

3. Pingree, "The Diffusion of Arabic Magical Texts in Western Europe," 58.

4. Cf. Delatte, *Herbarius.*

5. Copenhaver, "Scholastic Philosophy and Renaissance Magic in the *De vita* of Marsilio Ficino," 530.

6. Camus, *Voyage au pays du magique,* 234.

7. Löscher, *De talismanibus vel signis,* §4.

8. Pliny, *Historia naturalis,* XXVIII, 29; XXV, 115; XXIX, 26 and 83; XXX, 138; XXXVII, 50–51.

9. Ibid., XXVIII, 36.

10. Thiers, *Traité des superstitions,* chap. 28, 291–301.

11. Grimmelshausen, *Das wunderbarliche Vogelnest,* chap. 25–26, in *Werke,* vol. I. 2, 631–45.

12. Reichelt, *Exercitatio de amuletis,* 1.

13. Cf. Lecouteux, *Charmes,* 91, with illustrations.

14. Schneider, *Eröffnung der vortrefflichsten Geheimnüsse in der Arzney-Kunst,* 93.

15. Schneider, *Eröffnung der vortrefflichsten Geheimnüsse in der Arzney-Kunst.*

16. Blumler, *Amuletorum historiam eorumque censuram publico examini,* 2 and 4.

17. Reichelt, *Exercitatio,* 33; "guttae Apollonis," "spermata Solis," "Iridis."

18. For Gaffarel (*Curiositez inouyes sur la sculpture talismanique des Persans*), the Chaldean word *tselmenaija* comes from the Hebrew *tselem,* meaning "image."

19. Löscher, *De talismanibus,* §21: Abrasax figura Die mali Basilidiani.

20. Cf. Reichelt, *Exercitatio,* 29–30.

21. Cf., for example, Saintyves, "Talismans tombés du ciel," 50–63; Gaffarel, *Curiositez inouyes,* 15.

22. Cf., for example, Bonner, "Amulets Chiefly in the British Museum."

23. Belin, *Traité des talismans ou figures astrales,* 20–21. The book has another
    title, *Les Talismans iustifiez,* and is often cited this way by seventeenth-
    century authors.

24. Thiers, *Traité,* 303.

25. For astrological talismans, see Löscher, *De talismanibus,* §21.

26. Koblig, *Disquisitio antiquaria de talismanibus,* §4.

27. Sperander, *A la Mode-Sprach der Teutschen,* 722.

28. Cf. *Kyranides* (L, 9), in Mély et al., *Les Lapidaires de l'Antiquité et du
    Moyen Âge,* 102.

29. See section IX in vol. 3 of Luzel, *Contes populaires de la Basse-Bretagne.*

30. Cf. also Saint Augustine, *De civitate Dei,* VIII, 23–26. Arpe provides a
    summary of Saint Augustine's argument (Arpe, *De prodigiosis naturae et
    artis operibus talismanes et amuleta dictis,* 79).

31. Tertullian, *De idolatria,* 3.

32. For more on Ephesian letters, see Wolff, *Curiosus amuletorum scrutator,*
    453; Arpe, *De prodigiosis naturae,* 14, 44, 81, and 176. Wessely has put
    together a fine body of work in "Ephesia grammata aus Papurusrollen,
    Inschriften, Gemmen, etc."

33. Placet, *La Superstition du temps reconnue aux talismans figure Astrales, &
    statües fatales,* 40. Cf. also Arpe, *De prodigiosis naturae,* 46 and 174.

34. *Capitulare incerti anni,* cap. 10.

35. Cf. Lecouteux, *The Book of Grimoires,* 181–187.

36. Ibid., 57–62, in which numerous illustrations of this theme can be found.

37. Bodin, *De la démonomanie des sorciers,* 51 r°.

38. Cf. their reproduction in Lecouteux, *Charmes,* 22.

39. Thiers, *Traité,* chap. 29, 310.

40. Al-Kindi, *De radiis,* chap. VII. The edition by Alverny and Hudry appears
    in *Archives d'histoire doctrinale et littéraire du Moyen Âge,* vol. 41, 139–
    260; French translation in Matton, *La Magie arabe traditionnelle,* 77–128.

41. Al-Kindi, *De radiis,* chap. VII.

42. Ibid., chap. X.

43. William of Auvergne, *De legibus,* chap. 27, in *Opera,* vol. 1, 89b.

44. See Oresme, *Livre de divinacions,* chap. 2, in Coopland, *Nicolas Oresme
    and the Astrologers.*

45. One example out of hundreds: Georg Pictorius Villinganus, *Epitome de
    magia,* chap. 26.

46. For this entire exposition, see Weill-Parot, *Les images astrologiques au
    Moyen Âge et à la Renaissance,* 395–97.

47. *Tractatus brevis,* in Bacon, *Fr. Rogeri Bacon Opera quaedam hactenus inedita,* vol. 5, 6–7.

48. *Epistola frateris Rogerii Baconis de Secretis operibus artis et naturae, et de nullitate magiae,* in Bacon, *Fr. Rogeri Bacon Opera,* vol. 1, 526–27.

49. *Expositio super Theorica planetarum,* ed. G. Frederici Vescovini, in Hamesse, *Manuels, Programmes de cours et techniques d'enseignement dans les universités médiévales,* 137–182, here at 177.

50. Cf. Weill-Parot, *Les images astrologiques,* 623–26.

51. Trithemius, *Tratactus de reprobis atque maleficis.*

52. Saint Jerome, *Commentaires sur l'Évangile de saint Matthieu* IV, 23.

53. Cf. the section on "Bref" in Lecouteux, *Charmes,* 39.

54. Reichelt, *Exercitatio,* 76.

55. Ibid., 77.

56. For example, Johannes of Freiburg (Berthold von Freiburg), *Die 'Rechtssumme,'* 802, questions: "Utrum suspendere dia verba ad collum sit peccatum." Johann also speaks this way of brevets: "Item dicit quod illa brevia in quibus scribuntur quidam characteres et nomina inusitata sive nomine dei ineffabilia, et in quibus dicitur: quicumque super se portaverit istud *breve* non periclitabitur si vel sic. Aut illud vel illud bonum sibi continget, procul dubio reprobanda sunt nec portanda sunt. Et peccant qui scribunt ea aut portant aut donant aut vendunt aut portenda docent." Nicolas Magni (ed. Franz, *Der Magister Nikolaus Magni,* 173), notes: "Stigmata vero et figuras adhuc eciam christiani faciunt et vocant brevia et in proprii corporibus, cartis, in aliisque rebus, ut videlicet metallis, que omnia ydolatria vera sunt."

57. Cf. Weill-Parot, *Les images astrologiques,* 567ff.

58. Thiers, *Traité,* chap. 32, 358.

59. Ibid.

60. Cited by Seignolle in *Contes, Récits et Légendes,* vol. 3, 1159.

CHAPTER TWO.
AMULETS AND TALISMANS IN MEDIEVAL CULTURE

1. Thorndike, *A History of Magic and Experimental Science.*

2. Albertus Magnus, *Opera Omnia,* vol. 10, 640b–643a.

3. Cf. Thorndike, *A History of Magic,* on Thebit: vol. 1, 664–66; on Belenus, to whom *De sigillis planetarum* is attributed: vol. 2, 234–35; on Hermes: vol. 2, 223–27.

4. Hartlieb, *Buch aller verbotenen Kunst.*

5. Ibid.

6. Cf. Pingree, *Picatrix: The Latin Version of the Ghâyat al-Hakîm;* the Arabic text was translated by H. Ritter and M. Plessner: *"Picatrix." Das Ziel des Weisen vom Pseudo-Magrītī* (London: Warburg Institute, 1962). Shortly after I concluded my own study, a good French translation of the Latin text was published by B. Bakhouche et al., *Picatrix, un traité de magie médiéval* (Turnhout: Brepols, 2003).

7. Augsburg, 1488; Carmody, *Leopold of Austria, "Li compilacions de la science des estoilles."* Large extracts from this text can be found in Reichelt, *Exercitatio,* 171–72.

8. Reichelt, *Exercitatio,* 17, which cites the Vienna edition of 1489, p. 194.

9. An important source of evidence is the manuscript Plut. 89 Sup. 38 of the Biblioteca Medicea Laurenziana, which gives us Thebit's *Tractatus de proprietatibus quarundam stellarum et convenentia earundem quibusdam lapidibus et herbis* in folios 1 r°–3 v°. The manuscript also contains the *Tractatus de imaginibus,* folios 3 v°–8 v°, *Ptolomei Tractatus de imaginationibus,* folios 9 r°–17 r°, and *Theyzelius Quedam imaginum secundum planetatas* [!] *extracte de quodam libello,* folios 282 v°–294 v°. For the anonymous *Livre des sceaux des planètes,* cf. the Halle manuscript 14 B 36, folios 160 v°–170 r°, 260 v°–265 v°.

10. Carmody, *The Astronomical Works of Thâbit b. Qurra,* 179–97.

11. Ibid., 170–72.

12. Still called *Liber aggregationum sive secretorum de virtutibus herbarum.*

13. His books were printed in Basel in 1539. The most important for our subject is *De physicis ligaturis.*

14. *De fato,* article 4, cited after Weill-Parot, "Pénombre ficinienne: Le renouveau de la théorie de la magique talismanique et ses ambiguïtés," 77.

15. Cited after Weill-Parot, *Les images astrologiques,* 354.

16. For more on Eleazar of Worms, see Trachtenberg, *Jewish Magic and Superstition.*

17. D'Agostino, *Il "Libro sulla magia dei Segni" ed altri Studi di Filologia Spagnola,* 46.

18. Madrid, manuscript of the Escorial h. I. 16; Alfonso X, *Lapidario and Libro de las formas & ymagines,* 151–78.

19. Cf. Alfonso X, *Lapidario,* 101ff.

20. Gilli, *Former, enseigner, éduquer de l'Occident médieval,* vol. 1, 282.

21. Le Braz, *La Légende de la mort chez les Bretons armoricains,* 370.

22. Cf. Ertlé, *Sorciers, Magiciens et Enchanteurs de nos terroirs,* 349–53. Ertlé points out other names of this grimoire: *Egremond, Egremos, Ar Vif, An Negromans et le Livre de l'igromancie.*

23. *Steganographia, hoc est: Ars per occultam scripturam animi sui voluntatem.* The best study on this book is Ernst, "Schwarzweiße Magie."

24. *Astronomia magna oder die ganze Philosophia sagax der grossen und kleinen Welt,* chap. VI, in Paracelsus, *Paracelsus sämtliche Werke,* vol. 7, 122–37.

25. Paracelus, *De la magie,* 41.

26. Ibid., 77–78.

27. "Die Große Wundarznei," chap. 8, in Paracelsus, *Paracelsus sämtliche Werke,* vol. 10, 124–28.

28. Cf. what Reichelt (*Exercitatio,* 33) says about the *Guttae Apollonis, Spermata Solis,* and *Iridis.*

29. For more on the natural cameos, see Placet, *La superstition du temps,* 54–56; Gaffarel, *Curiositez inoyes,* 149–52.

30. Paracelus, *De la magie,* 105.

31. Ibid.

32. See Bondi and Pisani's edition of Ficino, *De vita libri tres.*

33. For more details on Giovanni Pico dela Mirandola's work, see Weill-Parot, *Les images astrologiques,* 639 and 675ff.

34. For other authors and works, see Arpe, *De prodigiosis naturae,* 52, 58ff; Placet, *La superstition du temps,* 80–90, 100–101; Gaffarel, *Curiositez inoyes,* 232–36, 283.

35. Gorlaeus, *Dactyliotheca,* published with commentaries by J. Gronov.

36. Marcarius, *Abraxas seu Apistopistus,* published with Jean Chifflet's *Abraxas Proteus.*

37. Gori and Passeri, *Thesaurus gemmarum antiquarum astriferarum,* vol. 2, 221ff.

38. Origen, *Tractatus* III.

39. Cf. Kropatscheck, *De amuletorum apud Antiquos usu capita duo,* 39.

40. Saint Augustine, *De doctrina christiana* II, 20.

41. Sermon 286 in Migne, *Patrologia latina,* vol. 38, col 1300ff; cf. Zellinger, *Augustin und die Volksfrömmigkeit,* 9ff.

42. Comm. in Col., Hom. 8, 5, in Migne, *Patrologia graeca,* vol. 62, col. 357–58; Reichelt, *Exercitatio,* 26 (*de circumligantibus aurea Alexandri Macedonis numismata capiti vel pedibus*).

43. Reichelt, *Exercitatio,* 33.

44. Mansi, *Sacrorum conciliorum nova et amplissima collectio,* vol. 2, 569: "quod non oportet eos qui sunt sacrati, vel clerici, esse magos vel incantatores vel mathematicos vel astrologos, vel facere ea quae dicuntar amuleta."

45. *Decretum Gratiani* part 2, case 26, questio 5, canons 4–5.

46. Martin of Braga, *De correctione rusticorum.*

47. Caesarius of Arles, *Césare d'Arles: Sermons au peuple,* sermon 1, 12. Delage translates *caracteres* as "grimoires," which is inexact.

48. Ibid., *Sermons au peuple,* sermon 14, 4.

49. Ibid., sermon 50, 1.

50. Cf. King, "Talismans and Amulets," 29.

51. Cf. Dobschütz, "Charms and Amulets (Christian)," 424; Gerstinger, "Bulla."

52. Cf. Gerstinger, "Enkolpion."

53. King, "Talismans and Amulets," 30.

54. Gregory of Tours, *History of the Franks,* book IX, 6.

55. Glaber, *Les cinq livres de ses histoires (900–1044).*

56. Ibid., IV, 3.

57. Bede, *Histoire ecclésiastique du peuple anglais,* IV, 27.

58. Epistola 50 ad Zachariam papam.

59. *Dicta de singulis libris canonicis,* canon 22, §13. Cf. also Hugh of Saint Victor (died 1141), *Didascalicon,* VI, 15.

60. Latin text in Caspari, *Eine Augustin fälschlich beilegte Homilia de sacrilegiis.*

61. Titulus 10: *De phylacteriis et ligaturis.* The *Indiculus* is edited in *Monumenta Germaniae Historica, Cap. reg. Franc.,* 2, I, 222–23.

62. Canon 42, ed. in *Monumenta Germaniae Historica, Leges,* 3, II, 292.

63. Wasserschleben, *Die Bußordnungen der abendländischen Kirche;* for the penitentials cited, cf. 239–40, 272, 395, 596, 648.

64. *Decretum* X, 33, and XIX, 80.

65. English translation by the Fathers of the English Dominican Province. Online at www.sacred-texts.com/chr/aquinas/summa/index.htm (accessed Nov. 20, 2013).

66. Kramer and Sprenger, *The Malleus Maleficarum of Kramer and Sprenger,* II, 1; cf. also II, 2, 6.

67. Gui, *Manuel de l'Inquisiteur,* vol. 2, 20.

68. Thiers, "Traité des superstitions selon l'Écriture Sainte," 35.

69. Quoted in Grimm, *Deutsche Mythologie,* vol. 3, 413.

70. Berg and Kasper, *Das buoch der tugenden.*

71. The anonymous author follows the path laid down by Thomas Aquinas; cf. *Summa theologiæ* II, II, question 38, article 18.

72. Cf. Aquinas, *Summa theologiæ,* question 38, article 19.

73. Cited by Thiers, *Traité,* 27.

74. Cf. Lecouteux, *The Book of Grimoires,* 42–45.

75. Ibid., 36, 92.

76. Stephan von Landskron, *Die Hymelstrass,* folio 42 r°.

77. Wirnt von Grafenberg, *Wigalois,* v. 4428–29.

78. Bang, *Norske Hexeformularer og magiske Opskrifter,* no. 1084b and d, p. 480.

79. See Baumann, *Aberglaube für Laien,* vol. 2, 546; see also p. 538.

80. Ibid., 534–35.

81. Ibid., 546.

82. Ibid., 548–49.

83. Saint Augustine, *De doctrina christiana,* II, 24.

84. Cf. Baumann, *Aberglaube für Laien,* vol. 2, 548–49.

85. Ulrich von Pottenstein, *Dekalog-Auslegung,* 44 G.

86. Ibid., 44 G.

87. Ibid., 44 X.

88. Ibid.

89. Ibid.

90. Sermon published in *Zeitschrift für deutsche Mythologie und Sittenkunde* 1–4 (1853–1859).

91. See Thiers, "Traité des superstitions," chap. 5.

92. Ibid.

93. Gugitz, *Fest- und Brauchtums-Kalender,* 112.

94. On the word *ananisapta,* see Seligmann, "Ananisapta und Sator."

95. Herolt, *Liber discipuli de eruditione Christi Fidelium.*

96. Cf. also the *Lübecker Beicht- und Gebetbücher,* folio 5b; *Das Licht der Seele,* folio 25a; *Spegel des cristene mynschen,* folio B1b–C2b.

97. Kramer and Sprenger, *Malleus Maleficarum,* II, 1, 16. I have verified the translation from the 1487 incunabula.

98. Ibid., II, 2, 6.

99. Reproductions in Lecouteux, *The Book of Grimoires,* 128, 134–36.

100. Printed in Vercelli in 1579, III, 3.

101. Thiers, "Traité des superstitions," 357.

102. Ibid., 50.

103. Ibid., 311.

104. A reproduction of this short magic text appears in Lecouteux, *The Book of Grimoires,* 110–11.

105. Thiers, *Traité,* chap. 26, 275–82.

106. Ibid., chap. 9, 74.

CHAPTER THREE.
SOME CHRISTIAN AMULETS AND TALISMANS

1. Various scholars have touched on this subject in great detail (Placet, *La superstition du temps*, 111ff; Wolff, *Curiosus amuletorum scrutator*, 586; Gaffarel, *Curiositez inoyes*, 158, 166). The Cross and the name of Jesus are the most often mentioned talismans, for example, Placet, *La superstition du temps*, 118ff. and 121.

2. Clement of Alexandria, *Le Pédagogue* III.

3. Belin, *Traité des talismans*, 104–7.

4. Cf. Wolff, *Curiosus amuletorum scrutator*, 586.

5. Bang, *Norske Hexeformularer*, no. 1069, p. 471.

6. Dresden, Sächsische Landesbibliothek, Staats- und Universitätsbibliothek, manuscript C 326, folio 35 r°.

7. Bang, *Norske Hexeformularer*, no. 1070, p. 472.

8. Cf. Herkenrode, "Une amulette." For other examples, see Lecouteux, *The Book of Grimiores*.

9. Cf. Reichelt, *Exercitatio*, plate 4, no. 1, 2, 6, 9.

10. Evans, *Magical Jewels*, 236.

11. Ibid., 182.

12. Cf. Franz, *Die kirchlichen Benediktionen im Mittelater*, vol. 2, 266.

13. Peter of Spain, *Thesaurus pauperum*, VII, 113.

14. Text from Lecouteux, *Charmes*, 117–18. Cf. also Gompert, "Der Zacharí-assegen gegen die Pest."

15. The original Latin pamphlet was published a decade prior to its being banned. For more on this history, see Guéranger, *Essai sur l'origine, la signification et les privilèges de la médaille ou croix de saint Benoît*.

16. Cf. Jacoby, "Heilige Langenmasse. Eine Untersuchung zur Geschichte der Amulette"; Legros, "La Mesure de Jésus et autres saintes mesures."

17. Lecouteux, *The Book of Grimoires*.

18. Cf. Cilia, *Locupletissimus Thesaurus*, 125–131. This book was reprinted six times between 1709 and 1744.

19. Deonna, "Talismans chrétiens," 19–20. Similarly, Deonna, "Abra, Abraca: La croix-talisman de Lausanne."

20. Wolff, *Curiosus amuletorum scrutator*.

21. For more on this material, see Brückner, "Cera—Cera virgo—Cera virginea."

22. Illustrations of them can be found in Lecouteux, *The Book of Grimoires*, 86, 92–94, 116–17, 164, 180.

23. Cf. Lecouteux, *Charmes*, 18.

24. Hansmann et al., *Amulett und Talisman.*

25. Cf. also the Vinje "black book" (grimoire) in Garstein, *Vinjeboka*, 67, no. 10, in which the phrase appears in a charm intended to reveal the identity of a thief. In the *Médecin des pauvres,* a chapbook from the Bibliotéque bleue of Troyes, the phrase is highlighted.

26. In the Vinje grimoire (Garstein, *Vinjeboka*, 72, no. 14), the phrase reads: † *De viro vincit leo* † *de tribis Judae.* This phrase can be found in the *Geraldus falconarius* (thirteenth century), in a treatise on hippiatry for protection against worms, in a Liege medical work, and on the Stavelot tryptich, and is used even for protection against thunder! Cf. Abeele, "De arend bezweren."

27. Cf. Lecouteux, *The Book of Grimoires,* 37–38.

28. Cf. Garstein, *Vinjeboka*, 67.

29. Braekman, *Middeleeuwse witte en zwart magie in het Nederlands taalgebied,* 50.

30. Ibid., 63.

31. Karlsruhe, Badische Landesbibliothek, Donaueschingen 792, folio 138 v°.

32. Braekman, *Middeleeuwse witte en zwarte magie,* 96.

33. Aymar, *Le sachet accoucheur et ses mystères,* 341.

34. Braekman, *Middeleeuwse witte en zwarte magie,* 186.

35. Thiers, *Traité.*

36. Ibid., 405: † *Agla Pentagrammaton* † *On* † *Athanatos* † *Anafarcon* †.

37. Ibid., 406: *Barnasa* † *Leutias* † *Bucella* † *Agla* † *Agla* † *Tetragrammaton* † *etc. Conjuro vos omnia arma, etc. Obsecro te Domine Fili Dei, etc. Abba Pater, miserere mei, etc.*

38. Braekman, *Middeleeuwse witte en zwarte magie,* 199.

39. Haver, *Nederlandse incantatieliteratuur,* no. 679.

40. After Jehovah it reads: † *Ya* † *Adonay* † *Saday* † *Homousion* † *Esercheye* † *Increatus pater* † *enz.* Cf. Haver, *Nederlandse incantatieliteratuur,* 483.

41. Franz, *Die kirchlichen Benediktionen,* 569, no. 3.

42. Ibid., 573.

43. Haver, *Nederlandse incantatieliteratuur,* no. 1016.

44. Braekman, *Middeleeuwse witte en zwarte magie,* 465.

45. Dresden, Sächsische Landesbibliothek, manuscript M 206, folio 66 r°.

46. Dumas, *Grimoire et Rituels magiques,* 214. This extremely practical book is a collection of the primary magical grimoires.

47. Ibid., 35.

48. Ibid., 237.

49. Ibid., 64.

50. Ibid., 68.

51. Ibid., 42.

52. Ibid., 40.

53. Ibid., 38. Cf. also *Le Véritable Dragon noir* and *La Poule Noire,* which offers the same text, p. 149.

54. Cf. Brunel, "Versions espagnole, Provençale et française de la *Lettre du Christ tombée du Ciel*"; Delahaye, "Note sur la légende de la *Lettre du Christ tombée du Ciel.*"

55. My thanks to Emmanuela Timotin, who brought this text to my attention and translated it for me. It is from a manuscript of Brasov, written between 1659 and 1681 by Barbul Hoban.

56. A number of these can be found in Lecouteux, *The Book of Grimoires.*

57. Gaffarel, *Curiositez inoyes,* 287–88.

58. Arnaldus de Villa Nova, for example, writes: "If it [the talisman] bears Hebrew letters, it is very effective" (*si habet litteras hebraycas efficassium est*); *Opera Arnaldi di Villanova,* folio 256 v°.

59. Wolff, *Curiosus amuletorum scrutator,* 576 and 579; cf. also page 586.

60. Ibid., 557, also cites the use of the Qur'an in magic.

61. Hamès, "L'usage talismanique du Coran." This researcher does not appear to know about the *Preserved Book* I mentioned.

CHAPTER FOUR.
THE MEDICINE OF AMULETS AND TALISMANS

1. Marcellus, *De medicamentis liber,* 624.

2. Cf. Galen, *On Simple Medicines,* XII, 874, and XIII, 256.

3. Plutarch, *Vie de Périclès,* 38.

4. Text in Reizenstein, *Poimandres,* 328ff.

5. Text edited in Ruelle, "Hermès Trismégiste"; and Pitra, *Analecta sacra,* vol. 5.

6. *De medicamentis,* XIX, 68.

7. Hildegard von Bingen, *Hildegard von Bingen's Physica,* 143.

8. The texts on this subject were published by Ideler in *Physici et medici graeci minores,* vol. 1, 387–96 and 430–40.

9. Bodin, *De la démonomanie des sorciers,* 32 r°.

10. Ruelle, "Hermès Trismégiste"; Pitra, *Analecta sacra,* vol. 5. See also Fachan, *L'homme-zodiaque.*

11. Lecouteux, *Mondes parallèles,* 117–18.

12. Herr, *Das neue Tier- und Arzneibuch des Doktor Michael Herr A.D. 1546.*

13. Sébillot, *Le Folklore de France,* vol. 3, 125.

14. Ackermann, *Quinti Sereni Samonici De medicina praecepta saluberrima,* 150–51.

15. Wolff, *Curiosus amuletorum scrutator,* 529.

16. Haver, *Nederlandse incantatieliteratuur,* 125.

17. In Constantinus Africanus, *Constantinus Opera,* 317–21. The text can also be found under the following title: *De incantation et adiuratione collique suspensione epistola.*

18. *Liber sanctus Hermetis ad Asclepium* (botanical), in Ruelle, "Hermès Trismégiste."

19. On the knowledge of melothesia in the Middle Ages, cf. Martinez-Gazquez, "*L'homo astrologicus* du manuscript 2052 des archives capitulaires de la Seu d'Urgell," 71–81.

20. *La Révélation d'Hermès Trismegiste,* vol. 1, *L'astrologie et les sciences occultes,* 141.

21. Reichelt, *Exercitatio,* 20, 55; Arpe, *De prodigiosis naturae,* 120.

22. Cf. Bernand, *Sorciers grecs,* 297.

23. Text edited in Kühn, *Claudii Galeni Opera Omnia,* vol. 10, 792ff.

24. Ibid., 207.

25. Cf. Halleux and Schamp, *Les lapidaires grecs,* Socrates and Dionysius, §§31, 32, and 35.

26. The full title of the book is *Inventorium sive collectorium partis chirurgicalis medicinae.* It was translated into French by the famous physician Laurent Joubert (1529–1583) under the title *La grande chirurgie* and edited by Éduard Niçaise in 1890.

27. Cf. Arpe, *De prodigiosis naturae,* 13.

28. For more on all this, see Delmas, "Médailles astrologiques et talismaniques dans le midi de la France (XIIIe–XVIe siècle)," 449ff.

29. Ibid., 452.

30. Arnaldus de Villa Nova, *Opera Arnaldi di Villanova,* folio 394 v°.

31. Aries: Ps. 8; Taurus: Ps. 19 (18); Gemini: Ps. 7; Cancer: Ps. 9; Leo: Ps. 43 (42); Virgo: Ps. 44 (43); Libra: Ps. 27 (26); Scorpio: Ps. 57 (56); Sagittarius: Ps. 59 (58); Capricorn: Ps. 70 (69); Aquarius: Ps. 80 (79); Pisces: Ps. 132 (131).

32. For more extensive details on these virtues, see Weill-Parot, *Les images astrologiques,* 482; Delmas, "Medailles astrologiques," 446.

33. Cf. Evans, *Magical Jewels,* 185.

34. Cf. Seignolle, *Contes, Récits et Légendes,* vol. 3, 758.

CHAPTER FIVE. AMULETS

1. Kühn, *Claudii Galeni Opera Omnia,* 22 vols.

2. Dioscorides, *De materia medica libri quinque.* On the use of plants and so forth in amulets, see vol. I, 138, 5–10; 15; 161; III, 91ff. Dioscorides mentions around fifty stones used in remedies.

3. Cf. Wirbelauer, *Antike Lapidarien,* 10.

4. Cf., for example, *Historia naturalis,* XXVIII, 228; XXX, 110.

5. Kropatscheck, *De amuletorum apud Antiquos.*

6. Delatte, *Textes latins et vieux français relatifs aux Cyranides;* with *Hermes,* 241–75; *Enoch,* 277–88; and *Livre des secrez de nature,* 297–352; Greek text in Kaimakis, *Die Kyraniden.*

7. Cf. Albert-Lorca, *L'Ordre des choses.*

8. Cf. Lecouteux, *The Book of Grimoires,* 57–62.

9. Delatte, *Textes latins,* 137–38.

10. Arnaldus de Villa Nova, *Opera Arnaldi di Villanova,* folio 217 r° and 215 v°.

11. Cf. Evans, *Magical Jewels,* 181.

12. Howald and Sigerist, *Herbarius pseudo-Apulei.* The text is cited by chapter and paragraph.

13. Arnaldus de Villa Nova, *Opera Arnaldi di Villanova,* folio 215 v°. Cf. also Diepgen, "Arnaldus de Villanova De improbatione maleficiorum," 385–403. In folio 217 r°, Arnaldus states that the mugwort should have a few seeds and will deflect the evil eye.

14. This is edited in Halleux and Schamp, *Les Lapidaires grecs,* along with the *Lithika* of Pseudo-Orpheus, the *Kerygmes Lapidaries,* the *Nautical Lapidary,* and the lapidary of Socrates and Dionysius.

15. Marbode of Rennes, *De lapidibus.*

16. Sloane manuscript 1784, folios 8–9.

17. See Halleux and Schamp, *Les Lapidaires grecs,* 80–123.

18. Ibid., 125–297.

19. See Delatte, *Textes latins,* 293–352.

20. Leonardi, *Les Pierres talismaniques.*

21. Robert, *Opera minora selecta,* volume 7, 24.

22. Fifteenth-century lapidary conserved in Rawlinson manuscript D 358, folio 81, Bodleian Library.

23. The lapidaries of Ragiel, Chaël, Solomon, Hermes, and Leonardi can be found in Leonardi, *Les Pierres talismaniques.*

24. On the properties of the cross, cf. Gaffarel, *Curiositez inouyes,* 158.

25. Cf. Arpe, *De prodigiosis naturae,* 142ff.

26. Marcellus Empiricus, *De medicamentis*, VIII, 56–57.

27. Papyrus: Marcellus Empiricus, *De medicamentis*, X, 34–35; cf. Pliny, *Historia naturalis*, XVIII: 29.

28. Delatte, *Textes latins*, 108, 9–10.

29. Letter no. 50 in *Monumenta Germaniae Historica, Ep. 3 Merowingici et Karolini aevi*, I, II, 309.

30. *Homilia de sacrilegiis*, chap. 15 and 19, in Caspari, *Eine Augustin fälschlich beilegte*.

31. Cf. Mansi, *Sacrorum conciliorum*, vol. 2, col. 569; vol. 20, col. 454.

32. Bluhme, *Leges Burgundionum*, in *Monumenta Germaniae Historica, Leg.* III, 497–630, chap. 34, 3; Eckhardt, *Lex Salica, 100 Titel-Text*, 24; Wohlhaupter, *Gesetze der Westgoten*, VI.

33. Mansi, *Sacrorum conciliorum*, vol. 10, col. 1200.

34. See *Vita Eligii* in *Monumenta Germaniae Historica, Scriptores rerum Merowingium* IV, pp. 705–8.

35. *Lapidaire*, v. 771ff., trans. in Leonardi, *Les Pierres talismaniques*.

36. Marsilio Ficino (1433–1499) explores the value of astral amulets and cites numerous recipes connected to decanic medicine such as this: "The image of Venus made in the hour of Venus when the first decan of Gemini is rising cures fever attacks." In his theory, the planets possess the actual virtues, whereas the decans are merely indications of time and place, to which he concedes some power. In the sixteenth and seventeenth centuries, planetary and decanic amulets rivaled one another. Cf. Ficino, *De vita coelitus comparanda*, III, 18. For decanic amulets, see Reichelt, *Exercitatio*, 62ff.

37. Gundel, *Dekane und Dekansternbilder;* cf. also, by the same author, *Sterne und Sternbilder im Glauben des Altertums und der Neuzeit*.

38. There are books that list these planet by planet; I have a *Book of Mars* like this as well as others on Venus and Mercury.

39. Manuscript 793, folio 380.

40. Ibid.

41. *Picatrix*, II, 10, 20.

42. Joubert, *Des erreurs populaires*, vol. 2, 375–76.

43. Bang, *Norske Hexeformularer*, no. 1093, 485.

CHAPTER SIX.
THE CRAFTING OF TALISMANS

1. Belin, *Traité les Talismans*, 35–36.

2. Ibid., 54–55.

3. Ibid., 64–66.

4. Ibid., 66.

5. Ibid., 68.

6. Ibid., 69.

7. Cf. Weill-Parot, *Les images astrologiques*, 664–69.

8. Wolff, *Curiosus amuletorum scrutator*, 489.

9. Ibid., 495: *ligaturae physicae periapta dicantur.*

10. Halleux and Schamp, *Les Lapidaires grecs*, 233–34.

11. *Picatrix*, III, 3.

12. See *Hermes, De XV stellis, XV lapidibus, XV herbis,* and *XV imaginibus* in Delatte, *Textes latins.*

13. In Halleux and Schamp, *Les Lapidaires grecs.*

14. Notker Labeo, *Martianus Capella, De nuptiis philologiae et Mercurii,* 64–70; cf. *Martianus Capella* I in the same volume, 39–42.

15. Cited from Flamand, *Les Pierres magiques*, 158.

16. In Agrippa, *La Philosophie occulte*, vol. 1, 64–77.

17. Ibid., iii, 5.

18. Ibid., vol. 1, iv, 4.

19. Text edited by D'Agostino in Alfonso X, *Astromagia*, 242ff.

20. Cf. Arpe, *De prodigiosis naturae*, 180ff.

21. Synthesis based on the translation in Gundel, *Dekane und Dekanstern-bilder*, 379–83.

22. Original text, edited by D'Agostino, can be found in Alfonso X, *Astromagia.*

23. *Picatrix*, IV, 2.

24. Alfonso X, *Astromagia*, 142.

25. *Picatrix*, II, 12.

26. Ibid., III, 11.

27. Ibid., III, 7.

28. Ibid., III, 9.

29. See *Pro lexis de Plinio* in Alfonso X, *Astromagia*, 186ff.

30. These prayers are found in *Hygromancia Salomonis*, Cod. Graec. 2419, folio 246 r° (Paris, Bibliothèque nationale).

31. Gaffarel, *Curiositez inouyes*, 287–88.

32. *Picatrix*, IV, 4 and 6.

CHAPTER SEVEN.
THE USE OF AMULETS AND TALISMANS

1. Placet, *La superstition du temps,* 64; 92–93; Gaffarel, *Curiositez inouyes,* 250–52; Arpe, *De prodigiosis naturae,* 15 (Antioch); 23 (Naples); 26 (Byzantium); 32–33 (Rome); 43 (Constantinople).

2. Robert, "Amulettes grecques," 3–44.

3. *Kyranides,* in Delatte, *Textes latins.*

4. Mély et al., *Les Lapidaires,* vol. 3, 95.

5. Ibid., 99.

6. Cf. Tzetzes, *Historiarium variarum chiliades,* III, 60: talismans against mosquitoes in Antioch and storks in Byzantium; Placet, *La superstition du temps,* 27ff.: the statues of Constantinople. See also Dulière, "Protection contre les animaux nuisibles assurée par Apollonios de Thyane dans Byzance et Antioche."

7. Cf. Dagron, *Constantinople imaginaire;* Bresc, "Sépulcres suspendus et statues protectrices"; Faraone, *Talismans and Trojan Horses.*

8. I have borrowed the following texts from Ruska, *Tabula smaragdina,* 101–4.

9. I have used the French translation of Carra de Vaux, *L'Abrégé des merveilles.*

10. Gregory of Tours, *History of the Franks,* book VIII, 33. Translation from Thorpe edition, 467.

11. Comparetti, *Virgilio nel Medio Evo,* vol. 2, 76.

12. Gervasius of Tilbury, *Le Livre des merveilles,* 28. John of Salisbury mentions this fly in his *Policraticus,* written around 1159.

13. Thiers, *Traité,* chap. 29, 307–8. Cf. also Placet, *La superstition du temps,* 17–22; Gaffarel, *Curiositez inouyes,* 244; Wolff, *Curiosus amuletorum scrutator,* 633; and see Faraone, *Talismans and Trojan Horses.*

14. Grimmelshausen, *Galgen-Männlin,* in *Werke,* vol. 2, 772ff.

15. Mizauld, *Memorabilium sive arcanorum omnis generis.*

16. Photographs of these houses can be seen in Dominique Camus, *La Sorcellerie en France aujourd'hui,* 62–64. Cf. also Lecouteux, *Démons et Génies du terroir au Moyen Âge.*

17. Seignolle, *Les évangiles du diable,* 821.

18. Kramer and Sprenger, *Malleus Maleficarum.*

19. Kompert, *Aus dem Ghetto,* 43–44.

20. Thiers, *Traité,* chap. 5, 6.

21. Alfonso X, *Lapidario,* 151–78.

22. Cf. Lecouteux, *The Book of Grimoires,* with numerous illustrations.

BIBLIOGRAPHY

Abeele, Baudouin Van Den. "De arend bezweren. Magie in de middeleeuwse valkerijtraktaten." *Madoc. Tijdschrift over de Middeleeuwen* 11 (1997): 66–75.

Ackermann, Johann C. G., ed. *Quinti Sereni Samonici De medicina praecepta saluberrima.* Leipzig: G. Müller, 1786.

Agrippa, Heinrich Cornelius. *La Philosophie occulte.* Translated by A. Levasseur. 2 vols. The Hague: Alberts, 1727.

Albert-Lorca, Marlène. *L'Ordre des choses. Les récits d'origine des animaux et des plantes en Europe.* Paris: Comité des Travaux historiques et scientifiques, 1991.

Albertus Magnus. *Book of Minerals.* Translated by Dorothy Wyckoff. Oxford: Clarendon Press, 1967.

———. *Opera Omnia.* Edited by A. Borgnet. 38 vols. Paris: 1890–1899.

Alfonso X [el Sabio]. *Astromagia: Ms. Reg. lat. 1283a.* Edited by Alfonso d'Agostino. Naples: Liguori, 1998.

———. *Lapidario and Libro de las formas & ymagines.* Edited by Roderic C. Diman and Lynn W. Winget. Madison, Wisc.: Hispanic Seminary of Medieval Studies, 1980.

Alverny, Marie-Thérèse d', and F. Hudry. *Archives d'histoire doctrinale et littéraire du Moyen Âge.* Paris: Librairie Philosophique, J. Vrin, 1974.

Aquinas, Saint Thomas. *Summa theologiæ [Summa Theologica].* Translated by the Fathers of the English Dominican Province, 1947. Online at www .sacredtexts.com/chr/aquinas/summa/index.htm (accessed Nov. 20, 2013).

Arnaldus de Villa Nova. *Opera Arnaldi di Villanova.* Lyon: Fradin, 1504.

Arpe, Peter Friedrich. *De prodigiosis naturae et artis operibus talismanes et amuleta dictis.* Hamburg: Christian Liebezeit, 1717.

Augustine, Saint. *De civitate Dei contras paganos.* Latin text online at www

.augustinus.it/latino/dottrina_cristiana/index.htm (accessed Nov. 20, 2013).

———. *De doctrina christiana*. Edited by Klaus D. Daur and Joseph Matin. Turnhout: Brepols, 1962.

Aymar, Alphonse. *Le sachet accoucheur et ses mystères. Contribution à l'étude du folklore de la Haute Auvergne du XIIIe au XVIIIe siècle.* Toulouse: Edouard, 1926.

Bacon, Roger. *Fr. Rogeri Bacon Opera quaedam hactenus inedita,* vol. 1. Edited by J. S. Brewer. London: Longmans, Green, Longmans, and Rogers, 1859.

———. *Fr. Rogeri Bacon Opera quedam hactenus inedita,* vol. 5. Edited by Robert Steele. Oxford: Clarendon Press, 1920.

Baïkov, Nicolai. *Dans les collines de Mandchourie.* Paris: Payot, 2000.

Baisier, Léon. *The Lapidaire chrétien: Its composition, Its Influences, Its Sources.* Washington, D.C.: Catholic University of America, 1936.

Bakhouche, Béatrice, Frederic Fauquier, and Brigitte Pérez-Jean. *Picatrix, un traité de magie médiéval.* Turnhout: Brepols, 2003.

Bang, Anton Christian. *Norske Hexeformularer og magiske Opskrifter.* Christiania [Oslo]: Cammermeyer, 1902.

Barb, A. A. "Gemme gnostiche." In *Enciclopedia dell'arte antica,* vol. 3.

Bartholmäus, Anglicus. *De proprietatibus rerum.* Frankfurt: Wolfgang Richter, 1601.

Baumann, Karin, ed. *Aberglaube für Laien. Zur Programmatik und Überlieferung spätmittelalterlicher Superstitionenkritik.* 2 vols. Würzburg: Königshausen & Neumann, 1989.

Bede. *Histoire ecclésiastique du peuple anglais.* Translated by Phillipe Delaveau. Paris: Gallimard, 1995.

Belin, Jean-Albert. *Traité des talismans ou figures astrales: Dans lequel est monstré que leurs effets, & vertus admirables sont naturelles, & enseigné la maniere de les faire, & de s'en servir avec un profit & advantage merveilleux.* Paris: P. de Bresche, 1688.

Berg, Klaus, and Monika Kasper. *Das buoch der tugenden. Ein Lehrbuch des 14. Jahrhunderts über Moral und Recht, nach der Summa Theologiae, II-ii, des Thomas von Aquin und anderen Werken der Scholastik und Kanonistik.* 2 vols. Tübingen: Niemeyer, 1984.

Bernand, André. *Sorciers grecs.* Paris: Fayard, 1991.

Berthold von Freiburg. *Die "Rechtssumme" Bruder Bertholds.* Edited by Marlies Hamm and Helgard Ulmschneider. Tübingen: Niemeyer, 1980.

Bianco, Ludmilla, ed. *Le Pietre mirabili.* Palermo: Sellerio, 1992.

Bidez, Joseph, and Franz Cumont. *Les Mages hellénisés. Zoroastre, Ostanès et Hytaspe d'après la tradition grecque.* 2 vols. Paris: Les Belles Lettres, 1973.

Bissing, Friedrich Wilhelm von. "Ägyptische Knotenamulette." *Archiv für Religionswissenschaft* 8 (1905): 23–27.

Bluhme, F. *Leges Burgundionum.* Stuttgart: Vaduz 1965.

Blumler, Martin Frederick. *Amuletorum historiam eorumque censuram publico examini.* Halle, 1710.

———. *A History of Amulets.* Edinburgh: privately printed, 1887.

Bodin, Jean. *De la démonomanie des sorciers.* Paris: Jacques du Puys, 1580.

Boll, Franz, and Carl Bezold. *Sternglaube und Sterndeutung. Die Geschichte und das Wesen der Astrologie.* Leipzig: Teubner, 1918.

Bonner, Campbell. "Amulets Chiefly in the British Museum." *Hesperia* 20 (1951): 301–45.

———. *Studies in Magical Amulets, Chiefly Graeco-Egyptian.* Ann Arbor: University of Michigan Press, 1950.

Boot, Anselmus Boetius de. *Gemmarum et lapidum historia.* Lyon: Huguelan, 1636.

Braekman, Willy L. *Middeleeuwse witte en zwarte magie in het Nederlands taalgebied. Gecommentarieerd compendium van incantamenta tot einde 16de eeuw.* Ghent: Koninklijke Academie voor Nederlandse Taal- en Letterkunde, 1997.

Braz, Anatole Le. *La Légende de la mort chez les Bretons armoricains.* Paris: Champion, 1928.

Bresc, Henri. "Sépulcres suspendus et statues protectrices: Fragments d'apotélesmatique sicilienne." In *Histoires et société. Mélanges offerts à Georges Duby,* vol 1. Aix en Provence: Université de Provence, 1992.

Brey Mariño, María, ed. *Lapidario—Alfonso X, Rey de Castilla.* Madrid: Castalia, 1979.

Brückner, Wolfgang. "Amulett." *Enzyklopädie des Märchens,* vol. 1. Berlin and New York: Gruyter, 1966.

———. "Cera—Cera virgo—Cera virginea." *Zeitschrift für Volkskunde* 59 (1963): 233–53.

Brunel, Clovis. "Versions espagnole, provençale et française de la *Lettre du Christ tombée du Ciel.*" *Analecta Bollandiana* 68 (1950): 383–96.

Budge, E. A. Wallis. *Amulets and Talismans.* New York: Dover, 1978.

Caesarius of Arles. *Césaire d'Arles: Sermons au peuple.* Edited and translated by Marie-José Delage. Paris: Cerf, 1971.

Caiozzo, Anna. "Les talismans des planètes dans les cosmographies en persan." *Der Islam* 77/2 (2001): 221–62.

Camus, Dominique. *La Sorcellerie en France aujourd'hui*. Rennes: Ouest-France, 2001.

———. *Voyage au pays du magique. Enquête sur les voyants, guérisseurs, sorciers*. Paris: Dervy, 2002.

Carmody, Francis J. *Arabic Astronomical and Astrological Sciences in Latin Translation: A Critical Bibliography*. Berkeley and Los Angeles: University of California Press, 1956.

———, ed. *The Astronomical Works of Thâbit b. Qurra*. Berkeley and Los Angeles: University of California Press, 1960.

———, ed. *Leopold of Austria, "Li compilacions de la science des estoilees."* Berkeley and Los Angeles: University of California Press, 1947.

Carra de Vaux, Bernard, trans. *L'Abrégé des merveilles*. Paris: Sinbad, 1984.

Caspari, C. P., ed. *Eine Augustin fälschlich beilegte Homilia de sacrilegiis*. Christiania [Oslo], 1886.

Catimpré, Thomas de. *De natura rerum*. Edited by Helmut Boese. Berlin and New York: Gruyter, 1973.

Chauliac, Guy de. *La grande chirurgie de Guy de Chauliac, chirurgien, maître en médecine de l'Université de Montpellier composée en l'an 1363*. Edited by Édouard Nicaise. Paris: Alcan, 1890.

Cilia, Gelasius de. *Locupletissimus Thesaurus, continens varias et selectissimas benedictiones*. Vohburg: Roll, 1709.

Clement of Alexandria. *Le Pédagogue,* book 3. Edited by Henri-Irenee Marrou, translated by Marguerite Harl. Paris: Cerf, 1960.

Comparetti, Domenico. *Virgilio nel Medio Evo*. 2 vols. Livorno: Vigo, 1872.

Constantinus Africanus. *Constantinus Opera*. Basel: Petrus, 1536.

Coopland, G. W., ed. *Nicolas Oresme and the Astrologers*. Liverpool: Liverpool University Press, 1952.

Copenhaver, Brian P. "Scholastic Philosophy and Renaissance Magic in the *De vita* of Marsilio Ficino." *Renaissance Quarterly* 37 (1984): 523–54.

D'Agostino, Alfonso. *Il "Libro sulla magia dei Segni" ed altri Studi di Filologia Spagnola*. Brescia: Paideia, 1979.

Dagron, Gilbert. *Constantinople imaginaire. Études sur le recueil des "Patria."* Paris: P.U.P.S., 1984.

Decretum Gratiani. Latin version online at http://geschichte.digitale-sammlungen .de/decretum-gratiani/online/angebot.

De imaginibus constellationum extra Zodiacum. Vatican, Codex Urbinas Latinus 1398, fifteenth century.

Delahaye, Hippolyte. "Note sur le légende de la *Lettre du Christ tombée du Ciel.*" *Bulletin de l'Académie royale de Belgique* (1889): 171–213.

Delatte, Armand. *Herbarius: Recherches sur le cérémonial usité chez les Anciens pour la cueillette des simples et des plantes magiques.* Brussels: Académie Royale de Belgique, 1961.

Delatte, Armand, and Philippe Derchain. *Les Intailles magiques gréco-égyptiennes.* Paris: Bibliothèque Nationale, 1964.

Delatte, Louis, ed. *Textes latins et vieux français relatifs aux Cyranides.* Paris: Droz, 1942.

Delmas, B. "Médailles astrologiques et talismaniques dans le midi de la France (XIIIe–XVIe siècle)." In *Archéologie occitane,* vol. 2: *Actes du 96e Congrès national des sociétés savantes, Toulouse, 1971, Section d'archéologie et d'histoire de l'art.* Paris: Bibliothèque Nationale, 1976.

Demonsablon, Philippe. "Note sur deux vêtements talismaniques." *Arabica* 33 (1986): 216–50.

Deonna, Waldemar. "Abra, Abraca: La croix-talisman de Lausanne." *Geneva* XXII (1944): 115–37.

———. "Armes avec motifs astrologiques et talismaniques." *Revue d'histoire des religions* 90 (1926): 39–97.

———. "Talismans chrétiens." *Revue d'histoire des religions* 95 (1927): 19–42.

Descombes, René. *Les Carrés magiques. Histoire et technique du carré magique de l'Antiquité aux recherches actuelles.* Paris: Vuibert, 2000.

Devoto, Guido, and Alberto Molayem. *Archeogemmologia: Pietre antiche, Glittica, Magia e Litoterapia.* Rome: Meridiana, 1990.

Diepgen, Paul. "Arnoldus de Villanova De improbatione maleficiorum." *Archiv für Kulturgeschichte* 9 (1912): 385–403.

Dieterich, Albrecht. *Abraxas: Studien zur Religionsgeschichte des späteren Altertums.* Leipzig: Teubner, 1891.

Dioscorides, *De materia medica libri quinque.* Edited by Max Wellmann. 3 vols. Berlin: Weidmann, 1906.

Dobschütz, Ernest von. "Charms and Amulets (Christian)." *Encyclopedia of Religions and Ethics,* vol. 3.

Dulière, W. L. "Protection contre les animaux nuisibles assurée par Apollonios de Thyane dans Byzance et Antioche. Évolution de son mythe." *Byzantinische Zeitschrift* 63 (1970): 247–77.

Dumas, François Ribadeau. *Grimoire et Rituels magiques*. Paris: Belfond, 1972.

Düwel, Klaus. "Buchstabenmagie und Alphabetzauber: Zu den Inschriften der Goldbrakteaten und ihrer Funktion als Amulette." *Frühmittelalterliche Studien* 22 (1988): 70–110.

Eckhardt, Karl August, ed. *Lex Salica, 100 Titel-Text*. Weimar: Bohlau, 1953.

Eckstein, F., and J. H. Waszink. "Amulett." In *Reallexikon für Antike und Christentum*, vol. 1.

Entzelt, Christoph. *De re metallica*, book 3. Frankfurt: Egenolphus, 1551.

Ernst, Thomas. "Schwarzweiße Magie. Der Schlüssel zum 3. Buch der Steganographia des Trithemius." *Daphnis* 25 (1996): 1–205.

Ertlé, Jean-Marie. *Sorciers, Magiciens et Enchanteurs de nos terroirs*. Paris: J. de Bonnot, 1996.

Evans, Joan. *Magical Jewels of the Middle Ages and the Renaissance Particularly in England*. Oxford: Clarendon Press, 1922.

Fachan, Zoe. *L'homme-zodiaque*. Marseille: Agep, 1991.

Faraone, Christopher A. *Talismans and Trojan Horses: Guardian Statues in Ancient Greek Myth and Ritual*. Oxford: Oxford University Press, 1992.

Festugière, André Jean. "Amulettes magiques. A propos d'un ouvrage récent." *Classical Philology* 46 (1951): 81–92.

Ficino, Marsilio. *De vita libri tres*. Edited by Albano Biondi and Giuliano Pisani. Pordenone: Biblioteca dell'Immagine, 1991.

Ficker, K. "Amulett." *Realenzyklopädie für protestantische Theologie und Kirche*, vol. 1, 1896.

Flamand, Elie-Charles. *Les Pierres magiques*. Paris: Courrier du Livre, 1981.

Franckenberg, Abraham von. *Gemma magica oder magisches Edelgestein*. Amsterdam: privately published, 1688.

Franz, Adolph, ed. *Der Magister Nikolaus Magni de Jawor*. Freiburg: Herder, 1898.

———, ed. *Die kirchlichen Benediktionen im Mittelalter*. 2 vols. Graz: Akademische Druck- u. Verlagsanstalt, 1960.

Froehner, Wilhelm. "Sur une amulette basilidienne inédite du musée Napoléon III." *Bulletin de la Société des antiquaires de Normandie* 4 (1866–1867): 217–231.

Gaffarel, Jacques. *Curiositez inouyes sur la sculpture talismanique des Persans, Horoscope des Patriarches, et Lecture des Estoilles*. Paris: Hervé Du Mesnil, 1629.

Garrett, Robert Max. *Precious Stones in Old English Literature*. Naumberg: Lippert & Co., 1909.

Garstein, Oskar. *Vinjeboka. Den eldste Svartebok fra Norsk Middelalder.* Oslo: Solum, 1993.

Gaster, Theodore H. "Amulets and Talismans." In *Encyclopedia of Religion,* vol. 1.

Gerstinger, H. "Bulla." In *Reallexikon für Antike und Christentum,* vol. 2.

———. "Enkolpion." In *Reallexikon für Antike und Christentum,* vol. 5.

Gervasius of Tilbury. *Le Livre des merveilles.* Translated by Annie Duchesne. Paris: Les Belles Lettres, 1992.

Gilbert, Emil. *Essai historique sur les talismans dan l'Antiquité, le Moyen Âge et les Temps modernes.* Paris: Savy, 1881.

Gilli, Patrick, ed. *Former, enseigner, éduquer dans l'Occident médieval.* 2 vols. Paris: Sedes, 1999.

Glaber, Rodulfus. *Les cinq livres de ses histoires (900–1044).* Edited by Maurice Prou. Paris: Picard, 1886.

Gompert, Ludwig. "Der Zachariassegen gegen die Pest." *Hessische Blätter für Volkskunde* 17 (1918): 37–52.

Gori, Antonio Francesco, and Giovanni Battista Passeri. *Thesaurus gemmarum antiquarum astriferarum.* Albiziniana, 1750.

Gorlaeus, Abraham. *Dactyliotheca.* Published with commentaries by Jacob Gronov. Leiden: Peter van der Aa, 1695.

Grabar, André. *L'Art paléochrétien et l'Art byzantin.* London: Variorum Reprints, 1979.

Gregory of Tours. *Histoire des Francs.* Translated by Robert Latouche. Paris: Les Belles Lettres, 1963.

———. *History of the Franks.* Translated by Lewis Thorpe. London: Penguin Books, 1974.

Grimm, Jacob. *Deutsche Mythologie.* 3 vols. Darmstadt: Wissenschaftliche Buchgesellschaft, 1965.

Grimmelshausen, Hans Jakob Christoph von. *Werke.* Edited by Dieter Breuer. 3 vols. Frankfurt: Deutscher Klassiker Verlag, 1989–1997.

Guéranger, Dom Prosper. *Essai sur l'origine, la signification et les privilèges de la médaille ou croix de saint Benoît.* Poitiers: Oudin, 1875.

Gugitz, Gustav. *Fest- und Brauchtums-Kalender.* Vienna, 1930.

Gui, Bernard. *Manuel de l'Inquisiteur.* 2 vols. Edited and translated by Guillaume Mollat. Paris: Les Belles Lettres, 1964.

Gundel, Wilhelm. *Dekane und Dekansternbilder, ein Betrag zur Geschichte der Sternbilder der Kulturvölker.* Glückstadt and Hamburg: Augustin, 1936.

———. *Sterne und Sternbilder im Glauben des Altertums und der Neuzeit.* Berlin and Leipzig: Schroeder, 1922.

Günzburger, Julius. *Medaillen Badischer Klöster, Wallfahrtsorte und anderer geistlicher Institute.* Nuremberg: Sebaldus, 1930.

Haage, Bernard Dietrich. "Dekane und Paranatellonta des Astrolabium planum in einem Nürnberger Fragment." *Archiv für Kultegeschichte* 60 (1978): 121–40.

———. "Ein Handschriftenfund zum Astrolabium planum des Petrus von Abano." In *Litterae ignotae. Beiträge zur Textgeschichte des deutschen Mittelalters: Neufunde und Neuinterpretationen,* edited by Ulrich Müller. Göppingen: Kümmerle, 1977.

Halleux, Robert. "Damigeron, Evax et Marbode. L'héritage alexandrin dans les lapidaires médiévaux." *Studi medievali* 15/1 (1974): 327–47.

Halleux, Robert, and Jacques Schamp, eds. *Les lapidaires grecs.* Paris: Les Belles Lettres, 1985.

Hamès, Constant. "L'usage talismanique du Coran." *Revue de l'histoire des religions* 218 (2001): 83–95.

Hamès, Constant, and Alain Epelboin. "Trois vêtements talismaniques provenant du Sénégal." *Bulletin d'Études orientales* 44 (1992): 217–41.

Hamesse, Jacqueline, ed. *Manuels, Programmes de cours et techniques d'enseignement dans les universités médiévales.* Louvain-la-Neuve: Institut d'études médiévales, 1994.

Hansmann, Liselotte, Lenz Kriss-Rettenbeck, and Claus Hansmann. *Amulett und Talisman. Erscheinungsform und Geschichte.* Munich: Callwey, 1966.

Harmening, Dieter. "Zur Morphologie magischer Inschriften. Der Donauwörther Zauberring und Formkriterien für seine Interpretation." *Jahrbuch für Volkskunde,* new series, vol. 1 (1978): 67–80.

Hartlieb, Johann. *Johann Hartliebs Buch aller verbotenen Kunst.* Edited by Dora Ulm. Halle: Niemeyer, 1914.

Haver, Jozef van. *Nederlandse incantatieliteratuur. Een geocommentarierd compendium van Nederlandse Bezweringsformules.* Ghent: Koninklijke Academie voor Taal-en Letterkunde, 1964.

Herkenrode, Léon de. "Une amulette. Légende en vers de sainte Marguerite tirée d'un ancien manuscrit." *Bibliophile belge* 4 (1847): 2–23.

Herolt, Johannes. *Liber discipuli de eruditione Christi fidelium.* Cologne, 1509.

Herr, Michael. *Das neue Tier- und Arzneibuch des Doktor Michael Herr A. D. 1546.* Edited by Gerhard E. Sollbach. Würzburg: Königshausen & Neumann, 1994.

Hiebner, Israel. *Mysterium sigillorum, herbarum et lapidum.* Erfurt: Birckner, 1651.

Hildegard von Bingen. *Hildegard von Bingen's Physica.* Translated by Patricia Throop. Rochester, Vt.: Healing Arts Press, 1998.

Holmes, Urban T. "Medieval Gem Stones." *Speculum* 9 (1934): 194–204.

Howald, Ernst, and Henry E. Sigerist, eds. *Herbarius pseudo-Apulei.* In *Corpus medicorum latinorum,* vol. 6. Leipzig and Berlin: Teubner, 1927.

Ideler, Julius Ludwig. *Physici et medici graeci minores,* vol. 1. Berlin: Reimeri, 1841.

Isle, Joseph Nicolas De L' [Charles Sorel]. *Des talismans ou Figures faites sous certaines constellations.* Paris: Antoine de Sommaville, 1616.

Ivanov, Jordan. *Livres et Légendes bogomiles (aux sources du catharisme).* Paris: Maisonneuve and Larose, 1976.

Jacoby, Adolf. "Heilige Längenmasse. Eine Untersuchung zur Geschichte der Amulette." *Schweizerisches Archiv für Volkskunde* 29 (1929): 181–216.

Jaenecke-Nickel, Johanna. "Schutzzauber im Jahre 1967." *Schweizerisches Archiv für Volkskunde* 64 (1968): 136–37.

Jerome, Saint. *Commentaires sur l'Évangile de saint Matthieu* IV. In Jacques Paul Migne, *Patrologia latina* 26, col. 168.

Joubert, Laurent. *Des erreurs populaires.* Lyons: Pierre-Rigaud, 1602.

Kaimakis, Dimitris, ed. *Die Kyraniden.* Meisenheim am Glan: Hain, 1976.

Kieckhefer, Richard. *Magic in the Middle Ages.* Cambridge, U.K.: Cambridge University Press, 1990.

King, Charles William. *The Natural History, Ancient and Modern, of Precious Stones and Gems and of the Precious Metals.* London: Bell and Daldy, 1865.

———. "Talismans and Amulets." *The Archaeological Journal* 101 (1869): 25–34; 149–57; 225–35.

Kircher, Athanasius. *Œdipus ægyptiacus.* 2 vols. Rome: Vitalis Mascardi, 1653.

Kluge, Karl Emil. *Handbuch der Edelsteinkunde für Mineralogen: Steinschneider und Juweliere.* Leipzig: Brockhaus, 1860.

Koblig, Johann Sigismund. *Disquisitio antiquaria de talismanibus.* Wittenberg: Schrödter, 1697.

Kompert, Leopold. *Aus dem Ghetto.* Leipzig: Max Hesses Verlag, n.d. [1906].

Kottek, Samuel. "Le symbole du Lion dans la médecine de l'Antiquité et du Moyen Âge." *Revue de l'histoire de la médecine hébraïque* 20 (1967): 161–68.

Kozminsky, Isadore. *The Magic and Science of Jewels and Stones.* New York: G. P. Putnan's Sons, 1922.

Kramer, Heinrich, and Jacob Sprenger. *The Malleus Maleficarum of Kramer and Sprenger.* Translated and edited by Montague Summers. New York: Dover, 1971.

Krause, Carl Christian, and Carl Christian Wagner. *Dissertatio de amuletis medicis cogitate non nulla.* Leipzig, 1758.

Kriss, Rudolf, and Hubert Kriss-Heinrich. *Amulette, Zauberformeln und Beschwörungen.* Wiesbaden: Harrassowitz, 1962.

Kropatschek, Gerhard. *De amuletorum apud Antiquos usu capita duo.* N.p.: Gryphiae Typis Iulii Abel, 1907.

Kühn, C. G., ed. *Claudii Galeni Opera Omnia.* 22 vols. Leipzig: Cnobloch, 1821–1833.

Kunz, George Frederick. *The Curious Lore of Precious Stones.* Philadelphia: Lippincott, 1913.

———. *The Magic of Jewels and Charms.* Philadelphia: Lippincott, 1915.

Laarß, Richard H. *Das Geheimnis der Amulette und Talismane.* Leipzig: Hummel, 1926.

Lambel, Hans, ed. *Das Steinbuch. Ein altdeutsches Gedicht von Volmar.* Heilbronn: Henninger, 1877.

Lambert de Saint-Omer. *Liber floridus.* Ghent Central Library. Codex 9. Twelfth century.

Lancellotti, Maria Gracia. "Médecine et religion dans les gemmes magiques." *Revue de l'histoire des religions* 218 (2001): 427–56.

Lecouteux, Claude. "Agla, Sator. Quelques remarques sur les charmes médicaux au Moyen Âge." *Nouvelle Plume* (Nagoya, Japan).

———. "Arnoldus Saxo: Unveröffentliche Texte, transkribiert und Kommentiert." *Euphorion* 76 (1982): 389–400.

———. *The Book of Grimoires: The Secret Grammar of Magic.* Rochester, Vt.: Inner Traditions, 2013.

———. *Charmes, Conjurations et Bénédictions: Lexiques et formules.* Paris: Champion, 1996.

———. *Démons et Génies du terroir au Moyen Âge.* Paris: Imago, 1995.

———. "Les pierres magiques et le merveilleux." In *Deutsch-französische Mediävistik. Mélanges pour G. E. Zink.* Göppingen: Kümmerle, 1984.

———. "Les pierres talismaniques au Moyen Âge." *Nouvelle Plume, Revue d'études mythologiques et symboliques* (Nagoya, Japan) 1 (2000): 2–19.

———. *Mondes parallèles. L'univers des croyances au Moyen Âge.* Paris: Champion, 1994.

Legros, Élisée. "La Mesure de Jésus et autres saintes mesures." *Enquêtes du Musée de la Vie wallone* 9 (1962): 313–37.

Leonardi, Camillo. *Les Pierres talismaniques (Speculum lapidum,* book 3).

Edited and translated with commentary by Claude Lecouteux and Anne Monfort. Paris: P.U.P.S., 2002.

———. *Speculum lapidum clarissimi artium et medicine doctoris Camilli Leonardi Pisaurensis.* Venice, 1502.

Lesses, Rebecca. "Ritual Practices to Gain Power. Adjurations in the Hekhalot Literature, Jewish Amulets, and Greek Revelatory Adjurations." Dissertation, Harvard University, Cambridge, Mass., 1995.

Libellus de sculpturis lapidum. Vienna, National Library, ms. 3408.

Licht der Seelen, Das. Lübeck: Ghotan, 1484.

Lippincott, Kristin, and David Pingree. "Ibn al-Hatîm on the Talismans of the Lunar Mansions." *Journal of the Warburg and Courtauld Institutes* 50 (1987): 57–81.

Löscher, Valentin Ernst. *De talismanibus vel signis, quae numi vel gemmae exhibent superstitiosis.* Wittenberg: Schrödter, 1697.

Lübecker Beicht- und Gebetbücher. Lübeck, 1487.

Luzel, François-Marie. *Contes populaires de la Basse-Bretagne,* vol. 3. Translated by Françoise Morvan. Rennes: Presses Universitaires de Rennes, 1996.

Mansi, Giovanni Domenico. *Sacrorum conciliorum nova et amplissima collectio.* 31 vols. Florence and Venice, 1757–1798.

Marbode of Rennes. *De lapidibus.* Edited by John M. Riddle. Wiesbaden: Steiner, 1977.

Marcarius, Johann. *Abraxas seu Apistopistus.* Antwerp: Moret, 1657.

Marcellus. *De medicamentis liber.* Edited by M. Niedermann. In *Corpus medicorum latinorum,* vol. 5. Leipzig: Teubner, 1916.

Marquès-Rivière, Jean. *Amulettes, talismans et pantacles dans les traditions orientales et occidentales.* Paris: Payot, 1938.

Martin of Braga. *De correctione rusticorum.* Edited by Claude W. Barlow. New Haven: Yale University Press, 1950.

Martinez-Gazquez, J. "*L'homo astrologicus* du manuscript 2052 des archives capitulaires de la Seu d'Urgell." In *Les Astres,* edited by Beatrice Bakhouche et al. Montpellier: Université Paul Valéry, 1966.

Massé, Henri. *Croyances et Coutumes persanes.* Paris: Maisonneuve, 1938.

Matton, Sylvain, ed. and trans. *La Magie arabe traditionnelle.* Paris: Retz, 1977.

Maury, Alfred. *La Magie et l'Astrologie dans l'Antiquité et au Moyen Âge.* Hildesheim and New York: Olms, 1980.

Megenberg, Konrad von. *Buch der Natur.* Edited by Franz Pfeiffer. Hildesheim: Olms, 1962.

Mély, Fernand de. *Du rôle des pierres gravées au Moyen Âge.* Lille: Desclée & De Brouwer, 1893.

Mély, Fernand de, M. H. Courel, and Charles Emil de Ruelle. *Les Lapidaires de l'Antiquité et du Moyen Âge.* 3 vols. Paris: LeRoux, 1896–1902.

Migne, Jacques-Paul, ed. *Patrologia graeca.* 161 vols. Paris: Imprimerie Catholique, 1857–1866.

———, ed. *Patrologia latina.* 221 vols. Paris: Migne, 1841–1865.

Mizauld, Antoine. *Memorabilium sive arcanorum omnis generis.* Cologne: Berkmann, 1574.

Montelle, Edith, and Jean Louis Kieffer. *L'Ondine de la Nied et autres contes.* Lille: Fol de Moselle, 1995.

Monumenta Germaniae Historica. All volumes online at www.dmgh.de (accessed Nov. 20, 2013).

Niedermeier, Hans. "Die Benediktusmedaille." *Bayerisches Jahrbuch für Volkskunde* (1960): 73–81.

Noguès, Abbé. "Pratiques empiriques." In *La Tradition en Poitou et Charente.* Paris: Librairie de la Tradition Nationale, 1897.

Notker Labeo. *Martianus Capella, De nuptiis philologiae et Mercurii.* Edited by James C. King. Tübingen: Niemeyer, 1979.

Nunemaker, Horace J. "An Additional Chapter on Magic in Mediaeval Spanish Literature." *Speculum* 7 (1932): 556–64.

———. "The Chaldean Stones in the Lapidary of Alfonso X." *Publications of the Modern Language Association of America* 45 (1930): 444–53.

Pachinger, Anton Maximilian. *Wallfahrts- und Weihemünzen des Erzherzogstums Österreich ob der Enns.* Enns: Musealverein "Laureacum," 1904.

Pagel, Walter. "Paracelsus and Techellus the Jew." *Bulletin of the History of Medicine* 34 (1960): 274–77.

Pannier, Léopold. *Les Lapidaires français du Moyen Âge des XIIe, XIIIe et XIVe siècles.* Paris: Vieweg, 1882.

Paracelus [Philippus Aureolus Theophrastus Bombastus von Hohenheim]. *De la magie.* Translated with notes and commentary by Lucien Braun. Strasbourg: Presses universitaires de Strasbourg, 1998.

———. *Paracelsus sämtliche Werke: Medizinische, naturwissenschaftliche und philosophische Schriften.* Edited by Karl Sudhoff. 14 vols. Munich: Barth; Munich and Berlin: Oldenburg, 1922–1933.

Pazzini, Adalberto. *Le Pietre preziose nella storia della medicina e nella leggenda.* Rome: Mediterranea, 1939.

Peter of Spain. *Thesaurus pauperum.* In *Obras Médicas de Pedro Hispano,* edited by Maria Helena da Rocha Pereira. Coimbra: University of Coimbra, 1973.

Pineau, Leon. *Le Folklore du Poitou.* Paris: Leroux, 1892.

Pingree, David. "The Diffusion of Arabic Magical Texts in Western Europe." In *La Diffuzione delle scienze islamiche nel Medio Evo Europeo.* Rome: Academia Nazionale dei Lincei, 1987.

———. *Picatrix: The Latin Version of the Ghâyat al-Hakîm.* London: Warburg Institute, 1986.

Pirmin, Saint. *Dicta de singulis libris canonicus.* In J. N. D. Kelly, *Early Christian Creeds.* London: Longmans, Green, Longmans, and Rogers, 1972.

Pitra, Jean Baptiste. *Analecta sacra,* vol. 8. Paris: Monte Cassino, 1882.

Placet, François. *La Superstition du temps reconnue aux Talismans, figure Astrales, & statuës fatales. Contre un Livre Anonyme intitulé Les Talismans ivstifiez. Avec la Poudre de Sympathie soupçonnée de Magie.* Paris: Gervais Alliot & Gilles Alliot, 1668.

Pliny the Elder. *C. Plini Secundi Naturalis historiae libri XXXVII.* Edited by Ludwig Janus. 6 vols. Leipzig: Teubner, 1865–1870.

Plutarch. *Vie de Périclès.* Translated by Jacques Amyot. Paris: Gallimard, 1951.

Poule noire, La. Avec les science des talismans et anneaux magiques. Paris: Bussière, 1997.

Rantasalo, Aukusti Vilho. *Einige Zaubersteine und Zauberpflanzen im Volksaberglauben der Finnen.* Helsinki: Suomalainen Tiedeakatemia, 1929.

Raspe, Rudolf Erich. *A Descriptive Catalogue of a General Collection of Ancient and Modern Engraved Gems, Cameos as Well as Intaglios, Taken from the Most Celebrated Cabinets in Europe and Cast in Coloured Pastes, White Enamel, and Sulphur, by James Tassie, Modeler.* 2 vols. London: Tassie, 1791.

Reichelt, Julius. *Exercitatio de amuletis, aeneris figuris illustrata.* Strassburg: Spoor & Wechtler, 1676.

Reinach, Salomon. *Pierres gravées des collections Marlborough et d'Orléans.* Paris: Firmin-Didiot, 1895.

Reizenstein, Richard. *Poimandres: Studien zur griechisch-ägyptischen und frühchristlichen Literatur.* Leipzig: Teubner, 1904.

Révélation d'Hermès Trismegistus, La. Vol. 1, *L'astrologie et les sciences occultes.* Translated by André-Jean Festugière. Paris: Gabalda, 1950.

Ritter, Hellmutt, and Martin Plessner, trans. *"Picatrix." Das Ziel des Weisen vom Pseudo-Magrītī.* London: Warburg Institute, 1962.

Robert, Louis. "Amulettes grecques." *Journal des savants* 1, no. issue 1 (January–March, 1981): 3–44.

———. *Opera minora selecta: Épigraphie et antiquités grecques,* vol. 7. Amsterdam: Hakkert, 1990.

Rose, Valentin. "Aristotles und Arnoldus Saxo." *Zeitschrift für deutsches Altertum* 19 (1875): 321–455.

Rouach, David. *Les Talismans: Magie et traditions juives.* Paris: Michel, 1989.

Ruelle, Charles-Émile, ed. "Hermès Trismégiste. Le livre sacré sur les décans. Texte, variantes et traduction française." *Revue de Philologie* 22 (1908): 247–77.

Ruska, Julius. "Griechische Planetendarstellungen in arabischen Steinbüchern." *Sitzungsberichte der Heidelberger Akad. d. Wiss., phil.-hist. Klasse, Jahrgang 1919, 3. Abhandlung* (1919): 3–50.

———. *Das Steinbuch des Aristoteles.* Heidelberg: Winter, 1911.

———. *Tabula smaragdina. Ein Beitrag zur Geschichte der hermetischen Literatur.* Heidelberg: Winter, 1926.

Saintyves, Pierre. "Talismans tombés du ciel." *Revue d'ethnographie et sociologie* 1 (1910): 50–63.

Schlumberger, Gustave. "Amulettes byzantines anciens destinées à combattre les maléfices et les maladies." *Revue des études grecques* 5 (1892): 73–93.

Schneider, Johann Daniel. *Eröffnung der vortrefflichsten Geheimnüsse in der Arzney-Kunst.* Dresden: Winckler, 1696.

Schnell, Bernard. "Zur deutschsprachigen Rezeption der naturkundlichen Schriften des Thomas von Cantimpré und Albertus Magnus. Zum Steinbuch der Salzburger Handschrift M III 3." In *Licht der natur. Medizin in Fachliteratur und Dichtung, Festschrift für Gundolf Keil,* edited by Josef Domes et al. Göppingen: Kümmerle, 1994.

Schwarz-Winklhofer, Inge, and Hans Biedermann. *Das Buch der Zeichen und Symbole.* Graz: Sammler, 1972.

Sébillot, Paul. *Le Folklore de France,* vol. 3. Paris: Guilmoto, 1907.

Seignolle, Claude. *Contes, Récits et Légendes des pays de France.* Vol. 3, *Provence, Corse, Langedoc-Roussillon, Alpes, Auvergne.* Paris: Omnibus, 2003.

———, ed. *Les évangiles du diable.* Paris: Laffont, 2003.

Seligmann, Siegfried. "Ananisapta und Sator." *Hessische Blätter für Volkskunde* 10 (1921): 1–25.

———. *Der böse Blick und Verwandtes. Ein Beitrag zur Geschichte des Aberglaubens aller Zeiten und Völker.* 2 vols. Berlin: Barsdorf, 1902–1910.

Sotto, Isaac del. *Le Lapidaire du XIVe siècle. Description des pierres précieuses* *et de leur vertus magiques d'après le traité du chevalier Jean de Mandeville.* Vienna, 1862; reprinted Geneva: Slatkine, 1974.

Spegel des cristene mynschen. Lübeck,1501.

Sperander [Friedrich Gladow]. *A la Mode-Sprach der Teutschen.* Nuremberg: Buggel und Seitz, 1727.

Stephan von Landskron. *Die Hymelstrass.* Augsburg: Sorg, 1484.

Studer, Paul, and Joan Evans, eds. *Anglo-Norman Lapidaries.* Geneva: Slatkine, 1976.

Tertullian, *De idolatria.* Latin text online at www.tertullian.org/latin/de_idolo latria.htm (accessed Nov. 20, 2013).

Thiers, Jean-Baptiste. *Traité des superstitions.* Paris: Dezallier, 1679.

———. "Traité des superstitions selon l'Écriture Sainte, les décrets des conciles, et les sentimens des Saints Pères et des theologiens." In *Superstitions anciennes et modernes: prejugés vulgaires qui ont induit les peuples à des usages & à des pratiques contraires à la religion,* vol. 1, edited by Jean Frédéric Bernard Amsterdam: Bernard, 1733.

Thorndike, Lynn. "De lapidibus." *Ambix* 8 (1960): 6–23.

———. *A History of Magic and Experimental Science.* 8 vols. New York: Columbia University Press, 1923–1958.

———. "Traditional Medieval Tracts Concerning Engraved Astronomical Images." In *Mélanges Auguste Pelzer.* Louvain: Bibliothèque de l'Université, Bureaux du "Recueil," 1947.

Timotin, Emanuela. *Legenda Duminicii.* Studiu monografic, ediție şi glosar. Bucharest: Fundația Națională Pentru Ştiință şi Artă, 2005 (with the edition of the Heaven's Letter).

Trachtenberg, Joshua. *Jewish Magic and Superstition.* New York: Atheneum, 1939.

Tricou, Jean. "Médailles religieuses de Lyon." *Revue numismatique* 13 (1951): 109–29.

Trinum magicum, sive secretorum magicorum opus, book 3. Edited by Caesare Longino. Frankfurt, 1663.

Trithemius, Johann. *Steganographia, hoc est: Ars per occultam scripturam animi sui voluntatem absentibus.* Frankfurt: Berner, 1606.

———. *Tractatus de reprobis atque maleficis.* Frankfurt am Main: Bassaeus, 1581.

Tucker, William Jewett. *L'astrologie de Ptolémée: Commentaire du Tetrabiblos de Ptolémée.* Paris: Payot, 1981.

Tzetzes, John. *Historiarum variarum chiliades.* Edited by Johann Gottlieb Kiessling. Leipzig: Vogel, 1826.

Ulrich von Pottenstein. *Dekalog-Auslegung. Das 1. Gebot.* Edited by Gabriele Baptist-Hlawatsch. Tübingen: Niemeyer, 1995.

Véritable Dragon noir, Le. Paris: Bussière, 1966.

Vincent of Beauvais. *Speculum naturale.* Douai: Baltazar Belier, 1624.

Wagner, Johann Christoph. *Disquisitio physica de occultis qualitatibus, et potissimum de sigillis.* Nuremberg, 1663.

Wasserschleben, Friedrich W. H. *Die Bußordnungen der abendländischen Kirche.* Graz: Akademische Druck- u. Verlagsanstalt, 1958.

Weill-Parot, Nicolas. *Les images astrologiques au Moyen Âge et à la Renaissance. Spéculations intellectuelles et pratiques magiques (XIIe–XVe siècle).* Paris: Champion, 2002.

———. "Pénombre ficinienne: Le renouveau de la théorie de la magique talismanique et ses ambiguïtés." In *Marsile Ficin ou les mystères platoniciens,* vol. 2. Paris: Les Belles Lettres, 2002.

Wellmann, Max. "Die Stein- und Gemmenbücher der Antike." *Quellen und Studien zur Geschichte der Naturwissenschaft und der Medizin* 4/4 (1936): 427–90.

Wessely, Karl. "Ephesia grammata aus Papyrusrollen, Inschriften, Gemmen, etc." *Zwölfter Jahresbericht über das k. k. Franz-Joseph-Gymnasium in Wien, 1885–1886* (1886): 1–38.

Wickersheimer, Ernest. "Figures médico-astrologiques des IXe, X^e et XIe siècles." *Janus* 19 (1914): 157–77.

William of Auverne. *Opera.* 2 vols. Paris: Pralard, 1674.

Winckelmann, Joachim. *Geheimnis der Talismane und Amulette.* Freiburg im Bresgau: Bauer, 1955.

Wirbelauer, Karl Willy. *Antike Lapidarien.* Würzburg: Triltsch, 1937.

Wirnt von Grafenberg. *Wigalois: Le Chevalier à la roue.* Translated by Claude Lecouteux and Veronique Levy. Grenoble: Ellug, 2001.

Wohlhaupter, Eugen. *Gesetze der Westgoten.* Weimar: Böhlau, 1936.

Wolff, Jacob. *Curiosus amuletorum scrutator.* Frankfurt and Leipzig: Groshuff, 1692.

Wolters, Paul. "Faden und Knoten als Amulett." *Archiv für Religionswissenschaft* 8 (1905): 1–22.

Zazoff, Peter. *Die antiken Gemmen.* Munich: Beck, 1983.

Zellinger, Johannes. *Augustin und die Volksfrömmigkeit. Blicke in den frühchristlichen Alltag.* Munich: Hueber, 1933.

INDEX

An "f" following a page number indicates a figure on that page.